GARDENING
GRIEF & GLORY

◆

Ed Lawrence
Answers Your Gardening Questions

A. KARSTAD.

with Liane E. Benoit

National Library of Canada Cataloguing in Publication

Lawrence, Ed, 1950-
Gardening grief and glory : Ed Lawrence answers your gardening
questions / Ed Lawrence with Liane E. Benoit ; illustrator, Aleta Karstad.

Includes index.
ISBN 978-0-9681210-1-6

1. Gardening. 2. Gardening--Miscellanea.
I. Benoit, Liane E. (Liane Elizabeth), 1956- II. Title.

SB450.97.L39 2006   635
C2006-906170-X

First Edition
Printed and Bound in Canada
by Friesens

Illustrations by Aleta Karstad
www.pinicola.ca

Cover and book design by Mike Sherwin
Cover photographs by Louis Molgat
Index editor: Holly Ebbs

Published under license from
Tatlock Woods Publishing Inc.
PO Box 146, Wakefield, QC, Canada J0X 3G0

Further copies of this book can be purchased at:
www.gardeningwithed.com

To the loyal CBC listeners
whose gardening challenges and triumphs
inspired this book.

ACKNOWLEDGEMENTS

I would like to acknowledge the professional and technical colleagues with whom I've had the pleasure of working to make this book a reality.

Michael Sherwin for his cover and book design, which beautifully took us to our final goal.

Bill Kretzel, for his priceless assistance in the preparation of the text.

Holly Ebbs who, as index editor, facilitated locating pertinent information in my sometimes rambling answers.

Aleta Karstad, for the sketches and illustrations that grace these pages, clearly depicting the intentions of my words.

Fred Schueler, who gave so generously of his time and expertise in reviewing the text.

Mrs. Butler, who insisted this book be done.

Loraine and Leonard Lee for their encouragement over the years and for Leonard's generous sharing of his invaluable knowledge and experience mentoring us in this endeavour.

Janet Podleski, for her time, advice and encouragement.

My friend and partner in this project, Liane Benoit, who persisted in her vision of producing this book. She convinced me that we should and proved herself right by ensuring that we did.

Louis Molgat, Liane's husband, was responsible for the cover photography and provided encouragement, patience and understanding on top of pitching in with anything else that was required above and beyond what could ever have been reasonably expected. And Sébastien, for sharing his mother with this project.

Ann Penman, my first producer at CBC, who convinced me to give it a try and taught me to absorb and reflect all that positive energy from the gardeners who called in.

Elizabeth Hay, Producer of "Ontario Today", for more than a decade of enthusiastic support and encouragement.

Dick Veerman, horticultural consultant and friend, who kept me aware of the reality of commercial greenhouse production and industry trends.

To my wife Kate who, through good times and hard times, helped me keep body and soul together at great personal expense. Without her support and encouragement none of this would ever have seen the light of day.

The paper used in this book respects the following
recognized environmental standards

Environmental Choice - EcoLogo
Environment Canada

Certification that identify ecological products. Considered criteria are the level of greenhouse gas emissions, water and energy consumption and the use of fibre.

Cascades is the only Canadian fine paper mill certified EcoLogo.

Process Chlorine Free (PCF)
Chlorine Free Products Association (CFPA)

Certification that identify that no chlorine were used in the papermaking process.

Cascades is the only Canadian fine paper mill certified PCF.

FSC Recycled
Forest Stewardship Council (FSC)

FSC certifications are promoting the responsible use of forest resources.

The FSC Recycled certification authenticates that the product contains 100% post-con-
sumer fibre, taking into account all transformation steps, from raw material to consumer product.

100% Post-consumer

Contains wood fibre that have been recuperated entirely from paper used by consumer
through recycling programs.

Permanent Paper

An alkaline paper that can resist more than one hundred years in standard
warehousing conditions.

Criteria and certifications are established by the American National Standard Institute
(ANSI).

Biogas Energy

Gas generated from the decomposition of waste buried in a landfill and transported at
the mill to power the paper production equipment. This green energy helps to reduce
considerably greenhouse gas emissions.

CONTENTS

FOREWORD

The gardening questions collected for this book are composites of the many thousands I have been asked over the past two and a half decades on CBC Radio's "Ontario Today" Monday gardening phone-in. While each and every gardening situation described by the callers is unique, the years have shown that some horticultural challenges, like certain plants, are perennial. It is these recurrent gardening problems that are identified and addressed within the chapters of this book and presented as vignettes that echo the question-and-answer format that has characterized my relationship with listeners throughout these years. The result is not a book that is exhaustive, nor is it a technical manual. There will no doubt be some vital areas that I have overlooked and perhaps some gardeners might have preferred a more formal and disciplined approach. But in the end I realized it was the random, un-programmed and eclectic nature of the weekly shows – the "never knowing what might come up next" aspect of them – that has been the essential element of their appeal. Hopefully we have successfully captured that essence in the pages that follow.

I had a wonderful chemistry teacher in high school who regularly told us "there are no dumb questions." I believed her and I hope that you too will find that she was right.

Ed Lawrence

JANUARY

A. KARSTAD

Perpetuating Poinsettias

How do I get my poinsettia to bloom again next Christmas? Can I prune these plants once the holidays are past or will that reduce the chances of them coming back red again next year?

When you get tired of looking at the coloured bracts of the poinsettia, go ahead and trim them back. Let the bracts that don't have any flower grow on, but if your plant looks a bit unruly, you can certainly trim off up to 25% of the plant without any danger of harming it. Keep the plant in full light.

The more light it has, the happier it will be. Give it thorough waterings and make sure it is drying down, but not drying out completely, between each one. If it dries out completely, it will flag very quickly. If you do find your plant completely wilted, soak it thoroughly and it will come back within a few hours. In terms of getting a poinsettia to flower again for next Christmas, the critical time to think about this is at the end of the summer when you bring it back indoors. Be sure that it comes in before any danger of frost. Keep it in full light throughout September. At the beginning of October put it on a strict schedule to get 10 hours of light and 14 hours of total darkness every day until it sets flower for you. Put the plant in a dark cupboard or closet for those 14 hours if you have to; just make sure that it doesn't get any light at all during that stretch. And don't forget the 10 hours of light daily as well. The plant won't set bud without the right amount of both light and darkness. Once you see the uppermost bracts starting to show a change in colour from green to red, or to whatever colour your poinsettia was, leave the plant out in the highest light you have available, preferably a south or west-facing window. Those coloured bracts and the almost inconspicuous yellow flowers will continue to develop on their own and should be ready just in time for the holiday season.

Money Tree Woes

My husband bought me a 3-foot Money Tree for my birthday and I think I over-watered it. Some of the stems are sort of shriveled and the leaves coming off of them are wilted. Most of the bottom leaves have fallen off completely. How I can save it?

The next thing you will likely see will be roots sprouting along the branches or along the nodes or stems. Humidity will do

that, as well as causing the wilting that you are concerned about. Stop watering and get it into full sun. Wait until it dries out completely before you water it again and when you think it is ready to be watered, give it another 5-7 days – that will likely be the right time. Then give it a very thorough soaking, let it drain thoroughly and put it back into its bright sunny location. Don't water it again until it dries down and keep it going on that cycle. Don't bother cutting off the rotted stems or leaves. Just let them be for now. They will probably either come back or shrivel up and drop off at a node, so it shouldn't be a problem. Try and keep it in enough light to get a red margin around the edge of the leaves. With enough sunlight at this size you should see it flower before too long. "Money Tree" and "Chinese Good Luck" plant are two of the common names for this jade plant, and don't we wish that it really produced both.

Recipe for Bonsai Mix

Can you recommend a good bonsai mix or how to make one?

The best combination is to take a normal soilless mix – any of the commercially available ones will do – and mix it with up to 40% clean sharp sand. The critical thing here is that you have enough organic matter in the soil-less mix to hold the moisture required to keep the roots from drying out, but enough sand to make sure there is not an overload of moisture constantly in the soil. In other words, you need a careful balance of moisture retention and drainage. It also means that you have got to be very careful and check the moisture levels in the pot daily, then water as and when required.

Flopping Cactus

I have an 8-year-old Candelabra Cactus that is about 7 feet high. It had grown taller but I had to cut off the top because it was getting too high for the room. Now it is falling over. It always stood nice and straight and pretty stiff but now, not only are the little branches on the main trunk falling over, the whole thing is coming down. I think I may not have watered it enough. Is there anything I can do to save it?

You'll need to put a long stake into the pot to hold it up at this point. You'll need something very solid like a larger bamboo stick or one of the metal-covered simulated bamboo poles. Tie it on with yarn, nylon stockings or some other soft material that is not going to cut into the stem. And watch the watering. The problem here is likely too much water rather than too little. Cut out the watering entirely for now so that it can stabilize. If a cactus gets too much water, typically it starts to flop. The cells actually rupture and that softens the stem so it just can't hold itself up any more. Just for insurance, if you have some good healthy tips on it now, take some cuttings in case the parent plant is too far gone. With the stem flopping over, too many cells may have ruptured for it to be able to renew itself. Put the cuttings into a dryish soil, or even straight sharp sand and keep them dry for about two weeks. That will give them a bit more of a chance to callus over and dry off at the bottom. After that, water them thoroughly but allow them to dry out between waterings.

Scales of Injustice

I have a beautiful 4-foot Benjamina that has developed brown scales. I have been using a screwdriver to try and pinch them off and in some places it's so bad that I have had to remove entire branches. I don't know how to handle it and the plant is really suffering. What should I do?

If you lift up that little spoon-shaped oyster shell cover or scale, underneath is a soft beige insect that squishes fairly readily.

But that is a lot of squishing for one plant, especially if it is a large infestation. What you want to do is mix up a solution of 40-parts room temperature water and 1-part liquid soap and add to that 8-parts rubbing alcohol. The rubbing alcohol helps by breaking down the waxy coating on the shell and lets the solution penetrate right down underneath. Spray the plant from bottom to top and make sure you get every scale that you see as well as in the crotches, along the stems and at the base of all the leaves. Spray to the point of run-off so that everything is thoroughly covered. It is best to do this in your bathtub so that the residue can go down the drain. After you spray, leave that solution on the plant for 5-10 minutes and then spray the whole plant again with clear room temperature water. Again, spray it from bottom to top and top to bottom very thoroughly. The scales are not going to fall off but the insects will die in place and when you touch them after you will see that the scales fall off quite easily. You will want to watch the plant closely after the treatment because some of the young ones will probably hatch and come back. If you see this happening, take a toothpick or a cotton swab, dip it in rubbing alcohol and touch the individual scale. That will kill it and should

be enough to control a small recurrence without having to repeat the spraying.

Revival of the Presumed Dead

I have another plant disaster. It is a dieffenbachia plant that was given to us – the previous owner suspected she had overwatered. She was right. This was a couple months ago and since then I think the root has rotted. The leaves were beginning to go brown and wilty and the roots were sort of soft and yellow. The plant fell out of the pot a couple of days ago and it smelled very bad. So last night we cut the mushy root stuff off, stuck the plant into a pot of fresh soil and didn't water it. This morning it is looking a little sad. All we have left is a single stock from the top and I was wondering if we can save it.

That root you cut off is perfect material to take right out to the compost and then scrub the pot well. To produce a suitable cutting from the stock you have left you must determine the lowest point where the rot has not penetrated to the centre of the stem. This may mean repeated cutting across the stem. Once you get to that point, make sure the cut is directly below the next closest node. If there are any leaves within a couple of inches of what you cut off, remove those. Take that cutting and put it in a glass or a jar with about an inch of water in the base. Get a hold of some English Ivy or willow cuttings and put them in the water with the dieffenbachia cutting. Leave it there in the water until you see roots about 1/2 - 1 inch long at the base of that stock. At that point you can pot it up into about a 4 or 6 inch pot. Don't bring the soil too far up the stem. You are probably going to need a support for it as well. Give it a thorough watering when you plant it up, but then be stingy with the water. Water only as needed thereafter – a thorough watering when you give it – but make sure it dries out between each watering. When the roots begin to grow out, move it up one pot size at a time. The establishment period is going to be the most critical. Once you have it potted up, it should be taking off within a month and looking vigorous again. But be very careful – make sure there are drainage holes in the pot and that the plant is drying down well. In fact, it can almost dry out completely to the point where the leaves do start to flag or droop. When they do that, soak it thoroughly. If you can catch it right before the leaves start to droop that would be ideal and the plant would waste a lot less energy. Interestingly enough they do root up most successfully in water.

Fertilizer Overdose

I think I have been given the wrong information by a prominent nursery here in town. They were telling me to give an application of 15-30-15, full strength, on my plants and to do this every week for the next 6 weeks. I think this is too much.

That is a heavy dose. To accurately recommend to anybody that they fertilize once a week is virtually impossible without knowing the condition of your plants or their location. If they are in a hot, dry greenhouse with a southern or western exposure and they have been growing vigorously, once a week may mean once every seventh watering because you have to water every day. That is very different than if you are only watering the plants once or twice a week. In normal indoor conditions those plants would be building up an incredible amount of salts with full strength fertilizing at that frequency. Cut that back to 1 teaspoon per gallon every fourth or fifth watering. That way you will be assured they are using all the nutrients available and that you are not getting any buildup of salts that could damage the roots. You will also avoid pushing the plants too hard, too fast. They will get a growth spurt as the light levels increase and their metabolism changes, so this way you are just providing a little more nutrient with your watering. If you are worried that they did get too much with that initial feeding, it is just a matter of giving them room temperature or slightly warmer water and letting that drain through them thoroughly to leach some of that fertilizer out and slow them down a little bit.

Fungal Attack

I am facing a personal plant disaster. Recently I have had a fungus attack on almost all the soil of my indoor plants. One of the big victims that had to be removed was a cactus. All the plants actually had little white wriggling bugs. So I went to the store and I tried "Trounce", and I tried insect dust, and now I have a re-infestation. I'm afraid that I might lose them all.

Let's try the non-chemical method. Scratch up the soil surfaces of all your plants and let that surface soil dry out completely. Lift each pot up both before and after you water to feel how heavy it is. Let them get down to about a quarter of that "wet" weight before watering again. It may mean that the frequency of watering drops off drastically for some plants. Separating the plants

will be helpful. Air circulation is going to make a big difference. If you are getting that kind of infestation around your cactus collection, get them away from the other plants. Don't water them at all for another 2 months and they will be very happy. When you think it is time for a drink, wait another week and you are more likely to be right. Then let them dry out completely before they drink again. Err on the side of dry with both cactus and succulents.

Pruning and Propagating Anthurium

Years ago we received an Anthurium plant that was in a little 2-inch pot on top of a fruit basket. Over the years it has never stopped blooming. It always has 2 flowers on it at a time. The only thing is that as it grows taller and puts out new leaves at the top, the ones further down drop off. It is over 2 feet tall now and about 18 inches of that is bare stem. It's beginning to look like a palm tree. What do I do about pruning it?

Don't prune it. They are a little difficult and I have found that if you cut back the top, the base often doesn't come back. If you can stake it, it is certainly worth holding on to. What you could try is a little air layering of the top of the plant. About 6 inches or so below the last set of leaves, at the 1-foot point, the stem should be at least as large around as your thumb. What you want to do is take a knife and vertically cut a thin strip off the stem that is about 1/8 inch wide and about 1/2 inch long. Just strip it down and take that little piece of the outer bark or exterior piece of the stem off leaving the cambium layer intact. Make at least 4 of those incisions at the same height around the stem – if you could cut 5 or 6, so much the better. Just try to space them equally as you go

around. Next, put a little #1 or #2 rooting hormone over the injured areas you have just cut. Get some sphagnum or peat moss, moisten it and wrap it around the stem to cover over those spots. Secure it with a bit of plastic wrap. Even a plastic bag cut up and secured with a twist tie will do quite nicely here. Make sure it's not tied so tight that it cuts off the circulation. An elastic band broken and then tied around it so it fits snuggly will also work well. The idea is to keep that moss damp inside. What should happen is you will start to get some root development on the stem. When you see the roots growing out through the moss to the point where they are

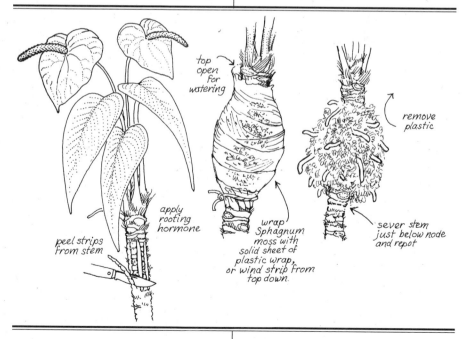

top open for watering

remove plastic

peel strips from stem

apply rooting hormone

wrap Sphagnum moss with solid sheet of plastic wrap, or wind strip from top down.

sever stem just below node and repot

clearly visible, cut the stem off below those new roots but making sure that you leave a node intact between the cut and the bottom of the severed top piece. That severed section with the new roots can then be potted into a new pot. That is the only safe way I have found to reduce these, if it works. If it doesn't work and no new roots appear after a few weeks, take off the plastic and moss. The worst that will happen is that the plant will heal over those injured spots and continue to grow on for you. It won't kill the original plant. If, on the other hand, it does produce new roots with the air layering, then you can safely sever it off and pot up the new section.

Shaping a Jade

I am wondering about cutting and pinching back my jade. It is in a 12-inch pot and stands about 2 feet high and 2 feet across. It's a bit wobbly and sort of polar and I'm hoping to give it a bit more shape. How should I go about doing that?

The pot size is certainly fine for the size of this jade. What you want to do with your jade plant is stand it or sit it somewhere where you can walk very comfortably around it and have a

A Seasonal Note

Winter is a perfect time to sit back and thumb through all those colourful seed catalogues that miraculously appear in your mailbox in the dead of winter. But remember to buy only what you realistically have time and space to plant on your property. You'll be less frustrated and happier with the results if you don't let yourself get overwhelmed with work later in the season. A successful strategy I've used for years to avoid the problem of too many seedlings at planting time — and one that still allows you to indulge that urge to plant in winter — is to arrange with friends and neighbours for each to start different plants which you then share with each other later on. That way no one ends up with too many of one variety and you can still let yourself get a little carried away. One last point that is often overlooked by even the most experienced gardeners is to start your seeds according to the directions for cold treatments, pre-soaking them etc., and to start them at the proper time. If the instructions say to seed 8 weeks before planting out, don't start at 12 weeks unless you're prepared to deal with oversized, floppy transplants for an extra month inside. Sometimes patience is the hardest part of gardening.

Jade

good look. A table that will allow you to work around it comfortably would be ideal. Start looking at the structure of the plant in terms of its overall form and type of balance you would like to see in it. If you want a tree-type form, as opposed to the shrubby form of the larger ones, start to take out anything that droops below the horizontal first. Once that is done remove the horizontals or anything that is sprouting up from the bottom. You want to end up with one central trunk and all of the growth branching up from it to give you the tree form. Ideally you'll want to hold your pruning to 25% - 30% at a time to encourage new growth but still not put too much strain on the plant. In terms of the timing of the trim, it's not necessary to wait until the plant has flowered – and if the plant has yet to flower, go ahead and prune it now. Don't expect

quick results but in a few months you are going to see a fair amount of new growth. Do the cutting with a very sharp knife, and cut just above the nodes. The nice thing about the jades is that the nodes are so clearly marked along the stem. Cut as close to the node as you can. If you leave a little bit there, don't worry about it – the bit that is left in front of the node will dry within a few weeks and then fall off leaving the callused node exposed. It will put out new leaves at the remaining nodes.

More Jaded Advice

I have a jade tree that is about one metre high with a stem about 20 centimetres thick. It is in a 30-centimetre clay pot. Should I re-plant it and if so, do I need any special kind of soil?

You might save yourself a big job here. Jade plants have a very fine root system and they do not like to be overwatered. As long as the top of the plant is balanced and can stand up in that pot without any chance of tipping, it is in the right pot for its size. The best way to avoid overwatering with any jade plant is to keep it in a smaller pot. They don't mind that at all. You are providing all the moisture and nutrients the plant needs right in that small pot. When you think it needs water, wait another week and you are probably going to be closer to the right time. That is to say, make sure that they dry down thoroughly in between the waterings. If you do decide to re-pot, I would recommend you amend a standard soilless mix with about 30-40% sharp sand so that it drains very freely and readily. The jade never likes to stand in water. A south window would be ideal for this plant and I would suggest giving it a 1/4 turn every day so it gets a very even exposure to light. After a month or so, you'll probably find a little red margin developing around the edge of the leaf. It's not at all unattractive. If you can give it that degree of light exposure, this will be enough to get it to set bud and flower for you. It should set sometime between the beginning and the middle of October next year and start flowering about the middle of November to December. The blooms look like tiny white stars but if you put something behind them to get a bit of a contrast, you will see a light tinge of pink. These 2-4 centimetre clusters of tiny, faintly perfumed flowers really are quite spectacular and well worth the effort to cultivate.

Encouraging Orchids to Bloom

I received an orchid in November and it bloomed beautifully for maybe 6 weeks or more. Every bud on it bloomed. The flowers had 5 petals and were sort of a pinky-mauve. But they are all gone now and I am wondering what to do with it?

It was probably a Phalaenopsis Orchid. They do extremely well. They cross or hybridize quite readily as well and the number of varieties available are growing almost daily. If you look down the main flower spike you will see bumps or buds along the side of it. Come down to the one just below where it last flowered

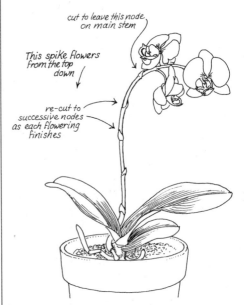

cut to leave this node on main stem

This spike flowers from the top down

re-cut to successive nodes as each flowering finishes

and trim the top off at that point but leave that last bud intact on the flower stem. Give it a reasonable amount of sun – behind sheer curtains would be ideal. The best way to water it is to soak it in another pot, allow it to drain and then put it back in its location. Do this every time it starts to dry down and it will be a very happy plant. It should come along and re-flower on those lateral stems within months.

New Growth on Overwintering Geraniums

Last year you mentioned it is possible to keep geraniums through the winter by digging them up and cleaning the roots, then hanging them in a cool, dark place and moistening the roots once a month. I have done that and now I notice after a few months that the geraniums have a little bit of new growth on them. Is that okay or should I take the new growth off?

It sounds like it's time to bring your geraniums out of the closet – that could be why you are getting the new growth. You'll want to pot them up and start them growing on. That new growth will certainly continue more vigorously as they come up into the light. Once they are potted, I would let them grow 4 or 5 sets of new leaves before you cut them back. When you do prune them, leave a couple of sets of leaves per new shoot on the original plants and that will encourage them to send out more new growth and get bushier. It will also give you fresh, very vigorous young cuttings that you can put into floral foam blocks and use to propagate other new plants.

Perpetuating the Dutchman

I have a very large Dutchman's Pipe in front of my house that is perhaps 75-100 years old and this year it had two seed pods. I brought the first pod inside about the first week of November and the other one I didn't find until I was putting up my Christmas lights in December. I had put the first one in the refrigerator and then when I discovered the other one, I took it out and saw that it was already opening, so now I have maybe a hundred seeds in total in a brown paper bag in my desk drawer. People have been asking me for slips off this vine for years and I have let them take some, but I tell them it won't work. What should I do with these seeds?

You are going to have to scarify these seeds a little first, assuming that their outer layer is still quite hard. If you threw them into a bag with a handful of sand and shook them around or put them into a tray with a piece of sand paper on the bottom and shook that tray back and forth for about five minutes so that they got scratched up, that would be easier than trying to rough up each seed individually with an emery board. Once you've done that, just sprinkle that mixture of sand and seed over some potting soil in a few pots and add a light dusting of soil over the top of that and keep it all moist. They probably had enough cold treatment from being outdoors so maintain the moisture in the soilless mix and put them on top of your refrigerator so they get a constant temperature through the soil. You will probably see germination in 6-8 weeks. If you get this going about the beginning of February, they should start to germinate quickly and that will get you to the end of March, at which point you would want to be pricking them off and planting the seedlings into individual pots or a maximum of 3 seedlings in a 3 inch pot. That will give them April and May to continue growing on before they get planted out near the end of May or in early June.

Hoping to Harvest Hops

I have been trying to germinate hops seeds. I bought a package last year and it says it takes 4-6 months for them to germinate. What would be the best method?

Hops need damp soil, warm conditions and a fairly constant soil temperature. The easiest thing to do is just sow them over the surface of the soil in a shallow pot or pan or even in a tray. Regular potting soil will work fine here or if you have some fine, well-rotted compost, a layer of that warmed up to room temperature and kept moist is an ideal media for sowing seeds. Keep things moist by putting a piece of clear plastic over the top of your pot or tray so that the evaporation slows down. You want to make sure the mixture stays moist but never soaking wet, so after an initial thorough watering, let things drain. You might even leave them uncovered for a few days to dry off the surface slightly and then put the plastic over top. Keep things reasonably moist on an ongoing basis. With hops, it is critical to keep a constant soil temperature in order to get that germination started. Placing the seeds on top of your refrigerator will provide constant heat – unless you have a very new refrigerator, in which case anywhere the temperature will remain steady would be fine. You should see the seeds start to develop in about 20 weeks.

Infested Orchid

I have a large bay window with about 20 or so orchids in it and I am having a real bad problem with scale. I have little dogs so I need to use natural methods to control it. I have tried treating them with some alcohol in the water but I am having no luck. Sometimes I have little black dots all over the bay window. Would that be scale?

No, it's probably not scale on your window. It may be fungus gnats that are coming out of the bark mixture that your orchids came in, in which case all you need to do to eliminate them is to allow the surface of that mixture to dry out thoroughly between waterings. If what you are seeing are elongated, black dots, then it could well be thrips. You would probably notice them on the orchid flowers as well. If you are not seeing them, just exhale directly on the flower. The warm, moist carbon dioxide in your breath will activate the thrips and you can actually see them start running about. Thrips damage the plants by piercing and sucking on the flowers, as well as being pollen eaters. On blue flowers, which they are particularly attracted to, you will see a whitening or a bleached-looking spot on the flower petal. If it is thrips, you can treat your orchids by spraying them with a very fine mist of a solution of 40-parts water to 1-part soap. Leave it on for 10 minutes and then flush the plant with clear water. If, on the other hand, you find it is scale, you can put some alcohol on a cotton swab and rub it on the individual insects. You have to put a little pressure on so that you are actually lifting that oyster shell scale a little and allowing the alcohol to get in underneath. You may well be killing the insects, but the scales won't fall off unless you brush or wipe them off. The alternative is to make the 40:1 mixture of water and soap and add 8-parts rubbing alcohol. Use a soft-bristled toothbrush and lightly brush that mixture onto the plant wherever you see scales. The brushing action actually shifts the scale enough to allow the mixture to penetrate in underneath and kill the insect. About 10 minutes after that application, rinse the plant thoroughly, bottom to top and back down again, with clear, room temperature water. This will avoid any damage to the plant that might be caused by the soap and alcohol mixture.

Cultivating Clivia

I have a clivia that has produced a big shoot with a large seed pod on it. It's been there for about 6 months and I have been wondering how I might propagate it.

You need to make sure that the pod is fully ripened and normally 6 months is more than enough time. The outside fleshy covering will turn a deep red colour when it reaches that stage. Once that happens you soak the seeds in room temperature water for 24 hours to help soften up the seed coat. Next, plant each seed to about its own depth in a loose soilless potting mix and keep it damp and well lit. You want a temperature in the range of about 22° celsius. Placing the pot on top of a fridge would keep that temperature quite nicely, assuming it is not a new fridge. Germination takes about 30 days. It is critical to keep that soil mix moist, so you may want to lay a plastic bag or plastic wrap over the pot. If there gets to be too much condensation, just lift it off once in a while. As soon as you see any germination starting, remove the plastic completely so that the soil doesn't stay constantly wet and then water as required. If you plant more than one seed per pot, separate the seedlings carefully once you see substantial root development.

Plant the individual seedlings into a 2, 3, or 4-inch pot and re-pot them into a larger size only after they have become slightly root bound.

Fuchsia from Seed

Last year a friend and I tried to grow fuchsias from seed but we were only partially successful. We potted them on the surface under grow lights. Most of the seeds germinated quite nicely and then we treated the soil for damp off. The plants got as far as their primary leaves and then just stayed that way for 3 or 4 weeks until most of them died off and we were left with only 2 plants. We thought we would like to try again. Have you any advice?

You have done everything right except for the first treatment for damping off. You can't stop damping off by applying a prophylactic or preventative treatment, so the one that you did was essentially wasted. I imagine when it appeared you probably thought it had already been treated so there was no point in treating it again. You are going to have to watch the watering with them once they start growing on and make sure that the surface is drying out. One way to help that process is to use fewer seeds in a pot or use a larger pot and sprinkle the seed a bit further apart.

Individual plants that get affected will be easier to prick off but you will also have more air circulation around them as they are growing on. Once they have germinated don't hesitate to help increase the air circulation by putting a small fan about 10 feet away to blow some air over the plants. Certainly the lighting from the grow lights is going to be helpful once they get going and 20° celsius temperature is ideal for what you want to do. If you are using fluorescent grow lights, there is little or no heat buildup from the tubes so keep your seedlings within 3-5 centimetres of the light. This gives them the ideal light intensity level. The light should be on for a 16-hour period every day. If you get problems with damping off, remove the affected seedlings immediately and apply the treatment. Remember to treat the soil, not the seedlings! You can certainly avoid the problem by spacing things out a little bit more and treating as it appears. And don't give up on them too soon. Even if they seem to stay at the same stage for 3 or 4 weeks, that is not a problem. They are establishing root systems during that time and that is critical to their success. If you can up the lighting after a week or two you will usually get more vigorous growth coming along as well.

Re-potting an Elephant's Foot

I have had a beaucarnea recurvata for about 20 years. It was probably about 2 inches in diameter and I have it now in the traditional plastic pot. The pot is about 9 inches across and the tuber only has an inch of soil all around but a year ago it sent out a new centre shoot which has grown about a foot. It is really quite amazing and I am wondering what kind of a pot I should move it into?

You can see why the name "Elephant's Foot" applies to this one. On the other hand, with that floppy head, "Ponytail" is not an uncommon name either. Transplanting this is something you don't want to have to do too often so I would recommend going up from a 9-inch plastic pot to a 12-inch clay pot. You want it at the same depth as it currently is planted in the old pot but to make sure you have enough watering space, bring the soil up no higher than the bottom of the rim at the top of the pot. That will allow you to give it a good quantity of water and let it soak down slowly into the soil without drowning the roots. Also be sure when you are taking your plant out of its old pot to tease the roots. Loosen up and let some of the roots out around the edges. You can get quite a length of root growing even in a pot that size. I had a blue pine in a 5-inch pot and when I teased the roots out that were wrapped around the bottom of the pot, they were over a foot long. Your plant had obviously been in that original pot for quite a while and was purposely put in that small a pot so that it could be sold and transported more easily. The critical thing now is to tease out that established root system so it can spread out through the new soil in that larger pot. Once you have it transplanted, give it a thorough watering, but make sure it dries down. The beaucarnea does not want to sit soaking wet all the time. That large elephant foot base on it is actually an excellent storage mechanism for holding a lot of moisture. You will avoid getting into any root rot problems if you water less frequently and let the plant's natural reservoir take care of the rest.

Cutting Cactus Down to Size

I have a very large cactus that is about 6 feet tall. It is one that has the arms that come out and it keeps having little arms that come out after that. It has gotten to be so big and so heavy that moving it now in the spring and fall is getting to be impossible.

Can I prune this? If not, some botanical garden is going to have a very nice donation.

Actually yes, you can prune. But first make sure that it is, in fact, a cactus that you have and not a euphorbia. There is a euphorbia that looks very much like a cactus with that typical arm shape, but the difference is that it does get small leaves that drop off. If yours has only small arms and no leaves, then it is very likely the cactus. You can prune it and it is just a matter of determining how high you want it to be coming up at the centre stem. You'll need a sharp knife and some good thick leather gloves because they do fight back. Decide what sort of size and form you want it to have before you cut and then trim the branches back. Taking up to 2 feet off the top and 6-12 inches off the sides, depending on the width now, would be about the maximum trim. Try to cut just above the aureole where the spikes or spines are coming out. When you are cutting back the arms, cut back to the joint and leave it exposed to the air for a couple of weeks. How far you trim it back is really going to depend upon the existing structure of the cactus and what the framework looks like. You don't want something that is obviously lopsided or asymmetrical so trim it back to leave a nice basic shape. Once you're satisfied, put it back in full sun and it should come along nicely.

Orchid Drowning

A friend was recently hospitalized and may be there for a long time. I offered to look after an orchid she told me was just ready to bloom. When I picked it up, I found the person looking after the plants had been over-zealous and the orchid was sitting in 2 inches of water. The stem with the blooms was completely brown and had a couple of nodes but there was no sign of anything that looked like it might flower. I cut that stem off. The plant is left with two fairly large green leaves that are quite soft and ridged. I took it out of the pot to replant it today and there are some roots – sort of a grey colour but reasonably firm. I cut away any that were soft and flabby. As well, the branch that would have bloomed has a couple of green nodes. I haven't told my friend of the disaster and hope to get the orchid on its way to a new life, but it looks pretty gloomy at this point. Can you suggest what I might do to encourage its survival?

Honesty is probably the best policy here. Let your friend know about the condition of the orchid when you picked it up. You don't have to make this all bad news however, since you can also tell her about the excellent care and close attention that you are giving her treasured plant. The over-watering was a serious problem only because the orchid was allowed to stand in water for too long. By your description of the plant, I assume it is a phalaenopsis or Moth Orchid. The grey colour of the roots is natural and in fact, when they are moistened, you can see the green colour of the chlorophyll beneath the roots' surface. These roots are normally exposed to both light and air and that grey exterior coloration protects the chlorophyll from sun burning, especially when the plant is dry. Leave the large healthy green leaves on the plant since it needs them in order to photosynthesize and produce the food energy required to stabilize the plant and start it growing again. The same applies to any green stems. The nodes you're noticing on the flowering stem are probably secondary flower stems which should bloom again after the plant re-establishes itself. Don't even think about feeding the orchid for another 2 months. Nobody feels like eating much when they are sick, plants included. Once the plant begins to re-establish, you can apply an organic, soluble, fish emulsion type fertilizer at 1/2 the manufacturer's recommended rate of application with every fifth or sixth watering. Put the orchid in a well-drained media such as unmilled Sphagnum peat moss, bark chips or even used wine corks cut into pieces. Soak the mixture thoroughly every time you water but ensure that it drains completely after soaking and is allowed to dry down, but not dry out, between each watering. Orchids much prefer rainwater or melted snow to most tap water, so if you can take the extra trouble to collect some it would be worthwhile. Just be sure to allow the water to reach room temperature before plunging the orchid into it for soaking. Hopefully, both recoveries will be completely successful.

Office Fern Dilemma

I keep buying these Boston ferns for my office and they keep dying on me. Somebody said you have to keep it wet, somebody else said you have to let it dry out and I don't exactly know what to do short of buying an artificial one. I'm facing east and the blinds are usually closed. Why can't I keep my Boston ferns alive?

They are all probably drying out in the office conditions. When you water it, soak it thoroughly. Make sure it's getting completely saturated, even if it means sitting it in a pail of water for a 1/2 hour. Let it dry down after that but don't let it dry out completely between each watering. Make sure it is not in the way of the office traffic where people will be brushing by it or bumping into it all the time, nor where there is air blowing on it constantly from a radiator or open door. Keep it away from the airflow. You do have an eastern facing window, so open the Venetian blinds and allow a little bit more light in as well. Ferns should be happy with that morning light and the indirect sunlight they get later in the day, and with proper moisture, they should flourish much better.

Forced Tulips with Freezer Burn

I have been trying to grow tulips on my second-floor balcony. I can root bulbs in pots but the trouble starts after that. First, I tried placing the pots in the freezer, but the bulbs turned to mush. I tried placing pots in the fridge or in a garbage can on my balcony containing potting soil and covered with leaves, but that also yielded fairly unimpressive results. What exactly do I need to do to produce the same beautiful, strong blooms that appear from bulbs planted in a yard?

The freezer will generate too severe a temperature for your

potted bulbs. In outdoor conditions, tulip bulbs are normally planted about 8 inches below the surface. This means that the cooling down and eventual freezing happens over a long period of time. The ambient heat lower down in the soil slows the process. If you put on heavy mulch, total freezing might never occur. In your freezer, the temperature of your bulbs drops rapidly from room temperature to well below freezing in a matter of hours. The result is burst cell walls and mushy, dead tulip bulbs. Unfortunately, placing the pots in a garbage can on the balcony with potting soil and leaves won't work well either, although this was a very inventive idea. A slightly slower rate of cooling happens in this case but it still allows a very deep penetration of the cold. The potential of getting into freeze-thaw cycles on warm winter days would make life very tough indeed for your bulbs. Placing the pots in a refrigerator is really your best bet, however you have to avoid having fruits in the same fridge as your bulbs. Ripening fruits give off ethylene gas that impedes or causes improper bulb development and aborted flowers. If your bulbs have to share airspace with fruit, you can overcome this problem by sealing your pots in plastic bags while they are in the fridge. Give your earlier flowering tulips 14 weeks in the cold, while later flowering bulbs will be happier with 16 weeks. Don't worry if you see the foliage start to grow in the fridge. Your best results will still be achieved if you respect that prescribed cold period. When you remove the pots, put them into a cool room, about 15° C being ideal, with indirect light for a week or so and then move them out into full sun and slightly warmer temperatures. The cooler the room, the longer the flowers will last. You can water as required to keep the soil constantly moist, but never let the pots stand in water. Don't try to save these bulbs for re-forcing. They can, however, go into a garden for naturalizing although it may take a year or two before they flower well again.

Hydroponic Amaryllis

I am growing an amaryllis hydroponically. At the moment it has two beautiful flowering stems on it, one that is in full bloom and the other with a bud coming up between two little leaves. I would like to be able to keep this bulb going and maybe replant it next year. Should I apply some liquid fertilizer now?

No, now is not the time to fertilize. Wait until the flowering has finished. If you start feeding it now, you will accelerate growth and the flowers will finish off much more quickly, so hold off on the fertilizer and just enjoy the blooms. If you want to prolong their life you can trim off the yellow anthers at the tip of the stamens so the flowers cannot get pollinated. That will make them last longer and you will avoid having any pollen staining on the flower petals. Once the flowers are finished, remove them, cut the stem back to an inch or two, and let the plant grow on. If you want it flowering for next Christmas, follow the usual routine, making sure it starts drying back by the beginning of August. Once it has dried back, cut off the dead foliage and let it sit in the sun for at least a morning and preferably a

day, just to dry off the neck, and then put it into a cool, dark location like a storage cupboard. The critical thing with growing amaryllis hydrponically is to make sure that the roots are going down to the water they want, as opposed to the water touching the base of that bulb. They rot easily and do not like to be soaking wet or in direct contact with water for any period of time. That being said, they will grow nicely in pebbles as long you have enough to support the bulb and the flower on the top. Make sure to keep the water level low at the bottom of the pebbles so the roots have to grow down to get to the moisture. If at some point you want to transfer this plant to a pot with soil, you can go ahead and do that without any problem at all.

FEBRUARY

A. KARSTAD

Perpetual Christmas

It is now mid February and I still have my Christmas tree. It's a 6-foot Balsam that we bought about a week before Christmas. It drinks about a litre and a half of water every day and seems to be quite happy. It's started to produce buds and I just can't bring myself to throw it out while it seems so alive. If I were to feed it with 10-60-10, would it root up so I could plant it in the spring?

Unfortunately, it is very unlikely it would root up no matter what you did. It would be so rare for the stump of a tree that size to callus over sufficiently to allow roots to develop. Obviously, it is in very good condition. I suspect it was fairly freshly cut before you purchased it and I would guess right away that you gave it a fresh cut before putting it in the water as well. That combination, along with keeping the water up, has brought it out of dormancy. It must be standing in a good sunny situation for this to work. Now, with the higher light levels of February, the tree has begun to expend the energy it had stored through the fall of last year to push out the new buds. It senses from the increase in light that the conditions are right – but it will only be able to go so far in sustaining those buds and itself. Eventually it will just give up. You can only trick the system so far – without a root base the tree cannot provide itself with all the nutrients it is going to need. Its metabolism must maintain a normal rate to sustain growth. Even if you were to add a 10-60-10 fertilizer, it would still need that callusing at the base of the trunk and a root system would have to start to develop – and that's just too much to expect at this point. With about 6 feet of height the base of this tree has got a very large surface area to callus over and normally they just cannot manage it. Generally, if Christmas trees are not freshly cut their pores start to clog up very quickly after they are put into water. Being fresh cut and put immediately into water, the clogging process is taking a lot longer with your tree and the fact that you are using treated city water, where the algae and microbes in the water are also reduced, means the capillaries aren't plugging up very quickly. At some point however, that will start to happen and eventually the tree will just lose its capacity to take up moisture. It's really too bad because wouldn't it be wonderful if we could replant all those millions of trees that are cut for the holidays every year?

Braiding Fuchsia

Somewhere I came across a fuchsia standard and I believe it was braided. I have finally found a white fuchsia, called Wedding Bells I believe, that I feel is worth encouraging but the stem seems very brittle to me. Is this a problem? How would I create a braided stem with this one?

There are a couple of things you can do with your fuchsia. The first is to take the existing plant and start trimming off the lower lateral branches to encourage upward growth and have a long stem develop. If the top has already been pinched, this is a little harder to accomplish but not impossible. Find an upright stem near the top of the plant that is growing straight. Stake it to keep it growing that way and then trim off the sides. Now if you want to have a braided stem, the process is a bit different. The plus in braiding is that you are getting a stronger, more rigid stem more quickly. To do that you would first have to take a number of cuttings. I would say to start with you would want at least an 8-10 centimetre or 3-4 inch cutting because you are going to have a couple of nodes beneath the soil surface. If you root them up in floral foam, you are going to want to put a minimum 3/4 inch of the cutting down into the foam. When these have rooted up, pick the strongest 3 and plant them tight in together in the same pot. When they get to be 6 or 8 inches tall, you start to braid them. Once you've got a few braids in, just tie them off loosely and leave the 3 tips to grow on. As they come along further and get long enough to bend a bit more, put a few more braids in. Keep this process up and when the stem gets to be a foot high or so, put a stake in there for sup-

port. Continue to develop it this way and when it gets up around the height that you want, that is to say, when you have braided up 2, or maybe even 3 feet of the stem, you can pinch off the tips to force some lateral growth and that will produce your crown. As the individual stems continue to grow and increase in diameter, they will start to self-graft or fuse together, eventually appearing as one stem.

Bulb Bonanza

I have a problem. Here it is only February and last night I was given a whole lot of tulip bulbs and chinodoxia that had been stored in a friend's garage, 180 in total. What is the best way to get these in the ground and have them bloom and produce this year?

I wouldn't be putting them outside quite yet. Six inch pots will work fine for the tulips. Put an inch or 2 of soil in the bottom, place the bulbs in and fill in with soil on top to about an inch below the top of the pot; 5 or 6 bulbs per pot should work quite nicely. Squeeze the bulbs gently as you are planting them. You may find that some of them go mushy as they warm up – discard them. After you plant, soak the pots thoroughly and put them into a cool, dark location. A temperature just above freezing is ideal so putting them back in a garage, if possible, would work well here. They are still going to need 8-10 weeks of cold at this point in order to develop a root system and start coming along. With your chinodoxia, a smaller pot would be fine but if you are using a 6-inch pot, don't plant them too deeply. Fill half the pot with soil, plant your bulbs and put an inch or inch and a half of soil over top. They'll need the same treatment though. Soak them and put them into a cool dark location. Even if the ground is workable in your area at this point, don't put them into the ground. If you do, they are not going to have the warmth that they need to develop the root system required to have any chance of flowering this year. If they go into a wet soil and stay damp and cold, some may just end up rotting, so it's much safer to do them up in pots and let them start coming along there. You can plant them out into the garden either after they have flowered or after all danger of frost has passed. When you do, plant the tulips so that the top of the bulb is about 25-30 centimetres or approximately 8-10 inches below the surface of the soil. The chinodoxia only need 10-15 centimetres or 4-6 inches of soil over top. You can, in fact, plant them out earlier, while there is still the

danger of frost, but only if you have hardened them off slowly by gradually introducing them to increasingly colder temperatures over a period of 2-4 weeks. Obviously they would be safer going out later. After they have flowered, plant them out if you haven't done so already, and let them die down on location in the garden. Leave them there and they will naturalize and come back the next year with no problem.

Treatment of Tillandsia

I have several tillandsia plants and I would like to find out how to make them flower. Currently they are sitting in holes that my husband drilled in some branches that broke off our maple tree. I stuffed the holes they are in with Spanish moss and put them in a south-facing window and I spray them once a week. I have heard that they are supposed to flower but mine aren't showing any signs of doing that. Is there anything I should be doing to encourage them?

A south-facing window is ideal. Tillandsias are in the bromeliacea family and what you probably have is a T. *cyancea*. Since they have little or no roots and absorb most of the moisture and food they need through their leaves, they're ideal for your log. You may have to pick up the spraying. Start with twice a week, at evenly spaced intervals. If that doesn't work, go to 5 times over a week and you should get improved results. Just give a light misting to get to the drip point with all of the foliage and that increase in moisture may be sufficient to encourage them along. Give them a few months to see if you are getting any results. If there are no results by then, what you may want to do is add in some soluble fertilizer to your water at 1/2 the recommended rate. Use a fertilizer with a low first number so you are not giving the plants too much nitrogen. Give them a fertilized spray with that followed by a couple of clear water sprays, and then one more fertilizer spray at a maximum. This will give them a little more nutrient and see what happens with the growth spurt. It likely won't get to that point. I think if you increase the frequency of the misting, that should induce the flowering on its own. Like their bromeliad cousins, which include the Pineapple, they only flower once, then put out offsets, and the parent then dies.

Geranium Growing Grief

I am attempting to grow geraniums from cuttings for the second year. Last year I was successful at it having them in a west-facing window after I took cuttings in mid February. When I put them out in mid May they did fine but didn't really flower profusely until about mid July. So this year I started in January – took the cuttings and let them dry for about 12 hours, then brushed rooting hormone on them and stuck them into the pots. I have them under grow lights but I am losing quite a few plants. The leaves have turned brown and died off and the stems themselves have just dried up. Others have done alright although I have taken off a lot of the leaves. Have you any idea why this might be happening?

Leaves coming off is not a big problem but something is going drastically wrong with them drying up like that. With the cuttings in individual pots it is a little hard to measure their progress. Personally, I like to start them in floral foam or in vermiculite where you can actually take them out to see what is happening and pot them up once you know that roots are coming along. With pots you have to make sure your soil mix holds sufficient moisture to encourage the rooting but doesn't stay waterlogged or you will get rotting. If you want to try again with these cuttings, re-slice at a slight angle through a node or just below a node on the stem, dip it into the rooting hormone and stick your cutting into a 1 inch cube of floral foam. You don't have to allow them to dry off, although I know some people prefer to do so – it does work equally well if you bypass that step. To make the cubes, just slice a piece about an inch thick off the end of a brick of floral foam and then cut that strip into 1 inch cubes. Soak these thoroughly, let them drain and then re-soak them. Room temperature water is fine. With a small sharp knife, pierce the cube at a slight angle through the centre and then stick the cutting about 3/4 of the way into the cube. Once it is in there, don't handle it by the cutting, handle it by the foam cube. Sit the cuttings in something like a shallow pan and keep the water about half way up the cubes at all times. When the roots start growing out through the cube and get to be about an inch or so long, pot them up into 4-inch plastic pots with your regular potting mixture. Give them a thorough soaking and watch them carefully. The biggest challenge with the geranium cuttings is often black leg, or they start to rot and get stem problems, but this seems to be virtually eliminated if you're using the floral foam. Just trim the top edge off the foam when you plant the cuttings and make sure the foam is covered with soil so you don't have it wicking moisture away from the roots at that critical intersection at the base of the stem.

Orchid Angst

There must be something wrong with my Phalaenopsis Orchid. I received it 2 years ago when it was in full bloom. When it finished blooming, I cut the stem right back to ground level and waited for it to grow a new one, but that has never happened. It grows lots of new leaves and lots of roots. In fact, some of the roots are about 10 inches long and are standing straight up. It makes the plant look very odd. At first the roots used to bend back down into the pot with the bark chips but not any more. I have the pot sitting above a tray of water in a south facing window where it gets diffused light. What am I doing wrong?

Phalaenopsis is from the Greek words Phalaina, or Moth, and Opsis, which means appearance or resemblance. Hence the common name "Moth Orchid" which most aptly applies to the white flowered species. This genus of orchid has about 50 species in tropical Asia. It is distributed from India south-east to the Philippines, with one species native to northern Australia. They are epiphytic, meaning they grow mainly on other plants, but are not parasites since they get no sustenance from their host tree or shrub. The advantage this gives them is to get a perch closer to the sunlight or above the competition from the other plants on the forest floor. Others may be lithophytes and grow on cliffs or rock faces instead of on other plants but the cliffs provide them with the same advantage of position and support. The phalaenopsis, not naturally being a plant that grows in soil, has very specialized roots which are often completely exposed to the air and enclosed in layers of absorptive cells called the velamen. This covering acts like a sponge, absorbing moisture and dissolved nutrients from the rain, dew and even the clouds in the high jungle canopy. You will notice that when the velamen is moist the roots show through and you can see that they are green. They are able to photosynthesize just like the leaves do. All of this background tells us a lot about what these plants need to be successful. All species of phalaenopsis grow well in pots or slatted baskets with a loose, well-drained, bark-based potting mix, or mounted on a slab of bark or natural cork. They do, however, require humid conditions, which you are providing via the tray of water, and prefer the diffused light that you describe. Good air circulation

around the plants is also essential as is a winter temperature of at least 15-18° celsius. They should be watered liberally throughout the year but fed only while they're in active growth and producing new leaves. Liquid or soluble fertilizer is best since it can be applied when you water, but use it at half the manufacturer's recommended rate of application for houseplants since orchids grow slowly. Since you're describing rapid and vigorous leaf and root growth, I suspect that you're feeding too often and that your fertilizer contains too much nitrogen. The result of an overabundance of nitrogen – the nitrogen content being indicated by the first of the three numbers on the fertilizer package – is the production of lots of lush, deep green foliage, at the expense of flower production. I suggest you feed it only during active growth, which is usually in spring when the light levels increase, and try a fertilizer with less nitrogen such as a 10-10-30. It is too bad that you removed the flower stem completely when the blooms finished. Often by cutting the stem back just as far as the next node down from the flower, you can have your phalaenopsis bloom again from the same stem. Having said that, with all the fertilizer I suspect this one has received, I suggest that you don't feed it again until it has re-flowered.

Potted Plants Used as Litter Box

My cat seems to prefer using the soil in my potted plants to his litter box. Have you any ideas about how to convince him to stop doing this?

The first line of attack is usually the application of a light dusting of baking soda to the soil surface to neutralize both the urine, which is acidic, and the smell which tends to bring the cat back to re-use the same spot. I also suggest using a mulch around the plant to cover the soil and make digging difficult or impossible. This would mean using something heavy enough, like marbles or pebbles. The other option is to place wire mesh or chicken wire over the surface. I've also had a couple of interesting alternatives suggested by others over the years that are worth sharing. The first is to place a layer of pine cones on the soil, which is a variation of the mulch idea and is aesthetically quite pleasing – certainly prettier than chicken wire or screening. The second novel idea was to place fresh orange peels around the base of the plant. Apparently cats hate the orange smell. By replacing the peels every few days to keep the orange scent fresh, cats will eventu-

ally decide the plant is no longer of interest. This one supposedly works with furniture as well, which could be especially helpful when training kittens, although you would certainly not want to put the orange directly onto the furniture. With any luck the litter box will soon start to appeal to your cat once again.

Cultivating Indoor Tomatoes

I have an Early Girl tomato plant about 2 feet tall that I am trying to grow in the house. It is in black earth with a couple fertilizing sticks and placed in a north-westerly window. It had a little withering on the lower leaves so I've removed them and just recently the upper leaves are starting to fold in a little bit. Can a tomato plant grown in a house environment produce tomatoes? If so, can you give me some tips on helping it along and what is the best way to start off a nourished tomato seed in an indoor environment.

The best way to start plants from seed next spring is to put some well-rotted compost into plastic bags this fall and store these in a garage or anywhere that you can get at them in the winter. When you are ready to plant, bring the compost in, warm it up to room temperature, and germinate your seeds in that. They will be very happy. They are going to grow nicely and you won't have to worry about feeding. With respect to your current Early Girl plant, I would suggest that you remove those fertilizer sticks. A south or a west window would be ideal – the north-west window is not likely to give it suf-ficient light to produce a flower. If it does flower for you, it is going to stretch out a fair amount to do so, so be prepared to support it. Either way, when it flowers, you are going to have to actually pollinate from flower to flower using a feather or cotton swab to mimic the cross-fertilization that would normally be done by insects or breezes outside. You

What is a Node?

A node is any place on the plant where a leaf joins the stem, where one stem joins onto the next branch or onto the main branch or trunk, or where there is an offshoot. Whenever you are required to cut off a plant for any reason, you will want to cut just in front of the node. There are two reasons why that is the ideal spot to cut. The first is that this is where the callous tissue will be formed and it will heal itself only at that point. The second is that it is also the point where the dormant buds form, so any new growth will initiate from there as well.

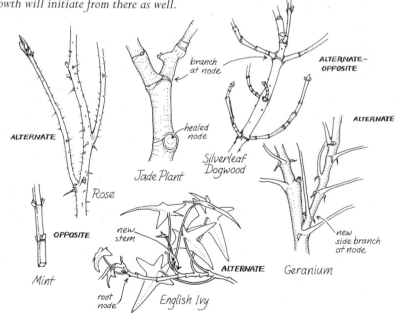

should be able to get your tomatoes to fruit – but be prepared for the fact that they won't taste like the greenhouse tomatoes grown in southern Ontario where the higher light levels and perfect temperature control produces a very tasty indoor fruit.

Rotting Lemons

I have 2 dwarf lemon trees that give me about 5 lemons every year. This year one of them has come up with a lemon that is brown at both ends and sort of looks as if it has no peel on it. It's the right size and shape but just very odd looking. What would cause that?

I suspect it is over-watering or perhaps it stayed waterlogged too long and didn't have full sun. When I have seen them go that way it is normally a moisture issue. We had a similar case in the greenhouse with one of the lemon trees a number of years back. We didn't realize that one of the overhead metal supports happened to be dripping on this plant and in fact, the lemons on the side with that excess moisture started browning at the tips on both ends and rotting. So do watch the watering. Don't mist or spray over the foliage and if you need to clean dust off the foliage, do it earlier in the day so that the

plant dries completely by the middle of the afternoon and doesn't stay wet going into the evening.

Tulip Bonanza

I planted a group of 18 tulip bulbs 6 years ago and have always let the leaves die back until I could pull them out without much resistance. Suddenly last summer, I had 3 times the number of tulips that I had planted. These tulips are thick and at least 2 feet tall or more. Did the seeds "take" all of a sudden or are there more flowers growing out of the bulb itself?

Oh, the joys of spring flowering bulbs, especially when we're thinking about them in the cold grip of a Canadian winter. What you're witnessing is tulip bulb multiplication which is accomplished by division. More simply put, each bulb is going through its natural reproductive cycle. As the bulb grows and develops, it produces small copies of itself within the layers of its body. Think of an onion. Each year, these new little bulbs continue to mature within the tunic of that parent bulb. The final stage of this natural vegetative reproduction cycle is when the offset, which is the horticultural term for these, reach the outer edge of the parent bulb and start growing on their own. They produce their own roots, foliage, and eventually, flowers. So the simplest explanation for your new bounty is that your bulbs have now produced offspring. I suggest that after allowing your tulips to die back this year as you normally do, you lift out and separate the new clumps. Re-plant the individual bulbs right away but give more space to allow sufficient growing room for each new plant. Once they come up, treat them as you would your other mature plants. A technique I use for removing the foliage once it has died back is to push down on the base of the stem before I try to pull it out. This breaks the stem off right at the bulb and avoids the disturbance that can be caused if the stem isn't quite ready to let go easily.

Of All the Gall

My daughter has a lovely ficus tree that lives outside in summer and comes in for the winter. Two years ago it developed a brownish growth around one of the stems. Now there are 4 of them, each about 2 inches in diameter. Two are quite high up on the stems; the other two are close to the soil and on larger branches. The tree is 5 feet tall and looks healthy, other than the usual drop of a few leaves during winter. Can you tell me what these growths are and how we should treat them?

These galls could be forming due to disease or insect infestation. If the ficus is doing well, there really isn't a problem other than aesthetics, so you could just leave them and do nothing. If you are anxious to remove them, you can start with the smaller affected branches in the crown and cut them off 2-5 centimetres or 1-2 inches below the gall. Before you cut, make sure that you place something underneath to catch any drips and avoid the sticky sap staining your upholstery or carpets. If you apply some dry peat moss to the wound it will absorb the sap and stop the bleeding more quickly. Assuming that you want to keep the larger branches, there is no need to remove them unless more growths appear further up in the crown, in which case you may want to cut off those larger affected branches as well.

MARCH

Amaryllis Offspring

My 6-year-old amaryllis has always given me 2 spikes with 6 trumpets and now it has also decided to sprout a bulb on the side. The bulb is about an inch in diameter and what I want to know is how I should separate it, and when, and once I have, when do I put them outside for the summer?

Ideally you'll let that offspring go through the summer with the parent bulb and then into dormancy in the fall. Allow the plant to dry down. Once it has done that, it is usually going to take at least 2, and maybe 3 months be-

fore you will get any regeneration on it. While it is in that dormant period, or just before you are ready to take it out again, take off that second bulb. While the plant is still dry, tease the roots apart, separate the bulbs and put the offspring into its own pot. That pot should be only about one inch larger than the "baby" bulb itself. Replant the larger "parent" bulb in its original pot and leave it dry and dark until it starts to show a flower bud. Once that appears, bring it up into the light and water only as required. Now back to the "baby". The nice thing about the young amaryllis bulbs is that

33

they are not going to flower right off so they don't need to go through the dormancy cycle. You can actually size them up more quickly by allowing them to grow year round in a sunny window. The next season, when you bring that young plant in at the end of the summer, it goes straight into that window rather than into a cupboard or closet to encourage dormancy. Water the young plant only as needed, making sure it is using all the moisture that is there before re-watering, and just keep it growing on. Feed the young bulb with a 1/3-1/2 strength soluble fertilizer every fourth or fifth watering year round. It will normally take 3 or 4 years of growing on this way before it produces a flower, so after the third or fourth summer outside, force it into dormancy as you are now doing with its "mother". As soon as the flower bud appears, bring it into the light and carry on with it as you would with any other mature plant.

Over-stimulated Begonias

I planted my Tuberous Begonias up in pots a while ago and they were doing famously. Subsequent to that, I read an article that said you should soak the tubers in a fertilizer before you plant them so I lifted them up again and soaked them in 15-30-15 overnight. By morning, they had absorbed all of the fertilizer and moisture and I replanted them. Two days later, all of the shoots and new growth fell off. Have I killed them or will they come back?

I hope they will come back, however I would be a little concerned about soaking them in water. This is not a technique I'm familiar with. I assume the fertilizer is meant to accelerate growth in the tuber prior to any root system or shoots developing. The concentration of the fertilizer may have been too much for the tuber but you may find that some dormant buds had not yet opened and you may still get some growth coming along. My recommendation would be to keep the soil moist but not wet because you now run the risk of the tuber starting to rot. Let it dry down somewhat on the surface. You are still going to have moisture below and the tuber will be capable of drawing the moisture from the soil as required and that will also help to encourage the root system back out. I have never heard of soaking with a fertilizer in that manner. Not to say that it would not work, but I believe the concentration may have been a problem here and in fact, drew moisture out of the roots and shoots that were already growing. Do not give up on them. It may just take a while for something to show up. In the meantime it is critical that they do not sit in soggy conditions, so no more water until they start showing growth again.

Stunted Leaves on African Violets

All of my African Violets have developed stunted leaves. Every single one of the 15 or more that I own are becoming crinkled and small and I can't figure it out. I don't see any bugs. I haven't done anything different than what I have done for years with them and now all of them are developing this problem. Have you any idea what it might be?

You have an infestation of cyclamen mites and they are tough to get rid of. They prefer cyclamen and they love African Violets, but they shouldn't affect any other plants you might have. The mites attack the crown – that crinkling and very hard stem and foliage is the reaction within the plant to the mites' feeding. You can get a measure of control with a soap and water treatment but predators would be more successful. Sourcing predators can be a little difficult but check your local garden centre or green house operation. If they can get you some mite predators, specifically for cyclamen mites, that would be the most effective approach. With a

hairy leaf like that, it is hard to get any penetration with the soap and water treatment. The African Violets like a bit dryer foliage and the mites certainly enjoy that as well. Treating them means wetting that foliage so you have got to make sure that you do it in the morning and that they dry out thoroughly afterwards. Spraying the plants is the most effective way. Use the 40-to-1 soap and water solution, leave them for at least 15 minutes or so coated with a good quantity of the solution and then rinse off with room temperature water. You are going to have to repeat that 3 times over a 10 day period. They'll be a little wilted after the fact, but they should pick up again. The alternative is a diazanon treatment, but that is really a heavy duty pesticide that you definitely don't want have in your home. Getting a predator insect to eat the cyclamen mites is much preferable – and don't worry about introducing the predators into your house because they are only going to last as long as there is a supply of mites. They will bring things into a balance and then disappear.

Caring for False Aralia

My favourite plant is a False Aralia and I desperately need some pointers on how to keep it. This is about my fifth one. I try and try but they always end up losing their leaves from the bottom up. I have my latest in a north window and it is about 18 inches tall but now it, too, is starting to drop leaves. I don't know what I am doing wrong.

Its real name, *Dizygotheca elegantissima*, is quite a mouthful! These plants don't like to be overwatered, so when you water them, water them thoroughly but make sure that they are drying down each time. That is critical or they will start to drop those lower leaves. The light level in a north window is also a bit dicey for them. If you can get them into an east window, that would be helpful. If you have a south or a west window, keep them a foot or so back or behind sheer curtains and that would be ideal as well. They can be in the full light in an east window without any problem at all. As the plants age, they will eventually drop those very fine serrated leaves and produce a wider, longer and rounded edge leaf. It's not quite as attractive as the younger leaves but still has the same palmate shape and certainly is an attractive green. This usually happens with aging and wouldn't show up until the plant is getting to be 3 or 4 feet high and growing on quite vigorously. At that point, you normally would have a combination of young deeply indented serrated leaves and these larger leaves towards the bottom. But the dropping wouldn't be ongoing. What you are describing here indicates two things: low light and too much moisture. Also keep in mind that a minimum temperature of about 60° fahrenheit or 15° celsius is essential.

How to get Bromeliad Blooming

My dear friend has had four generations of a Bromeliad plant and each one continues to propagate, however she has never had any flowers after the first one. Is there something she can do?

Yes, get it into full sun. All the light that you can give it is what will be necessary to bring it along to flower. The offsets come after the flowering and they don't generally produce until there has been flowering or the plant has become particularly pot bound, which must be the case here. Usually it is triggered only by the flowering. The flower comes along, then the pup or offset plant is produced. You can take those offsets and plant them. The parent plant most often will continue growing and give you more off- · sets, but it will not flower a second time. In order to have it flower successfully, you must keep that cup formed in the centre of the leaves filled with water. Other than that, full sun is what is required. If you are fertilizing, be careful not to give it too much nitrogen. A weak solution 1/2 -1/3 of the recommended strength would do. Fish emulsion fertilizers work well here but any of the solubles with a lower first, and higher second and third number will do.

Lotus Litany

A while ago I was given some advice on how to germinate and transplant lotus and so far, this is what I know: first, you scarify the round end of the seed with a file or emery board until the white layer underneath is just exposed and then you drop it into a gallon jar or aquarium lined with mud and stones and filled with room temperature water. The seed should germinate between three to seven days later and it prefers sunlight and warmth. After it germinates, multiple stems will reach up to the water surface and form tiny pads and the roots will grow down into the mud and stones. When this happens the seedling is ready to be transplanted. Assuming I can get all this to happen I'm wondering what needs to be done in the next stage?

Once the plant has started into fairly active growth it's time to transplant. Be prepared to dig down into the mud and rock to remove as much of the root system as you can without damaging it. The roots will migrate into all kinds of crevices so you are going to have to lift that whole section up and sort of flush things off carefully. I would suggest putting it into a 12-inch high, 10-inch diameter pot at this stage, using some gravel in the bottom to raise it up an inch or so. Put in your plant and fill the pot up with soil. This planting pot then goes into a larger jar or pot that is completely filled with water. You can put some gravel into the bottom of this second pot as well so the rim of the planting pot is sitting closer to the rim of the larger pot. Alternatively, you could submerge the planting pot right down inside the outer pot and put some heavier material over the surface of the planting pot so the water doesn't become murky and you don't get soil floating around. If you choose to submerge the plant pot, leave 2 or 3 inches free below the rim of the pot when you are potting, then add about an inch of clean sharp sand over the surface and another inch or so of pebbles, gravel or marbles to hold the sand down. Give it a few very thorough waterings before you put it into the second pot. This will rinse out a lot of the fine material that will cause the water to cloud up initially. That being said, after a few days in the outside pot, you can always lift out the plant pot and change the water to get clear water again. Be sure to water between the rims of the two pots, as opposed to watering over the top of the plant pot, whenever you need to top it up. This will help cut down on silting or murkiness in the water. The water should always be at room temperature so that you are not shocking the plant. There is also the question of fertilizer. I know Longwood Gardens down in Pennsylvania, where they grow some prize lotus and water-lilies, have developed a fertilizer made of manure pellets that they add to their plants dur-

ing the summer season. They also use compost and composted manure in the mix that they grow the plants in so there is a good quantity of nutrient in it to start with. If you can use compost in with your own soil mix, that is certainly going to be helpful. On top of that, you are going to want to do some fertilizing. Fish emulsion type fertilizers work quite nicely here, but don't go too heavy on the nitrogen. One with a low series of numbers to start with – something like a 3-5-3 – would be ideal. The plants should be kept in full sun and can go outdoors in the summer with the appropriate gradual acclimatization to the increased light level. That is to say,

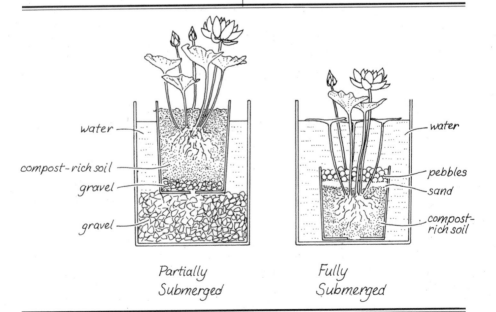

water — compost-rich soil — gravel — gravel —

Partially Submerged

water — pebbles — sand — compost-rich soil

Fully Submerged

put them in mottled or filtered sunlight and gradually move them into full sun over a 2 or 3 week period. Reverse this process to bring the plants indoors at the end of the season before the first frost.

Curbing an Avocado

Over the past few years my 6-foot avocado has been growing quite happily and has started branching out. I can see that soon it is going to be hitting the ceiling but I am not quite sure how to prune it to stop it from growing through the roof. Can I trim it without killing it?

You can easily trim this plant back just by pinching off the growing tip. This will stimulate growth in the dormant lateral buds and they will start swelling and growing out. The side branches that are there now will also get more energy as a result of the terminal bud being pinched out and they will start growing more and stretching out. If it starts to look unbalanced, you can pinch those back as well and you will get a much bushier fuller crown.

Eliminating Fungus Gnats from Seedlings

I am growing Tuberous Begonias from seed under lights over the

winter and even though I used a sterilized soil mix, I now find I am inundated with what I call fungus gnats. I tried using Vapona stripping in the area without any success. I want to know two things: do I need to worry about them, because there are a lot of them, and how can I treat them without damaging the seedlings?

With seedlings it is a little more difficult to control these infestations because the plants are usually very tight together. If they have reached a reasonable size, separating the seedlings into individual pots is certainly going to make a difference. Once you have given them an initial watering into the new pots, scratch up the soil surface so it will dry out more quickly than the rest of the soil beneath it. The disturbed soil will effectively work like a mulch and hold moisture a little bit longer below so you have to be careful about the watering. Drying out the soil surface means however that you are eliminating the environment these insects want and need to survive and that will cause a drop in the population. Check for soil weight before you water again because you are not going to be seeing a true representation of what is happening below once you scratch up that surface. In terms of using the pesticide strip, if you bag the whole area around the plants so that the strip is intensively off-gassing in a controlled environment you will certainly get a more effective coverage. You don't want any sunlight exposure while you are doing this because that would just heat up everything in the bag and bake your seedlings. Overnight will give you some effect but 24 hours in the sealed bag would be ideal. Be sure that everything is well ventilated when you take off the bag because you don't want to be breathing in that accumulation of toxic fumes.

Under-performing Petunias

My petunia seedlings have been up for about 3 weeks but they are still very small. This year I am keeping them at a more even temperature in an east window in the house which is 18-20° celsius on average, although there is some fluctuation. Last year I kept them in the conservatory and those plants were never really ready to go out. They were so small I could hardly handle them even in June. Is there anything else I can do?

If you could give them a little bottom heat, that would be helpful, but really, the tempera-

ture you are at is not bad. Temperature fluctuation does matter somewhat but light is also critical. If you could put them into that conservatory throughout the day, once the temperature is up above 10-12° celsius, and then take them out into the normal room temperature again as the sun goes down at the end of the day, they would benefit from that higher light. Don't put them in direct sun for the whole day initially. Full sun in the morning and then indirect light from midday on would be perfect. Once they get 3-4 inches tall, pinching out the growing tips will force them to branch out so you will get bigger and bushier plants.

Scourge of the Spider Mites

I have a large-leafed ivy plant that is quite beautiful and hangs from the ceiling to the floor in the kitchen. It is repeatedly attacked by spider mite even though I have sprayed it several times now. How far can I cut it back and will it return?

Let's play this one safe. Take a number of cuttings from the tips and dip them in the soap and water solution – that's 40-parts water to 1-part soap. Make sure they get a very thorough coverage. After about 10 minutes in that solution, bring them out and rinse them off with clear water. Put them in a glass or jar with a bit more water and they should root up beautifully. After that, cut away anywhere you see the mites. Spider mites are successful little devils and it has been shown that they will survive in the carpet in a dry office with no plant material around for up to 3 years. If you bring plant material back into that area, they come right back and thrive. So yes, they will be in the soil. One thing that really does help is to put your ivy outdoors during the summer months. If you can put it in bright light, but not full sun, that seems to cut down the population. A shaded area or balcony is fine. The indirect light that it receives indoors is still much less than it would get in shade conditions outdoors. When you are ready to bring your plant back inside in the fall, applying a soap and water treatment 2 weeks before should take care of any of the pests that might come back in with it. It will take 3 sprayings over a 10 day period to kill any successive batches of eggs. Spider mites are really quite interesting – their population increases exponentially with temperature and dryness. If the temperature goes up they multiply that much more quickly – not just a 2-4-6-8 increase, but 2-4-8-16 and so on. Conditions make a big difference.

Dryness is part of that equation as well so a light spray or misting of the plant with water on a regular basis will help give a measure of control.

Variations in an Orchid Stem

Three years ago I was given a Dendrobium Orchid that has survived despite my ignorance. Each year it puts forth one shoot of beautiful flowers. But now something strange is happening and I don't know what is wrong with it. At the highest end, the stem is about 1/2 inch in diameter but down toward the base it narrows down to about half of that. It looks like it could be knocked over very easily. Do you know why this might be happening?

Several things might have happened. It might have gone through a stressful dry period early on or there has been an increase in the amount of feeding to the plant at some point. Barring either of those and if the conditions around the plant have been reasonably stable, it may just be that it is now growing in better conditions than it had as a young plant before you got it. It has had some accelerated growth, possibly because it is getting more light, and that has caused the later growth to be more robust. In terms of the flowering, don't cut the flower spike off after you get that tress of flowers. Cut it back to the base of where the flower has started, in other words, cut at the beginning of the first flower spike. If you cut it back to that point, you will probably get a second spike coming along and with a plant that is 3-4 years old, if you cut it back again, you might even get a third. You will actually get more flowering from it by cutting it back. One of the great joys of Dendrobium is that they survive despite our ignorance and they are pretty tough. These are the ideal ones to keep as house plants if you are not really into the esoteric of caring for orchids. I don't think you really have much of a problem with this plant. With normal growth the leaves can still come out narrower at the base. If it is in better growing conditions now than it was before and there is more light out at the tips, you will sometimes see what seems to be a deviation in the leaf or stem form. It just means that not every-

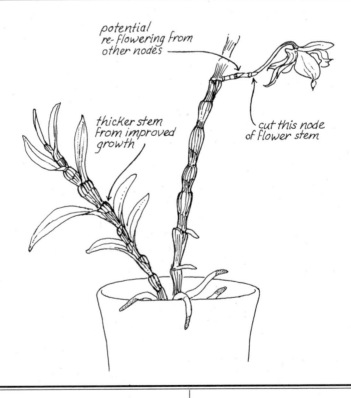

potential re-flowering from other nodes

thicker stem from improved growth

cut this node of flower stem

thing has always been ideal. Giving the plant a 1/4 turn daily to give a more even light to the entire crown is helpful but you likely won't eliminate the problem completely.

Time to De-cone the Roses

I pruned my roses back last fall and then covered them with large styrofoam covers and filled them with peat moss. Last week the snow was at the top of the cones and now it has melted so much they are sitting on bare ground. When should I remove the cones?

You should take them off right away as soon as the snow is gone. Most of the cones are white, so light will be reflected away and help avoid a build up of heat inside. But if you continue to keep them on with the daily temperature increasing, you will eventually get a lot of moist stagnant air trapped inside and this will provide the ideal conditions for certain diseases to start. If there is mulch built up around the base of the plant, don't remove that yet, but the cones should come off to let the branches get exposed to the air and light. It's a great sign of spring.

New Growth Creates Overpowering Odour

I own a "Corn Plant" that is now about 6 feet tall and suddenly a few weeks ago a new branch started growing out of the main stem. It was just like a piece of wood. Then little brown things began to grow on it. A couple of weeks later, I began to have a very overpowering perfume smell in my apartment. It was amazing, and quite frankly, overwhelming. I have had this plant for 10 years and this is the first sign of anything like this. What is it and what can I do to stop it?

These are the flowers and congratulations are definitely in order! Not many people get Dracaenas to flower indoors. You will probably notice large globules of what looks like crystalline honeydew around the flowers or the stock. It's a very sticky material and if you dab your finger into a little and taste it, it tastes like honey. It's wonderful stuff but it does stain. Warm soap and water will remove it from the carpet or upholstery if it does get on there. Once a plant has started this flowering, it will usually do it again. If you want to encourage that stalk to branch, don't hesitate to cut the tip back and if you do that after flowering, you will have a greater possibility of getting it to re-flower. Once the flower is finished, allow it to start drying back. On the other hand, if you don't like the smell, just cut the flower off and put it in the compost.

Tendril Outgrowth on Ivy

My ivy plant has been growing along really nicely, but on the parts of the ivy that are progressing most I have these little growths. They look like small clusters of green inch worms. Once the plant grows on and these little clusters are far enough back, they dry off and turn brown. They don't seem to be hurting the plant but they look really awful. What is causing this?

What you are looking at are adventitious roots. They are little nodules forming up along the stems that would actually root if they had the proper conditions. If the moisture conditions are favourable, the plant stops expending energy there and they stop growing. If the plant is trimmed back, the younger growth doesn't tend to put out as many root nodules. If it is watered a little more regularly so that it is not under any stress, that can also help. Otherwise, the plant thinks that it could take better care of itself and find more moisture if it could just put out a few

more roots. If it's getting enough moisture from the base roots, it doesn't tend to go to that effort.

Trimming Up Azaleas

I've had a red azalea for about 8 years and now it has these long thin twiggy arms. At the very end of these spindly bits they burst into a bunch of leaves and flowers. How can I get the foliage and flowers back into the centre?

What you are seeing here is more representative of the natural growth pattern and shape that the azalea would take if it were growing in the wild. The fact that you are getting less foliage along the stem may be related to the light it is getting. What you want to do is stimulate some new growth back along those stems, but if you cut everything back the capacity of the plant to produce food for itself will be so drastically affected that it would be forced to live on its reserves. To begin with I would suggest you target about 1 in 4 of those branches strategically around the plant. Cut these back about 50-75% of their length, making sure to open up the crown sufficiently so good light is getting in there. What will happen is you will stimulate some of the dormant buds left along the stem and they will begin to swell at the nodes and start into growth. As these develop and start hardening off, they will go from a pale green to a darker green colour and the leaves will get fairly thick again. This whole regeneration may take a couple of months. Once these pruned branches have re-established, do another pruning, this time taking off another 25%, again strategically around the plant. Bring those back and let them fill in and then repeat the process. The best time to start this pruning process is once 25% of the branches have finished flowering but before they have put out new growth at the tips. There's no point in having the plant waste energy out at the tips when you don't need the growth there, so if you can catch it right at that point, that would be ideal.

Dormant Oil/Lime Sulphur Conundrum

Spring is coming up quickly and I have been a bit confused by the conflicting instructions for this dormant oil-sulphur spray business. On the bottle the label says they are to be sprayed together. My gardening book says to do the dormant oil treatment three weeks before the sulphur treatment. I am wondering why the product label says to do it togeth-er and the book says to do it separately and to add an insecticidal soap. It also says on the bottle that if the temperature is below 40° fahrenheit – don't spray. Is that 40° fahrenheit during the day or at night? And lastly, the book says to apply lime sulphur and insecticidal soap. Should I do them separately or mix them together? If I am supposed to do them separately, which should go on first?

The attraction of that commercial dormant oil product is that the dormant oil and lime sulphur have been formulated in such a way that they are compatible – in other words, you can apply both at the same time and do away with one session of spraying. The products can be combined in the same sprayer and applied at the same time, but that doesn't mean they have to be. I think your gardening book is referring to a dormant oil treatment that is generally applied at an earlier stage in the development of the buds or when the tree is still dormant. That spray is intended to control the insects early in the season by essentially smothering them before they hatch out. The lime sulphur products are aimed at disease control, so there are two very different things being targeted. The spore development that the lime sulphur acts on usually happens a little bit later in the season. It is felt that if you do these as separate treatments that firstly, you will pay a bit more attention to the application of each one, and secondly, that you will be dealing with the specific problem at the time when that treatment will be most appropriate and effective. In terms of the combined dormant oil-sulphur spray, there is also less of a chance that the sulphur product will be washed off the tree before it is needed. With regard to the recommended temperature, the 40° fahrenheit or 7° celsius is a daytime temperature; however, I would also suggest people wait until it is no colder than -5° celsius at night, just for the drying. Certainly as a daytime target 7-10° celsius is fine – and preferably do it on a sunny, wind-free day. Try to spray early in the day so the mixture can dry as much as possible before the temperature drops. In terms of adding the insecticidal soap to the lime sulphur treatment, you can mix them together. All you need is a drop or two of the soap in the mixture and any liquid soap will work fine. It is only added as a spreading agent to break down the surface tension of the water so the sulphur spreads a little more easily. Mix everything up very carefully and make sure you are getting the right proportions. It shouldn't be making that sludge that some

people notice. You can avoid the sludge problem not only by mixing the proper proportions, but also using warm or even hot water for your mix. As you spray, the water will cool off so there is no danger of damaging the plant tissues with the heat. The solution will also get into suspension better if you mix it hot – and do keep shaking up the sprayer as you work to make sure it is continually being mixed. Otherwise you could end up with areas that receive either too much or too little concentration.

Overexposed Tomatoes

My tomato plants are growing under lights and unfortunately, thanks to a mistake made with the control timer, they have been getting 24 hour daylight for about 3 weeks. I kept wondering why they were growing so fast. They are slightly pale in the centre and there is a bit of a reddish tinge on the leaves. And they are certainly bigger than they should be. I wonder if you have any suggestions about what I should do with them now that I have got the light problem figured out?

If you can accommodate it space-wise, moving your tomato plants up a pot size – say from a 5-inch pot to a 6 or even 7-inch would certainly help. Put about a 1/2 inch of soil in the bottom of

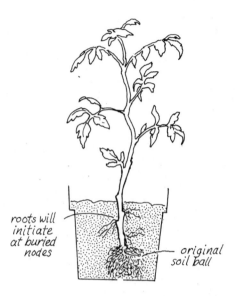

roots will initiate at buried nodes

original soil ball

the new pot, then pinch off the bottom leaves of the tomato plants and remove them from the 5-inch pots. Loosen up the edges of the soil ball and roots a little, put them in the new pots and fill in the soil around the plant and up the stem until you have only about a 1/2 inch of the pot rim showing. That should reduce the exposed stem by an inch or two. They will adventitiously root up along that section of newly buried stem so that you are going to get a much greater root system. With a shorter stem the plants are going to be much more stable when you do put them outside. Any feeding you do should be a light feeding only. And rather than giving them the 14-16 hours they would normally want under artificial light, you can cut that back

for a week or so to 12 hours on and 12 hours off. Pick it back up again to the 14-16 hour days after that. The transplant means they will have a massive root system and you will therefore have more vigorous plants so that when they do go outside, they will be ready to take off.

Cultivating Ginger Root

My mother had a ginger root on top of the microwave and one day I noticed it had started to sprout. I put it into a bowl of water and I can see roots coming out of the bottom and a green bud about half an inch long developing. I am wondering what I have to do to it to keep it going?

If you have normal potting soil, and one of the soilless mixes will work nicely here, you can pot it up at this point. Don't completely bury the root. Put it on the surface of the soil with the side that is sprouting roots facing downward and bury it to about half its own depth as you would with an

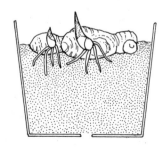

iris. Water it thoroughly and then be sure to let it dry down between waterings. A location with bright light is ideal for this, somewhere the plant can get full sun. As the roots start to fill that pot, be prepared to put it into a larger one. You will also have to stake it at some point because it is going to put up a stem that is 30-40 inches long at maturity. You may even see a flower on it that is quite pretty. It will throw off lots of offsets from the root as well, so you will be able to have fresh ginger root from now on once you get this one established.

Preferences for Pruning Equipment

There seem to be two types of pruning equipment: the bypass style and the anvil style. Why would you choose one over the other? Why are anvils so popular?

I would use the bypass in all cases. The anvil part on a bypass pruner actually holds the piece of wood or stem that you are cutting off and as the bypass blade comes down past that anvil, it slices cleanly. With an anvil style pruner

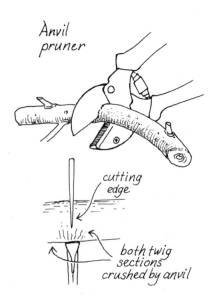

Anvil pruner

cutting edge

both twig sections crushed by anvil

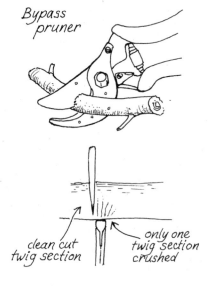

Bypass pruner

clean cut twig section

only one twig section crushed

the blade pushes down onto a flat surface causing both sides of the branch to experience a great amount of pressure. The cambium layer of that branch is getting crushed on both sides with the anvil type pruner, whereas with a bypass it is getting crushed on one side only. Make sure the damaged side is the one you are removing and that a clean cut is made on the piece of wood that remains on the tree, shrub, or plant. Anvils became popular because they were less expensive. This was before people realized that they were causing infection and opening up healthy plant tissue to diseases and other problems. There was also a time when florists would crush stems on woody material or batter them up on purpose with the idea that this would encourage better water uptake. The other benefit of an anvil pruner is that when you are cutting something, you can hold on to it more securely with the pruning shears and even use both hands if need be to cut through the tough stems. However, in terms of a clean or more surgical type cut and the general health of your plant, the bypass pruner is the one to go with.

Cultivating Kiwi

I was told that kiwi fruit will grow if you start them from the little seeds in the fruit. Would they grow outdoors?

You are never going to get any produce from the seeds of a regular kiwi. From the Arctic Kiwi vine, yes, but you are looking at a longer term investment. Kiwi vines need to be held up by an arbour-type structure where they can grow out in full light. You also must make sure that you have both a male and a female vine.

Eradicating Tomato Hornworm

Last year I had the dreaded Tomato Hornworms in my vegetable garden. Does it winter over in the soil? And how do I get rid of it before it does any major damage?

Yes, they do over-winter in the soil. They feed for 3-4 weeks, then crawl into the soil to pupate and emerge the next spring as a moth. That parent moth then lays eggs on the underside of the tomato leaves to repeat the cycle. We only get one generation here but in the southern U.S.A. they may have 3 or 4 generations per year. The best way to get rid of them is by monitoring the plants on a daily basis early in the season. The first sign of the worm showing up is usually some chewed up leaves and if you look very closely, you should find the culprit not too far away. If you do find one, just pinch it behind the head very tightly and lift it off the plant. That pinching should be tight enough to squash it. That is really the simplest way to control them. If you can get rid of them as soon as they show up, they won't go through their cycle of developing and cocooning and you avoid them reproducing and coming back the next year.

Premature Tulips

Temperatures have been all over the map this spring. At the front of our house, there is an area with no snow left at all. The tulips have come up about an inch and a half above the ground there and my concern is with the plummeting temperatures in the evenings. Is there something I can or should do to protect those tiny little shoots?

At this point, no. What you are seeing are the first leaves coming out and the actual flower stem doesn't start elongating until further along in the process. There is not an awful lot that you can do at this point that would be practical. Once the plants have been exposed to these temperatures, you may get some die back at the tips, but the rest of the leaf should still be fine and the subsequent leaves are hopefully going to be OK.

APRIL

Recommended Components of Compost

We live in the country and have a wood-burning stove. I also live on a lake and we pull a lot of vegetation out from there in the summer. I have access to horse manure and mulch my leaves in the fall and I am wondering what proportion of manure, vegetation and wood ash I should combine to make the right kind of compost for my vegetable garden and perennial beds?

The green vegetative material you are pulling out of your lake or garden has a high nitrogen content and doesn't need an awful lot added to it. You will want to mix in some drier material such as fallen leaves, stems and twigs to provide a bit of carbon in there as well. The essential thing is to let all of it break down sufficiently and then cure for 6-8 months after the breakdown has happened. The manure and straw is already an ideal combination. There you are getting a nitrogen source already mixed with organic matter. If you can combine the greens and the browns in a 50-50 ratio, you have a pretty good active compost. However, the ratio doesn't have to go that high for the compost on your vegetable garden. You can have less green, or nitrogen, in that compost without any problem. As for the wood ash, I would avoid using it at all in the compost. You can certainly spread it around your ornamentals or if you have a cedar hedge, for example, spread it underneath before you do an application of compost. Although wood ash will be a big plus for the trees, you don't want that ash going into your vegetable garden. The potential problem here is with the build-up of heavy metals like cadmium and lead in the ash. They can accumulate from the air into the "carbon sink" of the tree as it "breathes" and are incorporated into the wood. When wood burns the heavy metals are released but don't break down and are therefore part of the residue in the wood ash. You don't want these dangerous residues accumulating in your vegetable garden soil, or worse yet in your produce, so best to keep the wood ash away from any compost that's headed to your vegetable garden or fruit trees.

Grafting Over Damaged Trees

I have a magnolia tree that's about 10 feet high and this winter the darned rabbits have de-barked about two thirds of the *trunk all the way around. Is there any way to keep that tree alive? How can I keep the rabbits away from it next winter? I had tile on the bottom of it last winter but the snow just gave them a stepladder over it.*

What needs to be done is to build a bridge graft to bypass the damaged area so that when the tree comes out of dormancy, the sap and nutrients will still be able to run up through the cambium layer to feed the section above. First, you need to clean cut the edges around the area of the trunk where it has been chewed. To do that, take a very sharp knife and trace just above the ragged edge of the damaged area so that you create a clean, even edge. Next you want to cut 4 or 5 twigs from the same tree. They should be about a pencil width thick and long enough to bridge from the top of the damaged area to the bottom, plus about an inch extra at each end. Rabbits generally chew up and down as opposed to around the tree so they can take out a fair chunk. Take one of the twigs and split about an inch down at one end by slitting the end with a knife right down the centre of the twig and removing one side. Scrape out the wood centre on the side that's left until you reach the bright green cambium layer, so in effect what you create is an inch high "flap" of cambium and bark. Now do the same thing at the other end making sure that your flap is on the same side of the twig at each end. Place the 1-inch flap of one end of the twig just below the upper clean edge so that the flap overlaps the bark and the rest of the twig straddles the damaged area below. Trace around the flap with a knife or pencil to create an outline. Lift off the twig and cut away the bark from the inside of that outline so that the flap will fit back into it like a puzzle piece. You want to remove just enough bark to ex-

pose the cambium layer here as well. Next, fit the flap of the twig back into that cleaned-out area making sure that the inside cambium of the flap is against the exposed cambium layer on the trunk. Tack it in place with a very fine tack or a pin. Repeat the same thing at the bottom. Trace, cut away the bark and tack the lower twig flap to the trunk, cambium to cambium, finishing the "bridge". Build as many of those bridges as you can across the injured area, roughly an inch apart, all the way around the girdled section of the tree. Obviously, the bridges at the edges of the dam-

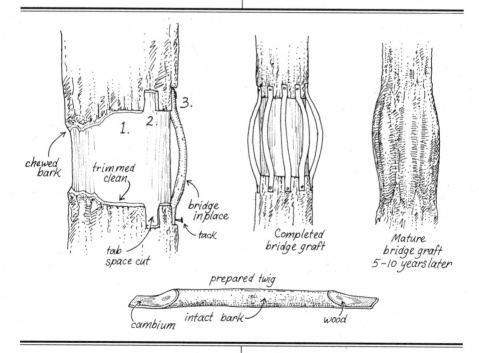

chewed bark

trimmed clean

1.

2.

3.

bridge in place

tack

tab space cut

Completed bridge graft

Mature bridge graft 5–10 years later

prepared twig

cambium   intact bark   wood

aged area may be shorter than the ones in the middle. Next take either grafting wax, which would be ideal, or beeswax, which also works well, heat it up and when it is liquefied, spread it over the grafted ends where you have attached the twigs to the tree so that you seal everything up. The wax will help hold the moisture in there. A light coating over the twig itself wouldn't hurt, but it is not essential. As the tree comes out of dormancy, give it a light feeding with a soluble fertilizer to stimulate a bit of new growth. One of the fish emulsion fertilizers would work quite nicely for this or any one with a balanced set of numbers. About a 5-5-5 would be fine. Be sure to give the tree a thorough soaking with that one application. You will have cleaned up the edge around the damage so you are pretty well eliminating any possibility of infection. By trimming back that edge you will also get a much better callus growth around the injury and hopefully you will get a "take" on some of your bridge grafts. As the tree continues to grow, it will eventually grow right over all of the grafting that you have done and seal over that injured section of trunk. You'll want to keep those rabbits out in future and the best way to prevent this from happening again is to wrap

chicken wire around the trunk of the tree from ground level right up to well above the snow line. Use a fine mesh chicken wire because mice can do the same type of damage to the tree as rabbits and that fine wire should help keep everyone out.

Recommended Fertilizer for Azaleas

We were given an azalea earlier in the spring that bloomed beautifully at that time but hasn't done a thing since. Is there any special feed that one has to use to get it to bloom again?

You can certainly use an acid fertilizer, one with a lower first number and higher second and third numbers, as you would for any fruiting or flowering plant. A tree or shrub fertilizer will also work as long as you keep a slightly acidic condition in the soil. That can be achieved by as little as breaking apart spent tea bags and spreading the used tea leaves over the surface of the pot. Just use the tea leaves as a mulch on top of the soil. Azaleas also want cooler conditions. If they are in a hot sunny location they will grow on and toughen up to it, but they will not produce flower buds. If you have it in a direct sun location, get it back from the window a little bit unless the room is particularly cool. A western window during the spring and summer months would be preferable. Water it thoroughly when you water it, making sure that it is drying down between the waterings – but don't let it dry out completely. It can go quite nicely into the garden in the summer but put it into shady or mottled light. Eastern light would be perfect where it will get a bit of direct morning sun, but partial shade through the rest of the day and then cooler conditions in the heat of the day from noon on, which is ideal for bud formation. And keep in mind, your azaleas will only flower once per year.

Getting a Seahorse to Bloom

I've had an orchid called a Seahorse for about 4 or 5 years and it has never bloomed. It has grown bigger mind you. I water it twice a week and spray it every day and I give it 25-10-10 fertilizer every 3 weeks. I put it in a bay window facing south and sometimes in the summer I move it 4 feet back from the window. The leaves are like a Day Lily and at the bottom of one of them there is a big sort of pouch thing. Is this orchid meant to bloom?

It's a Cymbidium Orchid and what it desperately wants you to do is put it outside in the summer and make sure it stays out until the first light frost comes along. Certainly bring it in before any heavy frosts but by all means give it cooler conditions through to the end of the summer and into the early fall before that heavy frost hits. It can take any lighter frosting with no problem at all. No more fertilizing for this orchid until it flowers for you. All the signals and care you are giving it is telling it that you like what it is doing for you right now with all this vegetative growth and that is what it's going to continue to do unless you change the pattern. There is too much nitrogen in the fertilizer you are giving it, which will encourage those wonderful leaves, but not any flowers. As far as the watering, use room temperature rain water or melted snow if possible, then give it a very thorough watering and let it dry down again. Don't bother with the spraying. If it's in a bright but cooler location it will be happier as well. Once it gets that nitrogen out of its system, I am sure you are going to see flower buds, and it should bloom successfully without any problem.

Woodpecker Worries

There was a Pileated Woodpecker around our backyard this win-

ter and we now realize it has drilled 6 or 8 holes in our maple tree about 20 or 30 feet up. Some of the holes are easily 3 inches wide. I'm not sure if I should get them filled in with cement this spring or just leave them alone. What would you recommend?

Cementing them up is probably not a good idea. If those holes are collecting water, you would need to be more concerned about drainage and that can often be treated by simply cutting an extended "V" on the bottom side of the hole. But do this if, and only if, you find the holes are collecting water. Otherwise, you want to minimize the amount of damage the tree will need to heal over around that hole. I can appreciate that with a hole 3 inches in diameter, you are concerned, but the biggest threat is if the heartwood starts to deteriorate. It might be worthwhile having a look inside those holes to start with. The fact that the Pileated Woodpecker came and started working on your maple tree is likely because something is in there to eat. It probably heard Carpenter Ants in there, went after them and then decided that your maple tree would make a good nest, especially if you are seeing a number of holes. Have a look in there and see what the heartwood looks like. If it is a bit soft, there has been an infestation and you may want to get in an arborist to examine the tree, make a decision on its soundness, and decide what needs to be done. You never know. Even with a 3 inch diameter hole in a tree, all the effort may have been for one grub. If woodpeckers are hungry and they know there's one morsel in there, they can be very determined.

Using Grey Water on Garden

We have set up a reservoir system that lets us reclaim water from household use and are hoping to use it this summer to water the gardens. What amount of shampoo, soap or laundry detergent would be safe to put on plants?

Any amount of soap or shampoo that you can tolerate on your body or in your hair at the normal dilution rate of a shower or bath is going to be fine for plant material. Even some of the harsher products like dandruff shampoo are still safe to re-use. You are not likely to be doing all of your watering this way and when it rains, any of these residues are going to be further diluted. Exposure to sun is going to break them down as well.

Where you can get residue build-up is generally on the surface of the soil. If you allow it sun exposure for a day and then scratch up the surface of the soil the next day, you really shouldn't have a problem. Even harsher products like chlorine that are regularly mixed in with detergent will break down with sun exposure and are usually so diluted in grey water that you are not going to have a problem. In fact, you may find you get a better penetration of moisture into the soil because the detergent or soap present in the bath or laundry water actually breaks down the meniscus or surface tension of the water as well as some of the tension around the soil particles. The water will actually penetrate more readily and there will be some slight nutrient content there from the soap, all of which is fine for the plant material. This is actually a very good use for it and has some added benefits for the environment aside from enhancing your garden. The soapy water put into our sewer system can cause major problems over time in terms of nutrient build-up or overload in our streams and lakes. This in turn causes an overgrowth of aquatic vegetation or algae bloom that takes up all the available oxygen in the water and can kill off fish and other aquatic life. Applying that same soapy water to your garden – where you want to encourage vegetation and where the plants can act as bio-accumulators and use these residues as food – helps reduce the amount of this water going into the sewers. So it is a great thing to do and there is no danger to your plants.

Preventing Mole Mayhem

My rock garden is full of perennials and shrubs that the mice and moles just loved over the winter. That area has a south-west exposure so it gets quite warm under all of that snow and they did quite a bit of damage. They chewed the bark off about 6 shrubs and I think they have eaten a fair amount of the roots on my perennials. I am wondering what I can do in the fall to deter them from living there again next winter?

Citrus rind can be helpful – get it down as late as possible in the fall before it snows. Cut up grapefruit, lemon, or orange rinds and sprinkle them liberally around all of the shrubs and at the base of the trees. If you have some slaked lime available, sprinkle some of that over the soil around the base of the plants. Tree trunks that are particularly susceptible to damage can be sprayed with a mixture you make by adding lime to very hot water. Knowing the right proportion is just a matter of adding the lime to the water until you can't dissolve any more. Filter that mixture – and here an old nylon stocking works well – and spray it right on to the trunks. A light spraying will do it or you can take a brush and paint it onto the trunks if you prefer.

To Mulch or Not to Mulch

I'd like to cover my garden bed with cedar mulch this year. I recognize the benefits of doing this for maintaining moisture in the soil and preventing weed growth, but if it's put down too early, won't it prevent my plants from coming up?

You will certainly get the benefits you mention from mulching, as well as the aesthetics and aroma in your garden from the cedar, but the application of any thick mulch will definitely impede germination and growth of all plants under its cover, not just the weeds. The proper timing of that initial application of mulch will vary somewhat depending on conditions. If the spring is hot and dry apply your mulch as soon as the soil has thawed out completely and has had a chance to warm up. The roots of the plants need that warmth to grow. On the other hand, if the spring is particularly wet, hold off until the soil has dried out, otherwise you will run in to all sorts of problems with rot or fungus. To allow some of your plants to self-seed into the bed, start your mulching around the shrubs, roses and the other perennials but leave other areas bare. Bring the mulch up to, but not in contact with, the stems of any woody plants such as hydrangea or forsythia. Likewise, mulch only up to the edges of your herbaceous perennials, not over the crowns. Once the plants that you want in your garden have germinated and started growing, you can finish mulching around them. Until that point you are going to have to weed in those exposed spots. Next year most of your self-seeders will germinate in or on the mulch, which may require you to gently lift the seedlings and plant them into holes in the soil in order to get them better established. Even if you ignore them, they will likely get their roots down into the soil eventually and take off successfully. Mulching will not prevent the weed seeds from germinating on top of the mulch but it sure makes pulling them out a lot easier.

Reviving "Dead" Cedars

After a cold winter with no snow, all of our cedars have turned or-

ange. Are they dead or will they come back and what, if anything, can I do to for them?

In years with minimal snow cover and therefore lots of dryness, plants just don't get all the moisture they need. Exposure to the wind and evaporation creates an awful lot of stress on plants and you end up with pretty miserable looking trees. How they do now will depend largely on just how successful this next season is in terms of the amount of moisture available in the soil. In some cases the cedars might be deformed from their conical shape, especially if the dieback has been strong, however the good news is that usually with a few good growing seasons you would never see the difference. They can fill in that quickly. With the spruce, pines and firs, it may take a bit longer, depending on how badly they were affected, but on the whole they too will come back. In terms of what can be done to help them along, if they are dry, definitely water them. Get some compost underneath them. Composted cattle manure would work as well but the manure should not be too fresh to prevent burning. Whatever you choose, make sure once you apply it to water it thoroughly to get those nutrients down to the root system as quickly as pos-

sible so that trees can pick it up and start using it. With lots of moisture and a bit of nutrient available your cedars should activate the dormant buds throughout their crowns and start back into active growth. The critical thing is to avoid any further moisture stress – so water well as required all season right up until freeze-up this fall.

What to Do with Bamboo

I bought four bamboo shoots about 5 months ago. They were about 3/4 inch across and different lengths and I was told to just throw them in some water and lo and behold, they started growing and have produced tons of roots. My problem is one of the four stems is now turning yellow on me and is starting to go a little bit soft. I am wondering what caused that? Is it reversible?

Regardless of what variety of bamboo you have there, the technique is much the same with all of them. They will throw shoots and root up quite successfully in water. Once you have a good show of roots, pot that stem into soil or a soilless mixture that has been amended with up to 25% sharp sand so that it will drain well. Bamboo wants those moist conditions though, so be sure to keep the soil or mixture constantly moist. Right now they are growing exclusively in water and allowing them to dry out would be too much of a shock to these plants. What I would recommend is that you not plant the yellowing one with any of the others. If you want them all together, I would plant 3 of them in one pot and leave the other in a pot of its own just in case it doesn't make it. Set them into a good bright location and they should do just fine.

Converting Turf to Flower Beds

Last fall we staked out the area of our lawn where we wanted to make a flower bed, put down multiple layers of newspaper and covered it over with mulch to kill off the grass. Now the question we are debating is whether we should pull all that off once the snow has gone or should we just put some top soil over it?

What I would suggest is that you can take the mulch off of the newspaper a bit at a time and start adding the soil over top. Leave the newspaper in place and plant right into the soil. If there is something that needs to be planted deeper than the layer of newspaper, just split the newspaper and plant into that hole. What you

will probably find is just a soggy mat where that newspaper was in any case. Once you have everything planted up and you are done, the mulch can go back on top. Bring the mulch right up close to the edges of your plants to control the weeds and prevent the grass plants from reappearing. It will also provide good moisture retention around your new plants and add to the appearance of your garden.

Mulched Leaves Still There in Spring

Last fall I put all my leaves onto my vegetable garden and I noticed that not all of them have broken down. I have already tilled once this season and I'm wondering if there is something that I could add to help the leaves break down?

If there was a bit more nitrogen present there, certainly things would break down more quickly. Adding some alfalfa pellets, usually sold in the form of rabbit feed, would introduce a bit more nitrogen, as well as add some more organic material to the soil. If the spring has been particularly dry, certainly watering would help accelerate the process. But if you have tilled already and broken those leaves up so more surface area has been exposed and they are well worked into the soil, I wouldn't worry too much. The worms will do a pretty fast, efficient job breaking down that old foliage, as will the micro-organisms in your soil, so I wouldn't go to any great effort at this point to feed them and bring them along. Just the fact that you have the organic material there is increasing the micro-organism population in that soil. I would let the leaves break down on their own at this point. If you can cut the leaves up a bit more in the fall – either by running a lawnmower over them before they go into the veggie garden or by tilling them well into that soil – they'll break down that much more quickly and completely over the winter period and your garden will be all set to go come spring.

Better Blooming Irises

Do I need to divide my clump of irises to get more blooms?

Yes, dividing should help. Do that division as early in the spring as possible, as soon as the soil is workable. Separate the roots so that you have a good section of root, each with a vigorous tip. When you are planting them up again make sure you place them so the roots are half above

and half below the soil. Dig your hole longitudinally so that it follows the direction of the rhizome, then mound the soil up a bit in the centre of that depression. A little bone meal and compost worked in is well worthwhile. Sit the rhizome on the mound and separate the roots so that they are trailing down on both sides. Backfill over the roots leaving the top half of the rhizome exposed above ground. The plants will do much better if they can be arranged with this type of exposure. Make sure this area drains well, especially if you tend to be planting into heavier, wet soil. If the rhizomes sit for any length of time in water they will rot. Repeat this process with each of the severed portions and you should see a whole new generation of blooms coming along very shortly.

Cracked Ash

A friend and I have been discussing what she and her husband might do with a mature ash tree in the backyard of the home she bought a year ago. It is quite a large tree and they hired a commercial outfit to trim it last year. That firm found a major crack in the foot of the trunk and suggested they have guy wires installed to anchor the tree. They opted not to do anything at that point and just wait to see what the trimming would do. But this spring that fork is weeping some sap, so we are wondering how much intervention is necessary to keep the tree healthy. They have a 5-year-old son and are not looking forward to having a whole bunch of guy wires coming down from this tree, but they'd rather not lose the tree either.

The guy wires would not be coming from the tree down to the ground. They would go from one side of that fork to the other, and possibly around elsewhere if there are other main branches. What they will do is to go through these major stems and bind the whole thing together as a unit. Here's the problem. If you can imagine looking at that fork with the wind blowing from the windward side, the outer branch is going to be pushed towards the centre, putting pressure on the crack and in effect, closing it, which is not a big problem. But if the wind blows on the leeward side, the windward side is going to be pushed away from the tree and will cause straining on that crack without the support of the other main branch to hold it up. If the wind moves around to the side, neither side of the fork would have support. So what they do with cables, either between two major branches or amongst a number of branches, is to make a

ring that ties the whole top together so that all the branches are getting the mutual support that would normally be there if there was no crack. In the interim, the injury at the fork that you see weeping gets a chance to heal over and callus and seal itself off, so you are not getting any water penetration. They will probably have a look at that situation at the same time as they install the guy wires. If the problem is severe enough, they may also put a threaded rod through the trunk to hold the whole bottom section to-

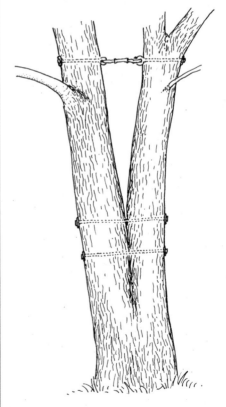

gether and try to alleviate any further pressure on it. Even with the rods in there, they would still have to do some cabling at the top. In either case, any cabling they do would stay up in the crown and would not come back to ground level. All of that being said, with a 5-year-old running around and the possibility of that tree splitting or breaking, if the professional advice is that the tree is dangerous, they should consider the child, if not the house or car underneath it, and take it down. If it breaks and injures someone or causes damage to a neighbour's property, they will be liable. If the advice is to try and save it, have them document the treatment and get a copy of any documentation for their insurance people. They are taking preventative steps and if ever something does happen, they can show that they had the required work done that was deemed necessary by the professional arborists and this would likely stand in their favour.

Transplanting a Large Magnolia

My mother will be moving this fall and she has a 10-year-old magnolia that she'd like to take with her. Its about 6 feet tall and 4-6 feet across at the crown. Can I dig it up and move it with her?

At that age the root system of the magnolia will have spread at least as far out as the tips of the branches. That starts to make a big root ball. It helps that you are not making the move until the fall though. You should start to prepare the tree 5 or 6 months before the move. Take a spade and drive it deep down into the soil around the perimeter of the tree out at the branch tips. Drive the spade in, remove it, skip one spade width and drive it in again. That means every second spade width you drive the spade full depth down into the soil and this cutting will prevent the roots from growing out too far. Repeat the process again 3-4 weeks later but this time, drive the spade down into all of the places that were skipped the last time. What you do when you stop the root growth outward is to force new growth between the trunk and the spaded edge you have established. Go around the area again in August and by mid September you are ready to give it a good soaking and dig the root ball created inside the spaded circle out. Take as much soil as possible with the roots, lift it and move it intact into the new location. Now that could be difficult without a large enough vehicle. The root ball must be protected, preferably inside a vehicle, but if that's not possible, wrap it up in burlap while it's being moved. Although it would be better to do this in the fall so the plant has a chance to settle in before the winter, the other possibility is to move the plant after freeze-up. Dig around it in the fall but don't lift the ball out. Make sure it is thoroughly soaked, allow it to freeze, and then move it later in the winter. If you transport it frozen, you don't have to wrap it. It will come out of dormancy in its new location in the spring and hopefully get established, but try for the fall if at all possible.

Alternate Native Ground Cover for High-traffic Areas

What alternative ground cover could you recommend that would function the same as a lawn? It should be native plants, something that is low maintenance and that will not need watering. One of our lawns receives full sun and the other is mostly under a tree and is shady until evening.

In both cases, you are not going to get the same degree of resilience to traffic with alternate ground covers that you do with turf. Grass stands up best, which is why it has been the traditional choice for lawns. If you still want to make the switch, either our native thyme or any cultivated thyme will do nicely in the higher-light location. Another alternative is ajuga, the bugleweed. It stands up very well and will take some walking on, but if there is regular traffic, you would be better to have stepping stones arranged so you can walk across the area without continuously crushing the plants. A big plus with the thyme, as opposed to ajuga, is that you will get a nice scent from it as it is walked on and crushed. You could also consider moneywort, which is a Lysmachia family plant, or lamiun. Remember however that these will not tolerate the kind of traffic that turf will. The smaller the leaf of the material you are putting down, the more resistance you are going to have to walking. Of the choices, the thyme will still stand up better to being walked on than the bugleweed or the lamium. In terms of the shade area, you could try periwinkle, the *Vinca minor*, or pachisandra, the Japanese Spurge. Even Lily of the Valley would work depending on how much walking you want to do on it. Hostas will also stand up in the shade area, but are not conducive to traffic. All of these have a fair degree of tolerance to drought but having said that, it is still best to mulch around them.

You are going to get a great deal of competition from those trees so if you can help hold some of the moisture at the surface by adding organic matter, the plants will do much better.

Japanese Imperial Blood Grass

I planted a small patch of Japanese Imperial Blood Grass last summer and was very pleased with the results. I was planning on planting more this year until I happened to see an article in a magazine that said it was very invasive in the south. I didn't notice that any seed had showed up on mine and so far, it seems to be pretty well contained. I was wondering if there could be a similar problem with invasiveness this far north?

The season here is not long enough generally to get full seed production, and even if you do get a full seed production one year, often the seed doesn't have time to ripen before it gets frozen. The result is that we don't have the same invasive problem with this grass. If you get a year where the season is extended and you are getting seed heads, cut them off before they get a chance to ripen. Other than that, it should not be a problem. You may find that it is spreading and getting

thicker, but it is not going to be as invasive as miscanthus, for example. The Japanese Blood Grass is a good ornamental plant and I wouldn't hesitate to use it.

Starting Over From Scratch

We moved into a house that had a swimming pool at one time, and then that area was back filled with what I suspect was not the greatest material. When we moved in it was infested with grubs, but we were really busy getting settled and couldn't do much to it. Now it's about 80% weeds, so I am trying to figure out a way of doing over the whole lawn. What I want to know is if there is a way of getting rid of the weeds without using herbicides and any advice you might have in terms of putting in a seed mix versus sod. If a seed mix is best, what mix should it be and do I need to put down some soil first?

It sounds like you would have to get some soil down there first or at least amend what is there with a good quantity of compost or well-seasoned manure. Mushroom compost or anything of that nature would work as well, but with the area you need to recuperate, whatever compost material you can find that involves the least amount of expense and trouble is likely going to work fine. Till the whole thing up as soon as it is workable in the spring, take out the weeds with a good stiff rake, roll it with a hand roller that is 1/2-3/4 filled with water, and then re-rake and re-level it so that you have got a decent seed bed. You will have to be able walk on that ground without leaving a footprint before you go on to the next stage, but it's fine to chew it up and get all of the dead material off there earlier in the season. You want to make sure the organic matter you are putting in is thoroughly mixed throughout the top layer – and I am talking about a minimum depth of 4-6 inches here and more if possible – so you get a uniform layer that will allow equal percolation or penetration of moisture down through the soil. Soil mechanics is fairly simple and specific when it comes to the transfer of moisture. Water will not move from one type of soil into another type of soil until the first one is fully saturated, so you want to be sure that the new soil and compost you are introducing is well and deeply mixed in with the soil that is already there. If you create a uniform layer of this new soil mixture down to that 4-6 inch plus depth, you are going to get even water penetration deep enough into and through the soil – which is what you will need to get good roots growing down through there as well. The effort you take to integrate that new material rather than just having the new layer sit on top is well worthwhile. In terms of a seed mix, it really depends on how much sun or shade you have. You will certainly want to get some hardy grasses in there and I would highly recommend that you mix in some clover as well. Trifolium repens or Dutch White or Creeping Clover as it is often called, or Strawberry Clover work well here. It starts out relatively low, covers a large area, and a 20-25% inclusion of clover in with your seed mix will fix enough nitrogen from the air to feed the entire lawn. That is all the nitrogen it will ever need, so there will be no more need for supplementary chemical feeding. Even without the clover, if you create a healthy active soil base with a good quantity of organic matter in there to start with, you will get enough microbial action going in the soil to sustain your lawn with only a light annual top-dressing of compost added. You will want to go with a grass mix that is reasonably drought tolerant and will also tolerate high and low light conditions. I would suggest a Creeping Red Fescue and maybe some of our native bluegrasses as opposed to a Kentucky Bluegrass. Go with something like a Poa trivialis, or the Annual Bluegrass Poa annua, a wild bluegrass we occasionally get here. Mix the seed thoroughly before spreading, then broadcast it in one direction from side to side across the width of the area, and again lengthwise across the area to get a very thorough seed coverage. Roll it with a light roller that is 1/4-1/2 filled with water or at whatever weight is sufficient to ensure that all of your seed comes into contact with the soil. Keep it moist until you get germination, which will probably take 7-10 days. Set your mower to a higher level – 2½ inches at a minimum – keep the lawn well watered and you should get some very good results there.

Three Methods for Multiplying Magnolias

The magnolia tree that I planted 30 years ago is called a Magnolia **kobus borealis** *and was supposed to be only marginally hardy. Despite that, it is now about 20 inches in diameter at the base, but I still worry. I would like to know if it is possible to propagate it so I can get a second one started just in case something happens. I tried air layering it last year but it didn't work. I may have started too late because it was already about the* *end of May. The tree produces lots of seeds and of course I tried planting them a few years ago but they didn't seem to germinate. Is possible to air layer it?*

I doubt that you would be able to air layer a magnolia, but it would be in an interesting experiment. If you were to try, I would suggest you do the nicking on it at the end of February or beginning of March before the tree comes out of dormancy. Pick a node at an active growing tip and go back maybe 6-8 inches from the tip. Injure it at the node but don't girdle it all the way around. Cut maybe 3 spots about as wide as your little finger and take out maybe 1/8 by 3/4 inch. Put a little #2 rooting hormone on and wrap some moistened sphagnum moss around it. Wrap plastic around that to keep the sphagnum moist. You don't want a great heat build up in there so wrap some aluminum foil around there as well, leaving a gap between the foil and the plastic. The foil should be bulged out a bit with the reflective side out to reflect the light and heat. That should keep the area dark and cool and avoid any greenhouse effect that would bake the section that is covered. Unwrap the foil occasionally to see if it has started to callus and root up. Once the roots are about an inch long you are ready to sever the rooted shoot. Remove the foil, plastic and as much of the sphagnum peat as comes off easily without damaging any roots. Using sharp pruners, cut the rooted tip off the parent branch directly below the node where the roots initiated. Remember to re-cut the parent branch just ahead of the next node down the branch so that it too can heal over properly. Pot up the rooted cutting in a 4-inch pot and add some rock phosphate or bone meal to the soil. Water thoroughly and place it in a warm, bright location, but not in direct sunlight for a couple of weeks. When the cutting is well rooted and growing vigorously, plant it out into your garden making sure that the new tree is well watered as needed. This method would certainly be worth a try but you would likely be as successful taking a few cuttings. First I would suggest that you get some willow cuttings or buy some pussy willow or corkscrew willow fresh from a florist. Cut the stems again, put them into water and let them sit for a week. Then add cuttings from the magnolia to the same water to see if you can get the rooting going that way. Don't forget to cut just below the node on the cuttings since that's the only place where roots will initiate. Now as a third option, these trees will throw an offset from the root

system. You can try to provoke this by exposing a root out past the drip line of the tree. Open up the area and injure the root slightly. Cover it back over and keep an eye on it. If you get a shoot coming from that point, uncover it again and cut the root cleanly leaving the section toward the tree intact. Then take out as much of the root system as you can with that new shoot. If this is a graft or a hybrid tree, obviously neither the seed nor the root cutting is going to reproduce true to form, but I think you have a variety that should be alright.

Clover Alert

I am interested in your suggestion to replace the traditional grass mixture with clover as a ground cover. However, I am concerned that the clover will attract bees and my son is allergic to them. The area I want to cover is in shade all day. Do you have an alternative ground cover suggestion that I could combine with thyme?

You are right to forget about the clover since the flowers may attract bees and that will put your son at risk. At the same time, forget about using thyme in this area since all varieties of thyme require full sun. As alternatives to grass in a shaded area, I'd suggest periwinkle, *Vinca minor*, which is about 2-5 inches tall with dark green foliage, or hostas, which come in a range of colours and sizes, anywhere from 4-20 inches tall or more and with a similar spread. Either or both of these would add variations in colour and foliage to your landscape and would do well in a more shaded situation.

Elm Ailments

Seven years ago I planted a Camperdown Elm that was about 2-3 inches in diameter at the time and it has grown considerably. After the first year the leaves lost their green and turned brown and papery but then the tree managed to come back. Each year I try something different like dormant oil or malathion or some other pesticide because I'm worried about an infestation of bugs. I've made sure that underneath the tree was clear; I sprayed the ground; I didn't spray the ground; I've tried everything. What should I be doing?

One thing that all elms are susceptible to if they undergo any heat or moisture stress over the summer is showing early fall colour and drying out. To avoid this, when you do the watering ensure that it is long and slow, a few hours or overnight, so that you get a good deep penetration of the moisture. Any infestation you might experience is likely to be beetles but that is only part of the problem, not the whole problem. The problem is wilt. Dutch Elm disease is a fungal growth that plugs up the pores, or conducting tissues, in the plant. The insect is the vector so it carries the fungus and infects the plant as it burrows into the tree. The fungus then starts to grow in the xylem, phloem and the conducting tissues of the trees. Camperdowns have shown some resistance to Dutch Elm disease but they are not immune to it. If the tree keeps coming back however, I would say that you do not have Dutch Elm disease and the problem is probably moisture stress and poor soil. There should be nothing growing under the tree. Mulch the soil with approximately 4 inches of mulch around the base but be careful not to pile the mulch up against the trunk of the tree. With enough nutrient and moisture your tree should be able to fend off any infestations without resorting to sprays of any kind.

Benefits of Wood Ash

Can I use wood ash to improve my soil? My grass is growing on a clay base. Would it be beneficial to spread over my lawn?

Yes it would. You can also add the ash to the other organic material in your compost or combine it with leaves or grass clippings. It's fine to apply the ash alone or in combination around your ornamental plants – but be careful not to use it on your vegetable garden or around fruit-producing trees and shrubs. With ash there is always the chance that it will contain heavy metals that could have accumulated in the wood as the tree grew and then concentrated in the ash through the burning process. You want to keep it away from anything that you might consume because vegetables and fruits can take up that concentrated residue with the other nutrients from the soil and become quite contaminated with high levels of the heavy metals. So avoid those areas of your garden where produce is growing. With that caution in mind, it would be best to spread the ash over your lawn just before mowing so that as you cut, the ash is forced downward with the blade action and into contact with the soil. Also, you will find that the nitrogen from the grass clippings in combination with that wood ash will make more nutrient available to the soil in short order. Do make sure however, that there are no nails in the ash, especially if you will be running a lawnmow-er over the grass after its spread. They make nasty projectiles and can do some awful things to cutting blades, windows, car finishes, plants and you!

Pruned Rotten

The apple tree in our yard is about 25 years old and has 4 different varieties on it. Over the years we have had different people prune it. Recently some branches were pruned into a more or less horizontal cut and I have noticed rot has started at one spot. There is a decayed section about 2 inches round where one of the branches was severed from the tree. Is this going to be serious?

What has probably happened is that the branch was trimmed too close to the main stem and rather than callusing over and starting to heal, it is trapping moisture and starting to rot. It would drain freely under normal circumstances except for the depression that has been created by that close pruning. If this happened recently, that decay has probably not gone too far down. The best thing to do now would be to trace around the injured area, preferably in the shape of an inverted tear drop. Cut that pattern with a very sharp knife, back into the healthy bark, and make sure that it tapers to a "V" at the bottom. Cut out what is wet or punky inside. Any wood that is solid in that heartwood is fine. Once you've cleaned that out, leave it open and exposed so that it will air dry and drain if any water does get into it again. The fresh cutting around the edge should stimulate some callus growth. If you can clean this area back to solid wood and make sure that it drains freely and easily down and out of that cavity, it should heal up nicely and not affect the health of the tree.

Fertilizing with Fido in Mind

I have a large maple tree, a linden tree and an ash tree in my backyard. I also have a dog. We take care of the dog's output very quickly so that is not a problem, but ever since we got the dog, I have stopped putting any kind of fertilizer onto the grass. And now in this past year, my back lawn has suddenly gone straight downhill. Is there anything that I can use that is non-toxic and that would encourage the grass to come back so that I don't have this mud pile out back?

Yes there is. If you feed the soil, it will take care of feeding both the turf and the trees.

Both also require great quantities of water. The roots of those large trees draw the moisture away from the surface and down deep into the soil, and that usually means the soil at the top is a lot drier than the turf can tolerate. What you'll need to do is to get some organic matter into the soil. I would suggest first thing in the spring, as soon as you can walk on the grass without leaving a footprint, give your lawn a thorough raking. Start in one direction, say north-south, and rake thoroughly, and then go perpendicular to that, so an east-west rake across the other way. A good stiff fan rake works fine. Don't worry if you see a quantity of matter come away with this raking – anything that will pull out in a vigorous raking in the spring probably shouldn't be there anyway or isn't going to do very well. Once you've raked, top-dress the whole area with either a fine compost or a composted cattle manure. Put about a 3/4 inch over the surface of everything. If after that you find the lawn is still not responding, that's a pretty good indication what is in there was probably not very strong to start with. If the overall quality of the turf is only low in certain areas, you may have to think about over-seeding those areas. You also have some practical considerations with your dog. If you are not looking for a fine, manicured-looking lawn but rather a more natural, environmentally friendly one with at least a reasonable surface to walk on – and one that the dog can be using quite comfortably – what I would recommend would be to over-seed through the whole area with Dutch White Clover or Creeping Clover, Trifolium repens. It spreads quite nicely and does not need cutting as often. With the clover you are also going to be adding nitrogen to the soil and fixing it there, and along with that top-dressing, encouraging the micro-organisms in the soil to get active again. You will bring a lot of life back into the soil and that will include earthworms, which will work through the earth and de-compact it. The other critical factor in rejuvenating this lawn, especially if the summers are dry, is going to be giving that whole area supplementary watering. Normally, to have a good turf lawn, you need full sun and 1-2 inches of water per week. With trees there, that water requirement increases appreciably. If you are not getting the rainfall that's needed, the trees will certainly respond by slowing down, but the grass doesn't like to do that and when it is forced into dormancy from a lack of moisture it starts to brown off

leading to those bare spots. Then when it does rain, the turf is too dead and the soil is too hard and compacted to absorb the moisture properly and the area just gets muddy. You will get much better coverage of the surface with clover there to hold some of the moisture in, but those supplemental waterings will be essential to keep everything going.

Ridding of Rabbits

Is there any humane way to discourage rabbits?

Smell and taste are important to rabbits. They are vegetarians. They don't like the smell of blood and they don't like meat, so blood meal is sometimes helpful. If you can side-dress around your plants with it, and you keep enough of the scent there, it helps keep the rabbits back. It's not a guarantee though. If they are hungry, they will keep coming in regardless of the odour. If you want something a little stronger, you can get a perfumey-type smell from any of the scented liquid detergents. You don't have to go to a 40-1 concentrate. Just put enough soap in the solution to make things smell and taste bad. A light spraying over the foliage of lettuce should help but do remember to wash it well before you eat it because there will probably be some residue. If you want an even stronger deterrent, wet the foliage with the light soap and water solution and sprinkle on a little bit of cayenne pepper afterward. It will make the plants even less attractive. The challenge with this method is that you have to reapply the soap spray, or soap spray and cayenne, after any heavy watering or rain. The good news is that once you start making their food less inviting, the rabbits will likely start looking elsewhere and change their existing eating patterns, hopefully to somewhere other than your garden patch.

Protecting Trees from Livestock

I am looking to fence in a wooded area for our horses that would give them some shade in the summer and a wind break in the winter. I might possibly have some free-range pigs in there as well. Quite a variety of trees would be growing in the enclosure and without fencing off each individual tree I want to protect them from the livestock. Is there some way to manicure them, especially the pines, so the animals won't rub up against them and get covered in sap?

You really would have to put up a physical barrier to sepa-rate the trees from the animals. Now if an animal has been near to an electric fence and has come to recognize and respect those wires, you can use a similar-looking wire around the tree and it doesn't have to be electrified. Get it up around the tree at the usual height and that should solve the problem with the horses. Free ranging pigs however, are not going to respect the fence in the same way and certainly would be going underneath the wire. With the evergreens this shouldn't be too much of a problem but you can watch to see if it becomes one. With the deciduous trees you can get internal bark injuries caused by something gnawing away at it – or you can get a lot of abrasion from animals scratching up against it repeatedly and this could, over time, put stress on those trees. Select the trees that are most important, usually the largest specimens, and get some physical barrier in place so that the pigs are not going at them. On the whole it should not be a large problem and in the long term it may actually be a mutually bene-ficial relationship. If you can keep enough mulch and organic material on the ground around the trees, combined with the ma-nure contributions from both the horses and pigs seeking shelter there, this may actually be a plus for these trees. You could have a nice mutual exchange happening there. In terms of when to go ahead and do some of the trimming, late fall or winter would be ideal. If there are maples, make sure you have a good 6 weeks of winter left before the spring thaw in late February or early March before you cut. If you don't, they will probably bleed like crazy. If you can't get the cutting done in that timeframe, wait until the maples are out in full leaf in the summer and then trim up some of the bits that you need to take off.

Tree Recommendations for Wet Location

Our backyard slopes down and at the far end flattens out into a park. Water tends to pool in that lower section, especially in the early spring, and I would like to plant a flowering tree or shrub that would do well in those conditions. What would you suggest?

Pussy Willows would be in their glory down there. Dogwood does beautifully and you can let the shrub grow to the size and shape that you want. You can go with either the Red Twig or Yellowtwig Dogwood. Both will give your yard some interest through the winter, both get fairly dense and they are both quite

happy with the wetter conditions you have down there. Those would be ideal. You might want to come back up the slope just a little when you plant depending on how much light you are getting down there, so that their feet are not constantly in water, but with full light they should be fine. Lilacs would also do very well in that situation but again, it would be best to come back up the slope a bit so they are not constantly in water. With adequate light and moist conditions they will stand up quite nicely.

Plants that Like Their Feet Wet

I'm planning a small flower bed that will get 4-5 hours of late afternoon sun. Could you suggest some low annuals or perennials that do not mind wet feet?

Annuals would not be too successful. In terms of perennials, hostas will tolerate wetter conditions but if you can raise the soil level up approximately an inch so it is a little drier toward the surface and slope it slightly away from the centre to drain off some of the surface water, they will be much happier. Astilbes will also stand up quite nicely. Beebalm will survive in wetter conditions but its preference is still for a drier location. Cardinal flowers, our native lobelia, will do wonderfully. The Wild Iris *versicolor*, often called the Blue Flag Iris, prefers a wet location. Siberian Iris will stand up nicely also. Ferns will do well and there are a wide range of both native and cultivated varieties. Annuals typically do not like to have their feet wet all of the time – with the exception of Canna Lilies. Those that do like a fair amount of moisture are unfortunately also susceptible to rot. If you do raise the bed a bit, there are a number of things that will grow successfully from Fibrous Begonias or Waxed Begonias to impatiens and alyssum. If you raise it up, anything that is shallow-rooted should tolerate these conditions.

Protecting Flower Beds from Road Salt

My plan is to establish a 3 x 12-foot raised bed about 14 inches high and to put about three spireas and some annuals into it. The bed will be butted along one side by a row of large flat limestone rocks about the same height as the proposed garden. The problem is that it will be about 3 feet from a municipal road. How can I protect the perennials and annuals from salt and winter ploughing? Have you any other suggestions for any other perennial bushes I might try here other than spirea?

The end of your garden closest to the road may be a bit more of a problem in terms of salt and winter damage, so reserve that end for the annuals. When you prepare the bed, do mound it somewhat in the centre. This does mean it will be a little more difficult to manage in terms of getting good penetration when watering, but the benefit will come in winter when salt becomes a problem. If the bed has a slight angle the dissolved salt will tend to run off as the snow melts instead of seeping down into your bed. You may still get some damage but what is good about the spireas you have chosen is that they are fairly resistant and do shed their leaves in the fall, so these will not get burned by salt. Any new, tender growth will always get burned a little, but in a healthy bed that should not pose too much of a problem. You can also try screening in front of that bed. It may be worthwhile putting posts in at the four corners and half way down each side of the bed and wrapping burlap around the whole bed in the fall to cut down the wind damage and stop more snow building up than would really be desired. The other alternative would be to run a snow fence along the edge of the bed on that one side. In terms of other plants that might go in there, dogwood is quite attractive and will stand up fairly well to salt build up. The Red Osier, Silverleaf or Yellowtwig would do nicely – and all of these dogwoods give you the added benefit of a yellow or red bark on the twig during the winter months which adds another element to the landscape. Mock Orange would also do well here. The Burning Bush is attractive and there is also viburnum — most are native and have the added benefit of attracting birds. Try to avoid the evergreens. They have more of a problem with salt residue collecting on the foliage, so for that reason you are best to stay with plants that shed their leaves in the fall.

Recommendations for Shady Yard

We live in a house with the main window facing west, we have big trees in front and a small area where we can plant flowers but it is shaded by the trees and only gets mottled light. What are the best flowers and shrubs, preferably with blooms, to plant there?

Start with shade-loving plants first and go through the range of hostas. Is the tree deciduous or coniferous? If it is deciduous there will be lots of light first thing in the spring and then it will diminish as the foliage starts to come out, but that does allow you to have a full range of spring flowering bulbs and woodland plants that will do very nicely there with full exposure to sun first thing in the year and mottled sunlight thereafter. That would include some of the natives such as Trout Lilies and trilliums that can be commercially purchased as well. In the heavier shaded areas, ferns will stand up quite nicely. Dogwood would work well in those conditions as well. If you are looking for evergreens in that setting, Japanese Yews are a good option. In terms of flowering shrubs, the more light the more they are going to flower. Spirea will give you some reasonable production if they are planted toward the edges where the light levels are highest. You could look at things like Mock Orange and honeysuckle but once again, be certain to get them toward the edges because of the light levels. Astilbe will do nicely in damper conditions. If your trees are conifers, any of the Northern Light series of azaleas would do nicely, as would rhododendrons. The Helsinki series of rhododendrons will love you for being planted there as will other acid-loving plants like Erica or heather. Do mulch everything you are putting in. With large trees, either deciduous or coniferous, you are going to have lots of competition for the light as well as for the moisture and nutrients that are available, so mulching will be a plus in helping those bedded plants get their share.

Non-chemical Treatment for Arborvitae Leaf Miner

I need some advice on an effective, non-chemical treatment for Arborvitae leaf miner. We have a 20-25 foot high cedar hedge that is about 40 feet long. Two summers ago it was pruned back on one side, up maybe 15 feet from the ground. The next summer, arborists identified a leaf miner problem and recommended a mixture of Cygone and Malathion but since it was already the middle of summer, they said the spray wouldn't be effective. The loss of leaves continued over the winter. Now that spring is coming, I'm wondering if there is something we can use – other than the spray – that is not a chemical and as harsh to the environment.

A vigorous, healthy tree is going to be much better able to withstand any kind of insect at-tack. I think your concentration should be on the soil and the hedge health itself rather than on defeating the miner that is already well established in the cedars at this point. Compost on both sides of the root system and scratch it in around the base of the plants. A thorough watering when things get stressful, especially early in the spring, will get the trees moving into vigorous growth. That is going to do more to control the miner problem than the spray would. If you only treat the symptoms and the cedars stay in a weakened state, then even with the spray the problem will come back. Robust trees are going to be able to withstand this sort of in-festation much better and you will find that the natural predators will start to clean up the miner prob-lem up for you. There are a few things you can do to help nature along. The leaf miner maggots over winter in the tips of the leaves so an early season light trimming of your hedge will re-move them. Do it before the cedars start into growth and clean up and burn the clippings. Alternatively, you can collect them up in plastic garbage bags and leave them in the sun for a month or two to kill the maggots and then add them to the com-post. In mid June or early July when the eggs would normally hatch, watch your hedge for any small grey moths with a wing span of about 1/3 inch. If the moths appear, spray the trees with a 40-1 solution of water and liquid soap. Leave that on for 10 minutes and then rinse the trees with clear water. That, along with any improvement you can make to the general health of your cedars, should take care of the problem.

Choosing and Planting Hedges

No reflection on my neighbours, but I'm looking to plant a hedge at the side of my property. Could you suggest a fast-growing, hardy one that would allow for some privacy, preferably all year round?

Your best choice for year-round privacy would probably be an evergreen and the one used most often is the Eastern White Cedar. It can be clipped and shaped or you can just let it go to give a natural effect which is not unappealing. For a hedge, I would suggest that you go with field-grown cedars. If you can find a source of them, they are usually cheaper than nursery plants but also have the plus of being single-stemmed specimens, as opposed to nursery-grown which are now often multi-stemmed. A snow load on top of a multi-stemmed cedar tends to cause it to splay or spread apart, so I find the field ones are a better choice. For a privacy hedge, I'd put in a double row. Plant the

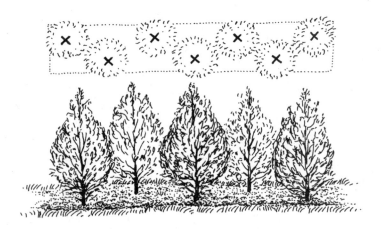

trees in each row about 2 feet apart from each other and the rows about a foot apart. In effect what you'll have is one plant and then another on an angle or diagonal and then the next in line with the first and so on in a sort of zigzag pattern. Eventually, as the trees grow, you'll have a few branches touching in the first row and in the blanks in between will be the trees from the next row, so you end up with complete coverage two deep all the way along. You'll want to create a nice soil bed before you plant, especially if you are in an area with very dry clay or rocky soil. In either case, you'll want to look at working in 30-40% compost. Before the hedge is planted, incorporate some rock phosphate, super phosphate or bone meal into the soil that will stimulate root development on the cedars as they are getting established. Give them a thorough watering after the installation and during that initial establishment period, then make sure they continue to get enough moisture throughout the first growing season right up until the soil freezes. If the plants aren't getting enough rain, you'll have to put some time and energy into watering until the hedge gets well established.

Transplanting Lilacs

We made a mistake by putting a lilac bush in an area that is too shady. It's about 6 feet tall now and we want to transplant it over to the front yard where it is sunny. What time of year do we transplant it and do we cut the branches back?

It would be best if you do not cut the branches back and wait until first thing in the spring, just as soon as the soil is workable, to do the transplanting. Take out as much of the root ball as you can and move that directly into the new location, planting it at the same depth as at the original location. Get some organic matter worked into the soil underneath it and adding some rock phosphate or bone meal to stimulate the roots will help. Water it in well so there are no air pockets left around the roots due to the transplanting. As it breaks dormancy and starts growing, it will be doing so at the new location. Be prepared to nurse it along for the first year as you would any new plant material. Try to avoid any unnecessary stress while it's re-establishing. If it's dry during the summer months, make sure the bush gets thorough watering. It should come along just fine and be all the better for the new location. That increase in sunlight should ensure you get a good flowering the next spring.

Controlling Sucker Growth

Every year we prune our plum and pear trees. The problem is that we get all these vertical shoots, maybe 4 feet long, coming out afterward and not from the bottom of the tree, but from the branches at the top. I know you are not supposed to prune a tree too much, but if you cut all these things off, they just all come back. How can I control them?

This is really where the balancing act comes in. If you can keep the initial pruning of the tree below 25% it will not produce as much of that sucker growth or what are known as water sprouts. If there are a number of water sprouts there, you can certainly prune them out, but keep that 25% maximum rule of thumb in mind. By limiting the amount you take off you will decrease the amount of re-shooting that is produced. Over a period of a few years that will allow you to bring the crown back to the size and shape you want. If you go past the 25% mark, you stimulate an awful lot of that sucker growth and they do tend to clog up the crown of your fruit trees. If that

happens, the tree will not produce well for you at all. You get less light penetration and the tree tries to put its energy into the sucker growth rather than fruit production.

Tent Caterpillar Offensive

My question has to do with army worms. I believe the proper term for them is tent caterpillars. I just moved into a place that has plum trees and crabapples and I was told by the former owner that she didn't get any fruit at all last season because these caterpillars had completely ravaged the blossoms and the leaves. The last thing I heard is that we are expecting them again this year. Is there anything I can do to stop them?

Yes. As soon as you start seeing the "tents" showing up, get out there with a long thin stick or small branch, preferably with a fork at the end, and just poke it into the tent and roll it around so that it winds up all the silk and picks it off. Then put the stick with that material onto the ground and step on it well. You might want to wear boots for this. Do it early in the day when the caterpillars are in there and you avoid the problem of having them out of the tent when you come by. Get them early in the season as well, for obvious reasons. The longer they're there, the more chance they have to spread and reproduce as well as damage the flowers and leaves. If you can't get at the tent with a stick, the other thing you can do is aim a good jet from your hose to burst the tent open, flush it out, and expose them. The tent is their protection and if they don't have that place to hide from their predators they'll get cleaned up pretty quickly. By getting that kind of control going you keep reducing the local population. You may not end up completely free of them, but you will certainly be far below the normal level for the garden. If this was a big problem last year, you may also want to alleviate some of the stress the trees have been under as a result. If you can make sure they don't dry out this year that would be a big plus. And certainly fertilizing with a side dressing of compost and mulching around them is going to be worthwhile as well. The most important thing is to make sure they don't go under any water stress this year, so if it starts getting dry, use the hose out there.

Rhododendron Won't Bloom

I'm not sure what to do about a very thick-leafed rhododendron in my yard. The first year I had it planted, it bloomed but then in the last few years I haven't had any. I noticed this winter that the bottom leaves are turning quite yellow and I was wondering if I am having a problem with it or not?

You will want to do some mulching around that plant. Before you add the mulch, scratch up the surface of the soil. Do this carefully and as early as possible in the spring. I say carefully because there is probably a fair amount of the fine root system near the surface, particularly if you've got clay soil. Start this process around the drip line of the plant and work in towards the centre. If you are finding too much root, don't bother scraping the surface but do get at least an inch, and preferably a couple of inches, of mulch down everywhere under the plant. Use an acidic mulch because you want to acidify the soil slightly here. Any old tea bags will help if you happen to be a tea drinker – dry them, break them open and keep the spent tea leaves in a container until you are ready to garden. Once you are out there, scatter the tea lightly over the surface of the soil under your rhododendron before adding the mulch. Barring the tea bag treatment, you can go with a pine bark or a cedar bark mulch which will have the same effect over the long term. If you have access to pine needles or cedar foliage, that would likewise be ideal as an acidic mulch.

All Flowers, No Fruit

I have a mature fruit tree in the backyard but I'm not even sure what it is because it blossoms every spring but never produces any fruit. Is there anything I can to do encourage it along?

Dryness after flowering will cause the abscission or abortion of the fruit, but not being pollinated can be a major problem as well. If you feel the tree is getting enough moisture and the issue isn't dryness, you could put some early spring flowering plants into your garden to encourage pollination. Get some flowering perennials or bright coloured annuals going out there. Pansies would be good or any other plants that flower early so that you can attract and keep lots of insects coming around. Get them in there before your tree comes into flower for obvious reasons. This will help ensure successful pollination and that is probably the critical thing. Your tree is producing flowers so it is obviously getting enough light and is happy with the growing conditions. Make sure it has all the moisture it needs. If conditions get particularly dry during or after flowering,

give it a thorough soaking. But the critical thing is to get insects into the area – if the flowers don't get pollinated they won't produce any fruit.

Chokecherry Infestation

We have a couple of choke-cherry trees in our back yard. Last year, after they flowered, one of our trees developed fruit that was shaped like a little pear. We cut it open and there were tiny orange worms inside. I am wondering if we have to use a soap and water spray or some other type of spray and if so, what kind?

What you have there is a chokecherry midge gall filled with chokecherry midges. You can avoid the use of any pesticide by making sure that any plant litter, either fruit, leaves or branches, is cleaned up around the trees in the fall. Once the chokecherries have gone into dormancy, apply a dormant oil spray. Spray them again with the oil before they come out of their dormancy in the spring. That should take care of any problem and unless you have a lot of wild cherries around, you are probably not going to see the infestation coming back. When you apply that oil in the spring, wait until it gets up to about 10° celsius through the day. Pick a bright, sunny day with no wind and try to get out there in the morning to allow as much time as possible for the trees to dry before nightfall. Spraying the dormant oil at that time of year will kill the insects in their dormant stage. It is also just before the buds come out so it won't cause any damage to the leaves.

Transplanting Roses

The large patch of heritage roses I have been growing for 6 or 7 years are now terribly overcrowded. I am hoping to move about 6 of them this spring. Do you have any advice on how best to do this?

It's best not to dig all of the roses out at once. Go at them one at a time, taking out as much of the root system of each rose as you possibly can. At the new location, dig a hole that is wider and deeper than the root ball of the plant you are moving, then add some organic matter and mix it well down into the soil. Move the plant to the new location, getting it in there as quickly as possible. Backfill with your amended soil, soak it in thoroughly and go on to the next one. Do make sure that you are burying the graft or bud union when you do the transfer, or if they are on their own root stock, that the initial joint is at least a few inches below the soil – 6 inches deep would be ideal. Don't forget to add some bone meal or rock phosphate to the soil in each planting hole to stimulate the new root development. The best time to transplant would be in the spring, as soon as the soil is workable. If you can move them before they break their dormancy and have them come out of dormancy in their new location, that will be the secret to success.

Black Spot on Roses

I have several Explorer Rose bushes that were ravaged by black spot last year. I removed all of the affected material but I am wondering how I can strengthen them this year to prevent that from happening again?

Keep an eye on them. If all the debris is gone from last fall, that is perfect. If not, do a cleanup this spring and take all the old leaves, petals and twigs away. You'll want to dig down into the top couple of inches of the soil as well, and to remove any infected leaf litter incorporated there. Scratch up around the entire area so that any litter or debris will dry out very readily on the surface around the roses. Anything you prune off, get completely away. A spray of baking soda and water at this point will help. About a 1-5% concentration of baking soda would be about right. You are not going to get a prophylactic effect but you will get some measure of control if any of the disease is still present. If the buds are starting to swell or the leaves are breaking out when you do the treatment, just let very large drips of the mixture go down the stem. Don't spray into the buds or you can get a bit of burning on the foliage as the buds open. This is not a problem with mature foliage however and sprinkling that mixture over the soil around the roses is also fine. Make sure you do the spraying when there will be a couple of days without rain or the solution will get flushed right off and won't have the effectiveness you want.

Gopher Grief

The first summer in our new home, I discovered a little gopher living in the backyard under my garage. I am wondering if there is anything you can suggest to plant in this area that the gopher won't eat.

Not really. Gophers will eat just about any seedlings. The hungrier they are, the more they are going to go after them. You can give your existing plants a measure of protection by applying a Tabasco or pepper spray right onto the plants. Add a few drops of Tabasco to a 40:1 water and soap solution or sprinkle cayenne pepper on right after a light soap and water spray. Just a light covering will do but you need to use something that tastes bad to deter them. The soap and water will leave an unpleasant scent for them as well. Unfortunately, this treatment is too strong to use on your young seedlings. The spray needs to be left on the plants to act as a deterrent and unfortunately, this will burn young plants. It is going to be difficult to get anything established unless you put chicken wire directly over it. You will need to create a bit of a cage about 6 inches high on each side of the seedlings and then over the top so that the gopher can't physically get at them. That should keep them safe until the plants get well established and then you can move on to the spray deterrent.

Hydrangea Blues

I have a beautiful plant with purply flowers that I purchased at the grocery store. I think it is a hydrangea. I am wondering if I can put that in the garden? Someone told me that if I do put it in my garden, I will never get those beautiful blue colours again.

I wonder why they said that? It's not entirely true. In places with a limestone base, hydrangeas tend a bit more toward the pinks or a purply blue. You can also help to encourage that blue colour along and its not that difficult to accomplish. Put a tablespoon of aluminum sulphate, which you can get from a local pharmacy or garden centre, into a gallon of water. Do a couple of applications of that solution early in the season just as the plant starts coming out of dormancy and another during the last 2 weeks of June. When the flower buds are about the size of a pea, do a final application and that should get the colour right back in there for you. Hydrangea usually do much better in a sunnier location but this one has been greenhouse grown and was developed as an interior plant. You will probably get some sunburn on the foliage when you put it out and that can result in a lot of reddening of the foliage. To avoid that, when you take it outdoors you could leave it in its pot for a week and place it in mottled sunlight, working it gradually into higher light over the next few days or weeks until you finally end up at the spot where you want to plant it. When you do dig it in, you might want to mix a bit of bone meal or rock phosphate in with the soil to encourage development of the root system. Be prepared to give this one good winter protection if you live anywhere below Zone 5.

MAY

So Much Garden, So Little Time

Over the years I have put a lot of time and effort into my ornamental gardens but I have a busier job now and less time and energy for the garden. I'd like to scale down but I also want my gardens to look cared for and beautiful. Can you advise me on how to make the best use of the little time I have?

I can certainly give you a few pointers. These are things that can be done at any time of the season and at a pace that suits your schedule. If you are planning on scaling back it would be useful to start by drawing up a site plan on a sheet of graph paper. Block in the elements that are there already and not likely to move like your house, garage, deck, driveway, or any other permanent structures. Make a list of all the trees and shrubs on your property. Note which ones are the most critical or desirable in terms of shade, protection or privacy and which ones need the most work to maintain. Identify the ones you want to keep and the ones you want to eliminate and plot the keepers on to your plan. Next list all of the plant materials that are in the beds now. Flag the ones that are doing well or are special favourites as well as those you find are too high maintenance or no longer suit. Plot these keepers on to the plan. Finally, draw up a wish list. This should include any new elements you may want to introduce such as lower maintenance or drought-resistant plants, statues, ponds, stone walkways or anything else that might replace the flowers or shrubs you have slated for removal. Plot those in as well. Drawing this plan up with different colours helps you visualize the changes and get some idea of how things might look over time. Then it's simply a matter of working toward that blueprint whenever you have the chance. The plants that you want to take out can be donated to local plant sales and charity events or given to friends. The new elements can be purchased and introduced as space opens up. Finally, there are a few one-time tasks that can help minimize the need for repetitive chores such as weeding and watering and these really help to improve the overall tidiness and appeal of your garden. One task that can really work wonders is edging. Just take an edging tool or sharpened spade and work your way around the outer contours of your beds so that you redefine those areas. This not only cleans up and highlights those spaces, it also helps with drainage and stops your turf from invading those beds. The effect goes way beyond the effort involved. The

next priority is to divide your perennials and give away any that are not needed. After that, prune back any shrubs that have grown out of shape. You can take off up to 25% of any plant, removing the parts that are dead, diseased, damaged or dangerous. Next clip off deadheads. It's another of those tasks that will give your garden a boost that goes well beyond the actual amount of effort involved. It will also promote new growth and more blooms, which helps to give your garden a more vigorous look. And last but not least, compost and mulch. Composting will ensure that your plants are well nourished and happy – and therefore much better able to fend off any infestations or diseases that might hit. Mulching will give the beds a cleaner look, help them retain more moisture, suppress the weed growth, cool the earth and as it breaks down will add more nutrient to the soil. Over time you should be able to create an aesthetically pleasing garden that requires far less work to maintain.

How to Preserve Seeds

What is the best way to preserve seeds?

It depends on the sorts of seeds. If you have tropical or subtropical seeds that you are using for annuals, they should not be frozen but kept in a cool, dry, dark location. The best thing to do is to put the seed packets inside a jar with a couple of pieces of dry paper towel and seal the jar. When you buy the seeds fresh you get about an 80% germination rate. That percentage will drop each year as the seeds age. In some instances you will drop down to 20% or less in the second year of attempted germination. The best approach is to use them as soon as you can. Seeds such as parsley, carrots, or any of our native or indigenous seed-bearing plants can be frozen because that is what would normally happen to them in their natural state. In fact, that freezing is sometimes needed to break the seeds' dormancy and allow germination. If you are freezing seeds for storage, bag or bottle them in clean, dry, sealed containers. Don't forget to label them – many seeds will look similar come next spring!

Vermin in the Composter

How concerned should you be about animals being attracted to your compost?

This should not be a big problem unless you live in the country and are putting a huge overproduction of apples into your compost, in which case the bears would likely be coming around to your property anyway. The stories you hear of compost piles being overrun by rats fall largely into the category of urban myth. You may occasionally get raccoons or skunks coming by, but they usually don't create too much of a problem. It's always best not to position the compost right next to the house for obvious reasons, but not so far away that you never want to use it. There are a number of good commercial composters on the market and some municipalities do offer them to their citizens free of charge or at a reduced rate to help get organic matter out of the municipal waste stream, but you can get by quite nicely with a simple home made structure. To build one, just place a number of cement blocks on the ground for support and lay a wire floor on top. A section of Frost fencing or the reinforcing wire used for concrete works well here and can be purchased at any building supply store. Next put a number of wooden or metal stakes in around the sides and then wrap some wire mesh around those. You'll need to cut a hole or two in the mesh at the bottom between the cement blocks below the wire floor so you can get a shovel into that empty space to take out the compost after it cures and falls through. Once that compost is up and running, work the fresh material down into the pile rather than simply throwing it on top to ensure it remains active – this will also discourage any unwanted visitors. If you find your compost pile is drying out water it liberally to re-activate the microbial population. A compost pile is well worth any time that it takes to build or maintain. The black gold it produces is really invaluable to any garden.

Preventing Wormy Carrots

I often grow nice carrots in my garden but they start getting wormy when I store them. I wonder how I could avoid that. I have heard that it's caused by a fly that lays its eggs on the carrots and I was wondering if I put white garden cloth over the plants, whether that would help?

The fact that you are getting wormy carrots in storage says to me that you do indeed have the Carrot Rust Fly. They attack celery, parsnips, and parsley as well. These flies eat small roots and tunnel into larger ones and it is their rust-red excrement that gives them their name. The adult fly does no damage to your plants but lays eggs on the soil surface in the late spring and early summer. The eggs hatch into an off-white maggot about 1/3 inch long

that feeds on and in the roots, then emerges as an adult in late summer. This new generation of adults lays eggs that hatch into maggots in late August or early September and these are the ones that come in on your stored carrots. So yes, laying out that garden cloth will prevent the flies from getting around the carrots to lay their eggs. Once you have seeded and there is enough warmth in the soil to get the carrots germinating, get them covered. The row cover has to go on early and stay on right through the growing season. It would be a good idea to try one of the spun row covers, just because they are less penetrable than the fine mesh. Obviously, you will need to lift it fairly regularly once the carrots are growing to do your weeding, but just replace it when you're done. It is not always 100% successful because some intruders are going to slip in when you lift the cover, but having your carrots protected most of the time is certainly going to be a major plus. Likewise, be sure to destroy any badly damaged plants to reduce the source of the next year's insect population. Another thing you could do is store your carrots in either dry sand or dry peat moss once they've been harvested. This will keep them cooler and provide a minimal but stable moisture level which prevents the carrots from withering and drying out, but be sure to inspect them carefully before storing them.

Mole Infested Lawn

I don't want my cottage lawn to be a city lawn but my problem is with moles and they seem to be getting worse. Short of buying a cat, which I refuse to do, what would you suggest to get rid of them?

If you know anybody who has a cat, get some of the spent kitty litter and put it into the holes. That scent will deter them and keep them away for a little while. If you are planning on leveling the lawn to get rid of all the burrows and tunnels, you can mix some of that dirty cat litter into the soil, but in the meantime, putting the spent litter down into the holes will help. The other thing you can do is mix up a solution of castor oil with 10-parts water to 1-part castor oil. Put a couple of ounces in various spots, ideally at the entrance to the tunnels and then down into them. Moles don't like the smell and it's sometimes easier to get this mixture down into the hole. If they are invading a garden area, planting some castor beans around the edge will give you the same effect as the castor oil. Winter poses another problem

because the moles and mice have free range under the snow. There are fewer predators looking for them and they have very favourable, insulated conditions. You can tell your problem is field mice if, come spring, you find the balls of grass and seeds they collect sitting in little piles on the surface of the lawn. The field mice can travel just under the snow, they don't even have to burrow into the ground, and they will nest on top of the soil with whatever they can put together. Normally, if you can deter them throughout the summer months, you usually won't get a big population through the winter. That being said, with a good snow cover, they can always move in from elsewhere. You can help the situation a little if you treat the area with the kitty litter and castor oil again late in the fall. A last cut of the grass going into the winter with the blade lowered to 1 or 1½ inches will also give them less to eat and may encourage them to move on to a more appealing site for winter.

Do's and Don'ts for Boston Ivy

I would like to grow Boston Ivy on the sidewall of a 2-storey brick house. How far apart and how far from the wall should I plant it? How high should the nurse stick be?

Over the long term, the tentacles of the Boston Ivy will eat away at the mortar of your wall, so it is preferable that it doesn't grow directly on the brick. You could use a trellis or wire for support to prevent this. In that case, you would plant the vines far enough away from the wall to allow room to get in and trim off anything that starts heading back behind or through your support system onto the wall. If you are planting without the aid of a trellis and letting them climb directly up the wall, put them closer, about 6-12 inches from the building. Let them run up onto the support sticks to start and once you get them up a few feet, they can start taking care of themselves. A nurse stick or support that is 1-1½ metres would help them get established. If you plant a vine every foot along the wall, you will have a lot of coverage more quickly. However, if you are willing to wait a bit longer, 2-2½ feet in between plants will be fine because the vine, once it is established, will continue to spread over the wall and give you very good coverage. If you want coverage quickly, start by planting them every 12-18 inches apart and as things develop, if you find it is

getting too heavy, start removing some of the in-between plants. In the long term, you will not have as much of a competition problem and you will get that initial coverage sooner.

Good Tree Choice for a Small Backyard

I am looking to plant a small decorative tree in the back garden of my townhouse and I am considering a Golden Chain Tree. Would you consider this tree to be hardy in a Zone 4 climate? If not, could you recommend an alternative?

The "Golden Chain" is a beautiful small-flowering tree but unfortunately the most common variety, the Vossi, is only hardy to Zone 6 in Canada. In a sheltered spot in Zone 5 you might get away with planting it, but not in Zone 4. If you were able to find a Scotch Laburnum you'd have a better chance of its surviving since it's hardy to Zone 5B. This one is smaller and has a broader head than the more common variety. It's been in cultivation as far back as 1596. The problem is that it is not as commonly available in nurseries and garden centres, which I find a great disappointment, so sourcing one might be a problem. Magnolia might be another option, but again, in that zone hardiness is an issue. That being said, the Yulan Magnolia, a native of eastern China, is hardy to Zone 5B and should be hardy in a protected site in Zone 4. I've also heard of gardeners having success in Zone 4 with Magnolia Galaxy, though it's only listed as hardy to Zone 6. The most common magnolia available in a small tree form is the Saucer Magnolia, but it is borderline at best. The Star Magnolia is hardy to Zone 5B but will take years to reach its maximum height of 3 metres and it needs protection from late frosts if you want it to flower successfully. Some other very good and extremely hardy options for smaller spaces in colder climates are the Amur Maple, or the serviceberry – also known as Juneberry, Shadbush or Shadblow. The Amur Maple can be pruned and maintained or allowed to become a large bushy plant. It's hardy to Zone 2 and has bright green three-lobed leaves that turn to bright red or orange in the fall. The leaves of the Allegheny serviceberry will also give you a nice orange and red colour in the fall as well as a show of white pendulous flowers in mid to late spring. It's hardy to Zone 3B, so it's a good choice for cold climates. As a native plant it also has the plus of being a good food source for many songbirds.

Alternatives for Under Pine Trees

I have a flower bed that is under a pine tree, so I would imagine very acidic. Last year I had pansies in there and they were beautiful until about the middle of August and then they died. This year I had impatiens in there and they didn't even grow. So what can I do?

Better to stick with the things that work. The pansies did not have any problem with the soil conditions. Their problem was the higher heat that comes along later in the summer. Under normal circumstances, if they have enough moisture they will start to flower again in the late summer as temperatures start to drop. Another one that would do nicely in conditions of partial shade and cooler temperatures is Primulas or the Polyanthus Primrose. Astilbe would work well if you are looking for a perennial. For some of the shrubs, you'll want to plant them towards the outer edge of the shade where they would get slightly higher light. You could try the whole Northern Lights series of azaleas which love those acidic conditions. Whatever you choose, the most critical factor in getting the results you want here is simply enough water for both the pine tree and everything else growing in the bed underneath it. That will always be a concern. The tree will take up a lot of moisture and the smaller flowering plants will dry out more quickly than the large pine tree. So make sure there is enough moisture available for everything. The pine needles do a great job of mulching the soil surface and that holds a little bit more moisture in, so on that count the needles are a plus.

Starlings and Grubs

It is clear that we have a problem with grubs. We dug around and found some and the starlings are certainly busy tearing at the soil. What do you think could be done without using heavy pesticides?

One thing you can do is to encourage those starlings. Despite the morning songs and the squawking, put up with them and learn to enjoy them. They are doing a marvelous job, and better the starlings than the skunks, raccoons or crows that all tend to chew the daylights out of things and tear up the turf. If your lawn does get damaged, rake it flat, put the turf divots back in place, pack them down, and wait until the starlings have finished their feeding. Top-dress after the birds are done, over-seed and things will come back in

quite nicely. Come hatch time, which is mid to end of June, if you are seeing a fair amount of hatch of either Japanese Beetles, European Chafers or June Beetles, that is the time to introduce some nematodes into the soil. Nematodes are tiny wormlike creatures that feed parasitically on grubs and are readily available at most garden centres. Make sure you check the date on the boxes. You'll want this year's product since I've heard that they don't store all that well. The nematode mixture has to be dissolved in water as per the manufacturer's directions. Your lawn and soil will have to be well watered and then once the nematodes are applied, maintained with a good high level of moisture in order to sustain them. If they dry out or if the soil is too cold, that is the end of them, so make sure all the conditions are right before they are introduced, otherwise you will never get the necessary population established. Needless to say, if the conditions are not right and most die off, the chances of nematodes clearing out your grubs will be severely compromised.

Impact of Road Salt

We live in a major highway corridor and this year I've noticed the pine trees are dying all along the road sides – big trees, small trees, pine trees of all kinds as well as the cedars. On some of the secondary roads you don't notice it as much. I was wondering if it is emissions from the cars? It looks like somebody has just taken brown spray paint and gone down both sides of the highway but it only seems to go back as far as the first or second row of trees.

Generally that dieback is caused by the penetration of spray from the passing cars and trucks. The salt is the culprit. On secondary roads, with fewer cars and generally slower speeds, there is less spray as well as less frequency of salting, so the trees are better protected. Some years are especially hard, particularly if there are a lot of small snowfalls rather than just a few big ones. Every snowfall leads to ploughing, salting and sanding, so it means that there are more regular applications of salt in the snowy years. If you get a number of clear sunny days between snowfalls, then you get the burning effect as well since there is more salty water on the road to spray up into the trees. That is likely what you are seeing and there is really very little that can be done as long as we are committed to having our roads cleared and salted throughout the winter.

Dog Days of Spring

I have about a 10 by 10 foot area in my backyard that the dog used for his business in the winter months. I cleaned and raked it up but I was wondering if I should re-seed it and what preparations to the soil I should make?

Start by giving the area a thorough soaking, loosen up the soil if it has compacted and top-dress a little if you need to level the area out. Compost will do fine for this. A sandy loam is ideal too and if you can mix them together, all the better. Level the area off and over-seed it. It shouldn't be a problem. The salts that have built up from the urine will normally be carried away fairly effectively with the spring runoff, either down into the soil or across the surface, so you don't have to be concerned with a big build-up. If you find there are areas that don't come back particularly well after seeding, you may want to give these another soaking or apply horticultural-grade lime on the soil at the manufacturer's recommended rate of application and then soak it and re-seed again. If it is a full-sun area, go with a general "park mix" of grass seed. Do wait until the temperature warms up to about 15° celsius and that should be sufficient for the seeds to germinate.

There should be no problem getting things re-established after that.

Home-brewed Insecticides

I heard somebody talking about natural substances that can be used for insect control. One was garlic crushed in the blender and added to water, and tobacco was another one. Do you know these formulas and what they are best used for?

I know that for deer and rodent control, garlic will certainly give you a deterrent effect. If you are looking at its specific properties, garlic is known to be useful as an antibiotic, but only slightly so, and it is an antiseptic, so if you have an infection, it can be used that way. If you use it as a deterrent, you want a solution strong enough to maintain its smell and obviously, the stronger the solution that you apply, the longer it is going to work. In terms of tobacco, commercial nicotine sprays are now off the market. You can brew some up at home and spray it on and it will kill most insects in the same manner that many other contact insecticides do. It leaves a toxic residue on the plant that will be consumed by the insects and act as a stomach poison. That being said, there is always a question of whether you want to be handling this sort of toxic product that can be absorbed through your own skin as well. I am not certain of the specific proportions you need to use when mixing this, but I have seen places where people just collected old cigarette butts, saturated them in a container with water, let it sit and steep for a few hours or overnight and then strained it and used it that way for caterpillar and insect control. You will also get some staining from the use of the nicotine, so do be careful if you are spraying it against any walls or painted surfaces.

Lawn Renewal

There are a few deciduous trees on my property, lots of weeds, some bare spots and the lawn has not been aerated or top-dressed in a long time. I have applied spring fertilizer and fall fertilizer occasionally in the past. When should I do a lawn renewal? What should I do? Do you have any ideas about what I can put in for ground cover other than using turf grass plants — something that is low maintenance and can handle human and dog traffic?

If your lawn has not been aerated and top-dressed in a long while, the first thing to do would be to remove as many of the weeds as possible, do an aeration and then top-dress over the whole area to level things out. I would recommend seeding it in the fall. You may need to do a touch up the next spring by over-seeding the area to fill in any bare patches. If you can get things established in the fall, they will take off that much better the next spring and you will have that much work already out of the way. Temperatures through the month of September and early October are generally conducive to germination of both grass plants and the alternatives. Seeding in with clover will reduce the cost of fertilizer because just 20-25% clover spread uniformly throughout the lawn will fix all of the nitrogen you would require to keep the turf plants healthy and vigorous. For a low-growing clover, the clover you should use is the Trifolium *repens* or Dutch White. Heavily over-seeding with this so that you go to 60-70% clover through the whole lawn area is not a problem and will reduce the amount of cutting that has to be done. It also stands up to traffic very well. If the seed doesn't germinate now, it will lay there dormant under the snow throughout the winter and come along next spring. The opportunity to get rid of the weeds and top-dress in the fall is a big plus but the whole process can take place anytime throughout the growing season. Obviously, in spring or summer you have to be prepared to water and stay off the area while the new lawn gets established. The fall/spring schedule is probably the one that will require the least amount of interruption in the use of your lawn. Given your circumstances, this is the ground cover solution that will best handle the human and dog traffic. If you want to reduce the amount of lawn you need to care for, you might want to consider creating or expanding planting beds. Another option for cutting back on turf is to remove the grass from underneath the trees and plant shade-tolerant perennials in there instead or simply remove the turf and mulch.

Transplanting Wild Orchids

Last year we bought a property up north on a lake. When I was clearing the land I found a beautiful little flower in the bush and later discovered that it was a Moccasin Flower, a member of the wild orchid family. Unfortunately, it is in the way and I tried to transplant it but found it has a very shallow root system between the soil and the top debris. Can I transplant this easily?

"Easily" is a relative term here. Orchids are very site specific and as a result, they are extremely good environmental indicators. Any change in their environment and they start to suffer or die off. So what that says is that you must duplicate the original conditions you found them in as closely as possible when you transplant – and that is a challenge. You also have to relocate as much soil and surface debris as possible with each one. That original soil is necessary because they grow symbiotically with the mycorrhizal fungi in that soil. Try to duplicate the soil type and conditions below the surface layer of organic debris as well as to ensure suitable drainage or moisture retention as the case may be. Taking a good quantity of the surface debris is a good start when transplanting but don't forget to add to it every year the way Mother Nature does each autumn.

Urban Squeeze on Large Trees

Our house is about 110 years old, faces west and the front lawn is about 10 feet by 10 feet square. In the very centre of that front lawn is a spruce tree that is about 3 storeys tall with a trunk that is about 10 inches in diameter and 30 inches in circumference. I just found out from the previous owner that it was planted 22 years ago after it arrived in the mailbox as a sapling in an advertisement supplement. The branches that are closest to our house are dying and I'm not sure what to do.

Here is the scenario. Late afternoon in the winter time, the sun pours down against the house and picks up all kinds of heat. When the sun goes down things get very cold but that heat from the house is still radiating. That heat building up in those branches closest to the house has caused a lot of that sap to liquefy. Then later it freezes fairly quickly and things start getting ruptured and the branches die back. They also dry out a lot more. The pores in the needles start to open up with that heat and are losing more moisture. The tree is probably taking up that entire front yard so there is a pretty limited area from which it can draw the moisture it needs to survive. Typically what happens with spruce in that situation is they start drying out from the bottom up and in this case, it is drying more on the house side because of the extra heat build up there. Unfortunately it is the wrong tree in the wrong place because it is always going to be too big for the location. That being said, there are a few things you can do to keep it going as long as you want it. Certainly trimming off the dead branches will make it more attractive. Making sure that it is well mulched underneath and thoroughly soaked on a regular basis will make all the difference in the world and that means watering it right up until freeze-up. That will alleviate some of the drying out but not all of it. With any luck you'll be able to get a few more years before it has to come down and be replaced by something a bit more appropriate to the location.

Battling Weeds

Every year I fight a losing battle with weeds. In spite of all my efforts, the offensive and unwelcome weeds return. Dandelions, thistles and burdock are the worst: they reproduce in abundance and seem determined to take over my lawn. I don't want to use chemicals. Have you any advice?

Any plant can be considered a "weed" if it is growing where you don't want it. Many plants that are perfectly acceptable and even beneficial from an ecological perspective can be a nuisance when they turn up in your lawn or garden. On the plus side, these plants do have some redeeming qualities. All of them have very long tap roots that draw a lot of nutrients up from deep in the soil.

The three you mention can anchor the soil and stabilize slopes. Thistles are a major food source for goldfinches who delay laying their eggs until late in the season in order to have a rich source of these seeds to feed their young. Burdock root is actually quite tasty. In spring the roots of the first year's growth can be peeled and eaten like radishes. You can also steam them like asparagus and season them with a little herb vinegar or lemon juice. The young leaves of the dandelion are edible and have a mild spinach flavour that is pleasant in a salad. The flowers are delicious battered and fried and taste a bit like mushrooms. Many of our grandparents may have made dandelion wine and some people still do. On the other hand, thistles can be painful on bare feet, dandelion sap stains clothing, and "burrs" cling to everything. They may be fine in a field but most of us would rather not have them in our gardens or lawns. So if you want to curb them, there are a few things you can try. At the very least, once they have seeded remove and destroy the burrs off the burdock and the thistles' seed heads. People have been known to vacuum the seeds from mature dandelion heads. A Shop Vac can work well here. With younger burdock and dense stands of thistles a regular mowing can be very effective. The more often you mow over their new growth, the weaker their root systems become until eventually the plants will simply starve and die. Once the thistles die off, turn up the soil, remove any stray roots and let that earth bake in the sun for a few weeks. Once that soil is "cooked", you can replant the area with more desirable material. New weed growth that pops up and other small infestations can be carefully dug out by working from the outside to the inside of the clump. It's best to loosen the soil with a fork before lifting the roots to try and minimize breakage because new plants can develop off any small pieces of root that get left behind. Covering an area with black plastic and then mulching over that will also be effective if you are trying to remediate larger areas. Dandelions pose a special problem because some forms can endure many mowings with little or no ill effect thanks to their extremely low leaves and a root system that is difficult to remove without wounding your turf. You can pull up young seedlings but the older plants tend to break off easily at the crown when you try to remove them and the remaining tap roots will callus over and re-shoot quickly. Try using a V-shaped weeder to pluck them out by their roots. Insert the tool downward and twist it to break or mangle the root, then use that forked end to pry out the upper part of the plant. You could also cut the roots diagonally with a knife, plunged at least 2 inches below surface, then pull out the severed plant. Top-dressing and re-seeding the areas where you have removed dandelions discourages germination of the weed seeds by creating greater competition for space and light. A weed-burning torch is another option that can be used to eliminate weeds from between the cracks in walkways or in driveways, but these propane flame-throwers need to be handled with care. Contrary to what you might think, the idea is not to destroy the plant with the flame. Simply burning off the top half of the plant will leave the roots intact and allow it to regenerate. What you actually want to do is to singe the weed to "melt" the waxy protective layer on the outside of the plant's leaves that prevents moisture from escaping uncontrollably from inside the plant. Once that waxy layer is gone, evaporation takes over, dehydrating the plant to the point where it can no longer survive. Weeds that transpire to death in this way generally disappear roots and all, but it takes some practice to apply just the right amount of heat to melt that "wax" without incinerating the plant. It's best not to try this method on your lawn because all of the desirable grass plants surrounding your weeds will get zapped too. The "perfect lawn" can be achieved, but it takes constant vigilance to counteract nature's tendency to mix things up. Nature always tends towards diversity, making the monoculture of our urban lawns a bit of an aberration. However, if you keep the soil well fed with an annual light covering of not more than a ½ inch of compost, maintain a 2½-3 inch grass length as a minimum, ensure your lawn has 1 inch of water per week applied all in one watering, not a bit at a time, and re-seed with a good quality grass seed when necessary, these will all help to keep "intruders" at bay without the use of chemicals.

The Lasagne Treatment

We have a lawn that we want to take out to turn into a flower bed. We had heard that we could do this by "the lasagne treatment". Can you tell us exactly what we need to do here, and when we should do it?

The "lasagne treatment" is a very good way to describe this process. It is a method of lay-ering material over the existing lawn and then planting into it. The first thing to do is to delineate the area you want to turn into a bed. If the grass is long or messy, put your lawnmower blade down as low as you can get it and run it over the whole space. Leave any clippings in place. Next start laying newspaper over the area. It needs to be about 10 sheets thick to be effective. Wet the newspaper down as you go and as you complete a section, throw a bit of mulch or compost over the top to hold it in place. Try not to overlap the newspapers too much or you will end up with some spots that are 20 sheets thick. You then have to decide if you want to raise the bed. This can easily be accomplished at this stage by adding soil on top of the newspaper. Put as much as you need to raise it to the desired height, then go ahead and plant right into that new soil. As the newspaper layer breaks down, the root system of your plants will penetrate through it. Your other option is to keep the bed at the existing level, in which case you need to put a slightly heavier layer of mulch over the whole newspapered area. Pull the mulch back from the location where you want to plant, cut a slit through the newspaper and plant directly into the soil below. Put the mulch back around the plant to further discourage any of the lawn from trying to poke through. The best time to do this conversion is in the spring: how early in the spring depends to some degree on the soil type you are working with. You don't want to be walking or working on that area before it has dried out sufficiently, otherwise you run the danger of compacting the soil. Obviously, a sandy or well-drained soil will dry out earlier in the season than a clay soil. Wait until you can walk over the area without leaving a footprint behind, then go ahead and start. There is no great benefit to getting at it any earlier.

Lawn Alternatives with Kids

We moved into our house last year with a large backyard but not a lot of grass. The majority of the lawn is one great big patch of mud and we have some large trees out there so it is very shady. I am not interested in creating a pristine lawn that requires a lot of water and maintenance. I am looking for an alternative that will still be "foot" friendly. It's got to be nice to walk on, especially for kids. I'm looking for something that will be resilient and not so unconventional that it will annoy my neighbours. Any suggestions?

Anything that is there that has turned to mud is undoubtedly pretty compacted, so it should be dug up and loosened to a depth of at least 4-6 inches. You may well be running into root systems from those trees so be prepared to dodge around them. Get a good quantity of organic matter on top of that soil and work it in well. The organic matter will help to maintain moisture and in combination with your soil, will help nourish whatever it is you are going to grow there. You'll also need enough moisture retention in the soil to supply the needs of the trees. The trees are going to take an awful lot of water, so there will always be competition. You'll need a ground cover that will be tolerant of shade, drought and low light conditions because those trees are always going to win that battle. In order to get that balance, I would go with a fescue grass. Creeping Red Fescue is probably the one that is generally most available. Sow about 20% Dutch White Clover mixed in with that – 20% is sort of a magic number because that proportion will provide all the nitrogen you'll ever need to feed that lawn area. If you want to go higher than 20-25%, that would not be a problem. The clover will stand up to the wear and tear of the kids, but you want to be aware: it's the clover that causes the stains kids get sliding on the lawn, so be prepared to do a bit more laundry if you put in a higher percentage of clover. Once you get your yard tilled up, level it off, sow the seed and give it a thorough soaking. Keep it moist until the seeds germinate. The kids will have to stay off for 3-4 weeks to let it get established. There's never a good time keep the kids off a lawn but

The Joy of Turf

Let's take a look at the positive side of grass as a ground cover. First, turf is the most durable of all the ground covers available in terms of its ability to take regular foot traffic. There are also several types of grasses that can respond to a wide variety of ground cover needs and conditions. Some grasses spread by a system of underground roots or rhizomes. Others spread by sending out ground runners at the surface of the soil. Still others form clumps with new shoots developing off the stems of the existing plant. The clumps tend to stay in place whereas the spreading types form denser sod and self-heal readily from injury by sending out new shoots to fill in the damaged areas. Each has advantages and disadvantages depending on types of traffic your lawn must endure.

Here are a few things to keep in mind when selecting the most appropriate turf for your lawn area. Kentucky Bluegrass of any type is out since it doesn't tolerate shade, wetness or extremes of pH. Perennial rye grass is not fond of shade and not very winter hardy so it tends to become patchy if used entirely on its own. More appropriate choices would be Creeping Red Fescue and Chewings Fescue. Both are widely used as lawn grasses but are somewhat different from one another. Creeping Red Fescue is a spreading grass and is preferable if your lawn will have to regularly self-heal from damage caused by traffic or heavy recreational use such as soccer, football, or baseball. Its ability to spread allows it to fill in any divots that may be inflicted and makes it much more forgiving of rough treatment. If self-healing is not an issue, Chewings Fescue, a clumping variety, would also work well. These fescues require less maintenance than other grasses, tolerate poorer soils, survive drought conditions, withstand heavy traffic, and most importantly for many homeowners, are the most shade tolerant of all turf grasses. Since you're rarely able to buy either one as a single species and may only find it as a pre-mixed product, I'd suggest you look for a "shade mix" grass seed. Find one with at least 60% Creeping Red Fescue. If you are in a very shaded area be prepared to re-seed again in the fall or spring as the weaker or less shade-tolerant species in the mix die out.

the best time to do this work in terms of the ground cover is in the spring. Seed a little more heavily than the recommended application. You are going to lose a bit of the seed to the birds initially and there may be few bare patches later on that you will have to re-seed. Buy about 50% more seed than the recommended amount for the square footage and that should be about right.

Rules for Pruning and Feeding Shrubs

What is the rule of thumb for pruning and feeding shrubs to encourage flowering?

Flowering shrubs will certainly benefit from a feeding to encourage vigorous growth. They will be just as happy, if not happier, with compost as the feed, as

---

Why Alternate Ground Covers?

When it comes to exploring alternatives to turf, the main incentive is usually the desire to reduce the maintenance that most lawns require, especially watering. Grass lawns are also the least environmentally friendly ground cover you can have. They all require regular feeding, usually through the use of a chemical fertilizer; disease and weed control, most often accomplished with synthetic pesticides and herbicides; regular, heavy watering that can seriously compromise municipal reserves; and regular mowing, normally done with a noisy, polluting power lawn mower. All in all, grass is not a plus in terms of environmental stewardship. Alternative ground covers, on the other hand, have several advantages. They add more variety, colour and interest to the landscape and they can be far more drought and pest resistant than any turf. They are best fed with compost, can be mulched to retain moisture and most importantly, don't need to be mowed. On the down side, an alternative has yet to be found that can stand up to heavy traffic as well as turf, so pathways usually have to be developed with stepping stones or gravel to accommodate any high-traffic areas. If you have kids, they need a natural surface to play on, and grass is likely still your best choice. Having said that, most homeowners can usually reduce the amount of lawn they have to manage by designating a play area and converting the rest of the lawn to alternate ground cover. Keep in mind that children are the most vulnerable to the health risks associated with pesticide exposure. In a limited area, weeds can easily be controlled by good maintenance practices. The play area requiring sod can be further reduced by installing a play structure and replacing the lawn underneath with sand. Properly planned, alternate ground cover provides an attractive, practical and almost maintenance-free landscape that will enhance the look and value of your property — and help reduce your environmental impact.

opposed to giving them a stronger dose of commercial fertilizer. Both the fungal activity and the insect activity will be breaking down the compost in the soil and putting it into a form that, along with the minerals in the soil, the plants can pick up and use. You have very little risk with well-aged compost, be it manure or straight vegetative matter, of giving the plant too much nitrogen and therefore affecting the flowering of your shrubs. If you are using a soluble or granular fertilizer, ensure that you have one for flowering and fruiting trees and shrubs which will have a lower first number, higher second, and higher third number or may have a lower first and second number and a higher third. Too much nitrogen will stimulate vegetative growth, often at the expense of flower production. In terms of pruning and shaping the plant, ideally all of them should be pruned right after flowering, allowing the maximum amount of time between the pruning and the flowering next year. That being said, if after coming through the winter you have dead or winter-killed material on the shrub, anything that is damaged or killed off can be cut out right away. Likewise, if branches are sticking out into a walkway or driveway or are in anyway dangerous, prune them

back. Shrubs that flower in the spring develop their buds during the subsequent growing season and hold them with the flower embryo intact through the following winter. Shrubs that flower later in the season usually develop their blossoms from the new growth. So if you always prune after the flowering, you should be successful in having your shrubs re-flower annually.

Landscaping Ponds with Cereal Grasses

Last summer we made a very pretty pond in the backyard. We want to give it a wilder look and I was wondering about planting cereal grasses like oats, barley or wheat. What would be the drawbacks or merits of doing that?

There are no drawbacks to planting grasses that I can see. As long as they are getting good full sun they should grow on and mature. That greenery of the grassy stage is really what you are after. You will also get a colour change with the seed heads as well as attracting a bit more wild life to your pond, specifically birds coming along and taking some of those seeds. If they don't get them all in the fall, try leaving them intact through the winter as an ongoing source of food. I think the grasses are worth a try. It sounds quite interesting.

Greening the Septic Field

What type of clover would you recommend as being suitable to plant over a septic bed? My local nursery carries White Clover seed. Would this do? Grass would be hard to grow on the type of soil that is on the bed and we don't want to add to our outside maintenance at the cottage.

Trifolium repens is the clover you are looking for. It is sold under various names such as White Clover, Dutch Clover, Dutch White Clover, Creeping Clover, and Strawberry Clover. You may also want to consider adding some native wildflowers to that area rather than having only one type of ground cover. Once they are planted, these wildflowers need very little in the way of maintenance. Some possibilities would be the Black-eyed Susan, Shasta Daisies, Oxeye Daisies and beebalm. They are all tough perennials that will add colour and help support many of the native insects and birds. Thyme would also be a good ground cover to mix in with the clover and would add yet another colour of flower to the mix. None of these plants have root systems that would go deep enough to af-

fect your septic tile field, so you can plant them in without any concern for the functioning of your system.

Wisteria that Never Bloomed

I have a 4-year-old wisteria growing east to west on a pagoda. It has never bloomed. Is there anything I can do to encourage it?

You don't mention how much direct sunlight that your wisteria gets. This may be the source of your problem. Wisteria does grow in shade, but to flower well it demands full sun. The plants prefer moist soil that is high in organic matter, although they will adapt to most soils as long as they can drain freely. They do poorly in hot, dry, compacted soils. When watering, saturate the soil deeply and try to keep it evenly moist from spring until the soil freezes in the fall. When the top 2 inches of soil dries out, it's time to water. Placing 2-4 inches of mulch around each plant in the spring will help retain soil moisture as well as keep the weeds down. If you already have mulch in place, pull it away from the plant first thing in the spring and then put it back in place once the soil warms up. If the plant is growing vigorously and has deep green foliage, it is probably getting too much nitrogen. This lush growth will be at the expense of flower production. I suggest you try a low-nitrogen fertilizer – the nitrogen being the first number of the three listed on the package, such as 5-5-15 applied first thing in the spring. One application of a soluble fertilizer at the manufacturer's recommended rate is sufficient. Once new growth emerges in the spring, prune out any branches that have died back over the winter. After the flowering period in early to mid July, prune to within 75 centimetres or 30 inches of the main stem and trim the new shoots back to 15 centimetres or 6 inches of the older branches. This will allow more light penetration to the remaining vine and encourage greater blooming the following year. Patience, though, is the essential ingredient in seeing wisteria bloom successfully. Plants started from seed or cuttings generally take 10-12 years of growing before they start flowering.

How to Grow Watermelon

I would really like to try to grow watermelon and wondered if you could give me some tips because the first time I tried it, not one of them grew.

We have a short season relative to the ideal heat and growing time normally required for watermelon, so if you can start your watermelon seedlings indoors, you are already on the right track. What you want to do is dig a large hole in your garden and put a good quantity of organic matter in there, preferably some cattle manure. It should not be absolutely fresh, but if it is, you can still use it down in the bottom of the hole with a layer of soil over top so that you have some heat being generated and the roots are working their way down into it, as opposed to the roots being planted directly into it. Put as much reflective material around the plant as possible to try and get the highest possible light and heat build up for it. Placing it close to a building would be extremely worthwhile in terms of providing a heat source. Also make sure that the watermelon plant never dries out. Alternatively, if you have a compost pile, it would grow beautifully in there as well. Just plant your seedling directly into the pile and water appropriately. Watermelons, or any melons for that matter, grow extremely well in a composter and the compost benefits from the extra moisture. Whichever method you choose, keep in mind that this is a long season plant – get it going indoors well ahead of time and ensure it has full sun once you plant it out.

Also be careful when you are transplanting not to damage the stem. That is really the death knoll for them. Just like your pumpkins, if the stem gets crushed the plant doesn't make it. The best way to prevent this is to sow the seeds in peat pots which don't have to be removed when its time to plant them out. As well as eliminating the danger of crushing the stem, the peat pots will also help prevent transplant shock. So if you can start your watermelons early, handle them gently and give them the heat and water they require, you should be able to achieve some measure of success. Creating the proper environment is key. A neighbour's daughter used an old tractor tire filled with compost quite successfully and I'm sure the heat of the sun on the tire was instrumental in her success!

Maintaining Cedar Hedges

I never know whether I should take the top off my cedar hedge or try to thin it out a bit. The trees are 8-10 feet in height. I'm really looking for some general "what I am supposed to do with this hedge" type of advice. I also need some suggestions on what works best to cut them.

If you are happy with that height of hedge, then trimming the tops back about 6 inches will help plump them up. Prune first thing in the spring and keep nipping them back as required until about the end of June, then let them go. The new growth that comes up will fill them out nicely, often within a year. To keep the height even while you're trimming, set up 2 or 3 posts and string a line between them to give yourself a guideline at the height you want

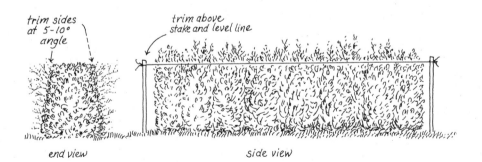

trim sides at 5-10° angle

trim above stake and level line

end view   side view

and then cut just a bit above it. As far as the sides go, it is better to keep the bottom a little wider than the top. Trim it on a slight angle so the slope is about 5-10 degrees in from the vertical and that will allow the sun to get at all of it. Hedge trimmers would do quite nicely for this but if there are rough bits or larger pieces that the hedge trimmers can't cut, use a pair of hand pruners to trim them off. If you are bringing the top down 6 inches, hedge trimmers should be able to do that as well. If you use an electric trimmer or a gas one, remember to treat it with respect. There is an awful lot of torque and cutting power in there so please keep your hands back inside the guards and on the handle. Never use a trimmer with only one hand and keep the cord back over your shoulder at all times. Cutting through the power cord is a shocking experience to say the least. Do wear ear plugs if you are using a gas trimmer. Do wear gloves as well. You don't want to lose control of the trimmer because your hand suddenly gets cut or poked by a branch. If you are working from a ladder, don't stand on top of it. Use a step ladder that is tall enough so you work comfortably without stretching and work only for a comfortable distance to either side of you.

It's better to climb up and down a few extra times than to lose your balance and fall when you're running that type of equipment. All that up and down is good for the waistline too, so at the very least both you and your hedge may end up a bit trimmer.

Moss in the Grass

We are desperate to get rid of moss in our lawn. What can we do?

Spring would be the best time to address this problem. Once the lawn is reasonably dry give it a good stiff raking with a fan rake moving in one direction, north-south, and then do it again east-west back across the whole area. Anything you pull out is probably not desirable in the lawn and can comfortably go into your compost. Once you've done the raking, aerate the lawn. One of the conditions that causes moss in lawns is compacted soil, and low fertility is another. If you aerate the lawn this will alleviate compaction and help air and moisture penetration into the soil. It will also help release the soil's nutrients more readily which are, in turn, going to sustain the grass plants. Break the plugs up and rake things out evenly after aerating. There is a possibility that the soil may, in fact, be rich enough; but it might be too acidic, so I would suggest a light application of agricultural or horticultural-grade lime over the whole area – one should be sufficient at the manufacturer's suggested rate of application. Top-dress the whole area with at least 1 inch of compost. There is a big plus there since you are going to be supplying some organic matter to the surface of the soil. The micro-organisms in the compost will help to keep the soil itself alive and in turn, that will release more nutrients for the grass. Once all this has been done, over-seed the area. You should get a good sword of grass established and the moss is not going to come back. Keep your grass tall and don't cut it any lower than a couple of inches. This not only conserves moisture in the soil but eliminates the essential light at the soil surface which is required for any other green plant growth... including moss!

Frustration with an Alpine Currant Hedge

For the past 4 years I have been trying to grow an Alpine Currant hedge across the front of my property – I've started calling it my "millennium hedge" because I think it's going to take a 1000 years to grow. I've tried trimming it back to make it come back bushier. I've tried lots of water, since it's in sandy soil, and I've put loads of compost on it. With all that, it's only about a foot and a half high; ideally, it should be about 4 feet high to provide some buffer from the road. Is there anything I haven't thought of that might help?

It's probably been reacting to transplant shock for the first year and a half and now it's into establishment mode. On sandy soil you are definitely going to have to worry about keeping this hedge wet for a while, but you can help alleviate your problem there by mulching over top of the roots. About a foot out on either side would be ideal if you can accommodate that much. The compost will certainly be a help and continue with the watering. Give it minimal pruning this year. Let it go up until mid summer before you give it just that fine pruning off the tips to even things up. If you do that about early July, let it grow through the rest of the summer and then just tidy things up again by trimming back any straggling shoots and branches after the first couple of hard frosts in the fall. Anything that would be susceptible to winter damage due to snow load should get trimmed back. Let it come through the winter again and grow on next year the same way so it gets a chance to fill out, put more growth on and develop before you do the pruning. As it gets older you are going to have to do the pruning a little earlier in the season to keep it in shape and then let it fill out in the summer. As a choice of hedge, Alpine Currant is one that generally needs a couple of prunings once it's well established to keep it in check during the summer. But for now, if you do it later in the season, you are going to get increased growth on the plant and

have it better established more quickly. I think you will find that it takes off this year.

Plug Pulling versus No Plug Pulling Aerators

My soil aerator pokes holes in the ground but doesn't pull the plugs out. Does this work as effectively as the type that pulls the plugs out of the ground?

In a sandy soil the type of unit that just pokes holes is acceptable, however it doesn't aerate

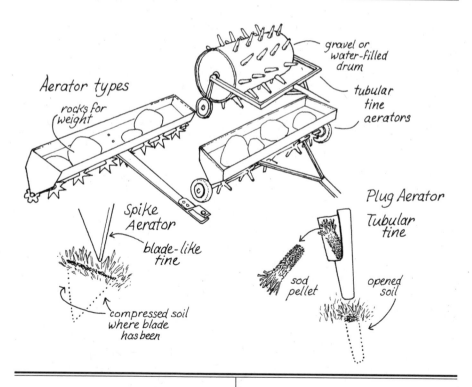

Aerator types

rocks for weight

gravel or water-filled drum

tubular tine aerators

Spike Aerator

blade-like tine

compressed soil where blade has been

Plug Aerator

Tubular tine

sod pellet

opened soil

the soil as effectively as those that take out a plug. When you pull a plug out of the soil you are creating space by physically removing a piece of earth. With the spike type aerators, those that just pierce down into the soil, you are in effect pushing the earth down and away and compacting it locally to open up the hole. On balance you are compacting the soil more than you are opening it up, so you are not getting the same effect at all. It is not totally ineffective, but it's not as useful as an aerator that will take a plug from the soil and allow the area around it to loosen up and breathe.

Suggestions for Covering Siding

Could you suggest some kind of plant I could use to cover a wall that has siding on it?

As long as the wall gets high light exposure a good number of things could go in there. If you are looking for a flower, a Trumpet Vine would be a possibility as would Climbing Honeysuckle. If you want something that will grow faster and cover up more of the siding, something like Wild Grape or Virginia Creeper would do nicely. Rather than growing it directly on the siding, use a trellis or suspension system placed a minimum of 4-6 inches away from the siding so the vine is actually climbing up onto something else. The trellis or wire lattice is really only going to be seen as the vine gets started. Once established, the support system virtually disappears and if you ever want or need to remove the vine no stain or damage will be left behind on the siding.

Encouraging Sweet Cherries

Back in the spring of 1999 I bought a Sweet Cherry tree and then transplanted it three years later. It is about 10 feet tall now and the trunk is about 2½ inches around. A few flowers appeared last spring but they didn't turn into cherries. I cut the first row of limbs off the trunk and it has been growing like crazy, but I'm still not getting any fruit. Is there something else I should be doing?

The fact that it is growing like crazy is a sign it has established itself quite nicely after the transplant. If you could put down an inch of your own compost or some well-seasoned cattle manure over the soil under the tree, right out to the drip line of the leaves, that would certainly be helpful. Once you've got that spread, put down a layer of mulch over top to about 3-4 inches deep. Be careful not to pile any of it up against the trunk of the tree. Keep it back at least 6 inches from the bark to make sure there is good air circulation around the trunk itself. Cherry trees must be 5-7 years old before they start getting into any serious flower and fruit production. The fact that you have already had flowers after 4 years is pretty impressive. I would say with the mulching you will definitely see fruit by next year unless something else is inhibiting that production. You say that you cut the first row or lowest branches off the tree and this suggests to me that the tree is on or near your lawn and the branches were probably cut to facilitate mowing. If that's the case, shield the tree out beyond the drip line before you fertilize your grass. The high nitrogen content in lawn fertilizer promotes vigorous vegetative growth on your cherry tree but at the expense of flower production, so keep it away from the tree roots.

Iris Borer

This morning we were lifting patches of irises and dividing them up and we found very live evidence of iris borers, some large ones and some tiny ones. I am wondering if there is some kind of an organic way to deal with these – and can we replant these irises in the same soil?

Isn't that the worst smell you have ever come across? And yes, there is a way to deal with iris borers without using any chemical application. After you remove the irises to divide them, cultivate the soil thoroughly at least 6 inches deep so the root systems can get back down in there. If you come across any grubs in the soil, just remove them as you go. Incorporate some organic matter into the soil while you cultivate. You are not going to do this every year and it may be a while before you get any compost down under these plants again. If you are in clay soil you will want to raise up the area a bit to encourage drainage so the irises are not sitting there wet. Divide the plants out and go through them all. Cut out and eliminate anything that has a borer. Don't take any chances. If in doubt, throw it out! Once this process has been accomplished, plant the irises back. Going through them and removing the affected areas is the most successful pesticide-free treatment. That new organic matter is really going to encourage good healthy vigorous growth and they will be able to stand up much better if problems do come back. And just a reminder when you are replanting the irises, a minimum of 1/2 to

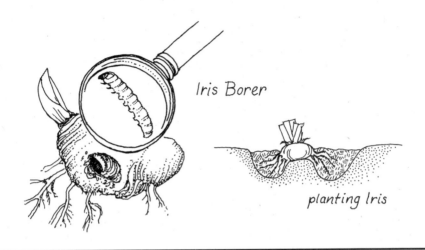

Iris Borer

planting Iris

2/3 of the rhizome needs to be exposed to the air. You will notice along the rhizome that the roots tend to come off either side. You want this part of the root fully covered. When planting them back in, the best way to make sure you get the rhizome well exposed but the roots buried is to make a ridge or hill in the centre of the hole by digging down at a slight angle on both sides. Sit the rhizome straddling the ridge and put the roots down on either side. The roots will get covered when you fill in but the rhizome stays up on the ridge. Be sure to encourage the root development by adding either rock phosphate, bone meal or a high phosphorous fertilizer into the hole before planting, and water them in well. Any and all bits and pieces of rotted rhizome and discarded foliage should be placed in a sealed plastic bag and left to sit in full sun to bake for a couple of weeks. After that you can safely incorporate them with other organic matter you have in your compost pile.

Defining Pesticides

What are the generally accepted definitions of pesticides, herbicides, and fungicides?

"Pesticide" is the general or catch-all term that is used to describe anything that kills pests of any sort. There are also sub-categories of pesticides, such as herbicides used to kill plant material, fungicides to kill fungi, insecticides for insects, algaecides for algae, rodenticides for rodents and aracnacides for spiders and mites. Any of those can be lumped under the term "pesticide". There are a few naturally occurring pesticidal compounds such as nicotine, pyrethrums, and the alkaloids in Rhubarb leaves, but the vast majority of commercially available pesticides are man-made chemicals that tend to persist in the environment or leave residues that bio-accumulate. These can also combine with other natural or man-made substances to create compounds that are equally harmful to human health – and pose a special risk to the health and development of children.

Restriction on the Cosmetic Use of Pesticides

Our municipality is debating a by-law to restrict the cosmetic use of pesticides and I honestly don't know what to think. The pesticide industry presents lots of convincing research that seems to show that these products are safe, effective and disappear quickly from the environment, so why not use them? On the other hand, those calling for the ban seem to have their own studies that show that these products are linked to serious problems, everything from birth defects to cancer. Who do we believe?

Well over 120 towns and cities across Canada, as well as the entire province of Quebec, have opted to reduce or ban the cosmetic use of pesticides, but I don't think I know of a case where that debate hasn't been long, ugly and pretty polarized. Essentially, the pesticide industry is fighting hard every step of the way to have us believe that we need their products in order to have pest-free gardens and healthy public green spaces. A lot of money is at stake. Good horticultural practices and alternative control methods, things like integrated pest management, will give you the same results, but these companies don't necessarily want you to know that. We've all used pesticides at some point and they work. It's only recently that researchers have begun to suggest that a neurotoxin designed to kill a bug might actually have an impact on our own nervous systems. Some of these toxins can build up and combine with other things in the environment to a point where they could become a threat to human health. A lot of the most common pesticides in use in Canada today were developed and certified back in the '50s and '60s before anyone suspected they might pose a danger or even knew which questions to ask. Many of these were "grandfathered" so they are not obliged to meet the burden of proof of today's tougher standards – but they are still out there in the market-place. One of the most popular lawn treatments in this country has been "under review" for more than 20 years. Even though they have yet to determine whether or not it is safe, you or I can go into any hardware store or garden centre in this country today, buy it, apply it and have our children play on that lawn the same day. So where do we turn for advice? One of the most objective, comprehensive and science-based studies on pesticides was produced by the Ontario College of Family Physicians in 2004. After reviewing all the scientific literature available on this subject, the researchers were surprised to discover how strong and convincing the medical evidence was regarding the potential health risks posed by the use of some pesticides. They had not expected so clear and conclusive a result. Likewise, the International Agency for Research on Cancer has also determined that some substances used in pesticides are known, probable or possible carcinogens. So you have to ask yourself, is it really worth the possibility of putting your health at risk for the sake of a few broadleaf weeds? A weed is a weed. Your long-term health, or your children's, is far more important. If you want to have a look at

the Ontario College of Physicians' study, you can find it on their website at www.ocfp.on.ca. Or pick up a copy of Theo Colborne's book "Our Stolen Future". It's a very approachable discussion of this issue and reads a bit like a mystery novel, but is based on real science. Both of these can be useful resources if you want to become better informed on this topic, minus the hype of the industry lobbyists or the "no spray at any cost" faction. In the end we all have to ask ourselves: if chemical-based pesticides are only being applied for "cosmetic" or aesthetic reasons, for the sake of appearances, are these chemicals really something we want to have in our parks and home gardens or should we consider achieving those same ends through alternative gardening methods?

Japanese Lilac is Stripped and Cracked

There is a beautiful white Japanese Lilac in our backyard that is about 30 years old, and the foliage is coming out nicely, but two disturbing things happened this winter. Many of the branches seem to be stripped of bark and it looks like the work of animals, although we don't see any animals doing it. And then the main branch seems to have a large crack going right around it. What is the maximum age for these plants and should we be putting a seal in where the bark has been removed?

Age should not be a factor until this plant is 40 or 50 years old. It's more likely a result of the freeze-thaw cycle throughout the winter which can cause frost cracks quite easily. The best approach is to position a plank south of the tree about 6 inches away from the trunk and leave it during the winter months. Last thing in the fall, put this plank up, tie it into place on top and bury the other end into the soil. This will cast a shadow on the trunk to keep the sunlight from heating it up. Otherwise, every day during the winter when the sun beams down that plant thaws and then later, when the sun sets and the temperature drops, the liquid inside freezes, expands and cracks the trunk or branches. Once this cycle has started, it is very hard to stop. The shade from the plank will prevent these extremes and the plants generally heal quite nicely. You don't have to worry about a sealant for the cracks that are there. In fact, it is preferable for these to stay open and air dry to prevent fungal growth and so the birds can get in there to go after any insects.

Tomato Troubles

Last summer we had a terrible time with our tomatoes. They all got some sort of blight, turned black and we got nothing edible out of them. We picked off all the tomatoes and threw them out so that they would not infect the compost, but we left the plants in the garden and they are still there. What should we do?

Take the plants out of the garden, then till the area thoroughly and add some compost. Plant the tomatoes somewhere else for the next couple of years but make sure it's a good bright sunny location. If you could divide your garden into 4 quadrants and rotate the tomatoes through a 4-year cycle, that would be ideal. If you can't do that, at least alternate the location every year – every 2 is even better and every 3 would be better still. Just be sure you have got good strong light for the tomatoes in each position because that is the biggest requirement they have. If all else fails and you can't get them into a bright spot elsewhere in the garden, put them into pots in a bright sunny spot. The only challenge with tomatoes in pots is that they are very thirsty, so you have to water them just about daily. In your case, you will want to plant them as far away as possible from the last location. Try and stress the plants as little as possible which means a good deep watering if we get a hot, dry period. To achieve this, dig a hole beside the plant large enough to accommodate a 2-litre plastic bottle, right side up with holes punched in the bottom. Take the twist cap off, put a funnel into the neck of the bottle, fill it up with water, put the cap back on and then let it leak slowly. You are getting 2 litres of water down into the root zone every time you water that way. The next year, if you are using the same pots, it is certainly worthwhile to replace all of the soil. The old soil can go into the garden or the compost as long as there hasn't been a problem. If you are not replacing the soil at the bottom of the pot, at least mix it thoroughly with the new soil. The interesting thing here is the soil mechanics. If there is a difference in the two types of soil, the top layer of new soil will have to become completely saturated before moisture will move further down into the pot and you can end up with waterlogged conditions on the top and dry conditions on the bottom. If you mix all the soil together to create a uniform soil, the water will flow much more freely. If you are using black earth in your pots, watch the nitrogen content be-

cause you will end up with lots of green plants but not much tomato production. Black earth is also fairly dense and holds a lot of moisture, so mixing in about 30% sharp sand to help open up the soil; compost in there should help with this as well. Make sure they are in full sun, water them well and you should have a good return this year.

Transplanting Asparagus

I came across some asparagus growing in a ditch along the side of a road. Although they have pretty much peaked at this point, some are incredibly large, up to almost 2 inches in diameter. What I would like to know is when would be a good time to transplant them and what kind of conditions should I put them into?

If the asparagus are doing well where they are, I would simply mark the location, leave them there and go back and collect the spears in the spring. You know that the spears are going to come along there and that way you don't have to go through the whole exercise of moving the plants. When they come up into foliage and develop through the rest of the season, everybody driving down that road still gets to enjoy them. Most people forget where they are when spring comes along but if you mark them off with some sign that you will recognize, you can be sure to get the harvest. One of the reasons asparagus does very well on the side of the road is that they were originally salt marsh plants, so the road salt that sprays over the edge of the road is actually quite beneficial to them. But they do want a deep, well-drained soil and it may well be that some sort of mulch ended up in that ditch or they may be picking up some nutrient runoff from a farm field. There must be some natural composting that's happened around them because they are obviously very old, strong plants. Having said all this, if you really want to move them, I would say wait until the end of the season. Let the asparagus die back and then dig them up and plant them into a well-drained, reasonably rich soil. Given the size of the plants, the root ball will probably extend a foot or so out from the clump all the way around and as far down as the height of the plants, possibly 30-40 inches, so this is a pretty major job to undertake. You would likely have to dig it out in pieces, but that would help rejuvenate after transplanting and shouldn't be a problem.

Rejuvenating an Aging Garden

My garden has been in the same area for over 20 years. I know I should move it, especially with cucumbers and tomatoes growing in there, but I never seem to get around to it. I've been told that you can add more soil. What kind of soil should I add? Unfortunately, I don't have a composter, but should I be adding fertilizer and bone meal as well?

What you want to do at this point is get a hold of some well-matured compost, something that is at least 1-2 years old. Composted cattle manure or sheep manure would be ideal here but whatever you choose, it is best if it is a year old rather than fresh. Carbon levels are a bit too high in fresh vegetative compost and it requires nitrogen from the soil to break down. This in turn would deplete the amount of nitrogen that would be available for your plants. So amending the soil with mature compost would certainly be your first step. Then as long as you rotate your plants into different sections of that garden each year, this is as good as putting them in another location. It's never a good idea to grow anything in the same spot year after year because the soil will be continually depleted of the same nutrients and elements. It would also be helpful to mulch in the rows between the plants. You could also sow Dutch White Clover down the walkways between the rows and let it grow. The clover will help fix some additional nitrogen into the soil. It's also a good idea to throw grass clippings on there. Sprinkle them between the rows, let them dry off and they will work very effectively as mulch. A very thick mat of them does a wonderful job. The other thing you might want to consider is coffee grounds. Some time back some big coffee shop chains announced that they would donate used coffee grounds to gardeners as a way to reduce and reuse their waste. Coffee grounds are marvelous for the garden because of the natural balance – the nitrogen content along with the carbon in the beans is just about perfect for producing compost. You can put the grounds into the composter or straight onto your soil. At the end of the season turn the whole thing over to mix things up and enrich the earth. You can add compost in the fall and mix that in well along with the green manure of the clover to keep enriching the soil that way. In terms of specific fertilizer requirements, you would have to have a soil test done to see what is there or what is missing. If you decide to have that analysis done, make sure to get samples from a variety of spots since different vegetables will deplete the soil of different nutrients. That testing should show any major deficiencies, but certainly amending the soil with the compost and any of the materials suggested previously will help ensure it remains viable. Well-fed soil will always be able to feed your plants adequately, regardless of its location.

Cilantro Woes

I like to grow a lot of herbs to use in my personal chef business, but I have had a terrible time trying to grow cilantro. It goes to seed and then I have coriander and that is not what I want. Is there something I can do to stop this happening?

The fact that your plants are going to seed means that you've got good, high light there. Get a good quality of organic matter into that soil, especially if there is clay, and mix it in very well. Make sure you keep the cilantro a little wetter than some of your other herbs as it is coming along, but not soaking wet. It's also best to grow cilantro in a slightly raised row that will allow good penetration of water as well as provide lots of warmth for the roots. Mulch would also be helpful to hold the moisture in the soil and give more vegetative growth.

Pollinating Pears

I have a Bosc pear tree. Do I need a pollinator?

Yes, you do need a pollinator and in order to get a good crop of pears, you need to plant at least 2 cultivars. However, not all varieties can pollinate each other. Bosc will pollinate well with D'Anjou, Bartlett and Clapp's Favourite for sure, but its always best to check with your local supplier, if possible, to find the most suitable mate for Bosc in your area. Don't plant your pear trees too far apart – 10-15 feet is the maximum separation for dwarf trees; 15-25 feet for full-size trees.

Potato Problems

We are getting ready to plant our potatoes and I still have several from last year that are a bit sunburnt but have good eyes. We had some scab as well but around here that's a perennial problem. I'm more worried about the fact that we had quite a few marbley potatoes. Could that be caused by insects or earwigs? Would the eyes from those potatoes reproduce new potatoes with the same kind of problem?

Not necessarily. Genetically you would not get the same problem but if the conditions that caused the marbling are still there and if you are going back into that same location, you could still see that same problem emerge. It could have been that the soil stayed too wet. You will often see that in a clay soil or with a very rainy summer. It could possibly be insects transmitting a viral disease. In this case, the insect – and it is usually aphids – would be working as a vector to transmit this disease and infect the plant as it passes through. Weed your potatoes since aphids often come from plantain and catnip, among other weeds, and keep an eye out for insects. If you see a problem, the 40:1 water and soap solution sprayed on to the plants should offer a good measure of control. If you do spray be sure to repeat with clear water after 10 minutes. In terms of the recurring scab situation, one thing you can do is to throw a handful of cedar or pine needles into the planting trenches and between the mounds. Anything acidic that can go in underneath along the rows eliminates the scab problem very quickly. In terms of the sunburnt potatoes, there shouldn't be a problem planting those as long as the eyes you are planting are healthy and disease free. You may want to try not planting your potatoes as deeply and mounding mulch up over top of them instead. Just pile 6-12 inches of dry mulch over top of your seed potatoes and as the plants grow up through it, keep adding more mulch. In a dry summer the mulch will also maintain that much more moisture in the soil. The spuds grow downward, but rarely much deeper than their own thickness, and the roots can still penetrate the soil just fine. You'll also find you don't have to dig as much when the potatoes are ready to harvest and they do beautifully. Often I just lift the mulch without disturbing the plants anytime I need potatoes and collect a few before the main harvest. The plants continue to grow on and produce more.

Pumpkin Patch Prescription

What is the ideal soil for pumpkin growth? The soil we have grown them in has a lot of clay and the pumpkins do not grow very well. What should we be doing?

With pumpkins, the more compost the better. In fact, the best place to grow them is right on the compost pile. All squash, which includes pump-

kins, grow best in compost. You could also put a few wheelbarrows full of compost on top of the clay. Make sure they get enough moisture but don't keep them soaking wet or you will get problems with rotting or fungus or just generally poor growth. Well-drained soil with lots of compost and full sun exposure are essential for success.

Companion Plants for Toxic Black Walnut

We have a Black Walnut with branches that pretty well cover our entire yard. I understand the Black Walnut is toxic to other plants, but is there anything I can plant underneath it that will live?

There are actually a good number of plants that will survive under your tree. The toxic property of Black Walnut comes from a chemical called "juglone" produced by the roots and then carried up and spread throughout the rest of the tree. Juglone does make the immediate area around the tree somewhat toxic to other plants. By killing off its neighbours this way, the Walnut hopes to eliminate a lot of the competition for moisture and nutrients it might otherwise get and give itself the best chance for growth and survival. The juglone content in your soil peaks in the fall. That's when the greatest number of leaves, twigs, and dead branches fall onto the soil, increasing the juglone content to far greater levels than you would get from the root system alone. If you can increase the depth of soil over top of that root system and make sure the area is cleaned up as the leaves fall, you have a pretty good chance of growing anything that will tolerate the shade that is there. The nice thing about Black Walnuts is that they are an open crown tree. They leaf out late so you can grow all kinds of spring flowers nearby. When you are adding that new soil, try not to add more than 6 inches over the existing surface because too heavy an overlay is going to impede the penetration of air and moisture and compromise the tree's root system. It's important to mix that new soil in well, so if you are putting down at total of 6 inches, start by putting 3 inches down, mix it in well, then add another 3 inches and mix again. You want to have a fairly uniform mixture of the new and old soil for at least those 9-12 inches. Do your planting into that making sure there is always enough moisture and nutrients for whatever you are planting underneath it as well as for the Black Walnut itself. This is a large tree and it takes up a lot of water. Literally soaking up a ton a day or 1000 litres of water is not unusual for any mature deciduous tree. It also needs lots of nutrient to support itself so a good quantity of organic matter in the soil will help keep it alive and vigorous. You also need a decent friable soil to get good penetration of moisture and nutrients down to the root system. It may take a bit of effort to maintain, but the value of a mature Black Walnut – in terms of the landscape and the cooling that it provides in the summer – far outweighs any headaches you run into with it. In terms of the type of plants that might go under there, Spirea will do quite nicely as long as it is planted around the outside edge of the tree where it would get the greatest amount of light. Even lilacs will bloom under Black Walnut, but again, adequate moisture is essential and they must be planted in the sunniest areas closer to the tips of the branches. Hostas will stand up in the shadier parts, or astilby, as long as they have a good quantity of moisture available. The range is really almost limitless. Follow the normal standards for planting. Be sure to incorporate some rock phosphate, bone meal or super phosphate when you are planting to get the root system of the new material well established.

And mulching over the surface certainly is well worthwhile to cut down the watering requirements for the plants. That way you are sealing the moisture in so it is not just evaporating straight out of the soil. Some things, you will find, do better than others and there will be a degree of trial and error. The one challenge is going to be the clean up, but it's usually not a big problem. The leaves can be lightly raked off the surface of the mulch or blown off with a leaf-blower and collected elsewhere. Don't forget to remove all the leaf stems, twigs or any branches that fall as well. In terms of disposal, walnut leaves take a long time to lose their juglone content, so these may be ones that you compost separately for a few years or put into a bag and discard.

JUNE

A. KARSTAD.

Vegetable Garden Turned Wedding Venue

Our home is in the country and we will be having our daughter's wedding reception in our garden. The only place that is large and flat enough to put the tent is over our existing vegetable garden. What would be a good thing to plant there this spring that would give a nice footing under the tent? We intend to turn it back into a vegetable garden next year. Could you also suggest some flowers that I could plant this spring that will be in bloom in early July and that would be nice for cut flowers?

The first thing that you will have to do is a proper level-ing and grading of the area you want to use for the tent. Once that's done you can put something down like an annual rye-grass. You certainly can get rid of that quite easily by tilling the soil before the next year's seed germi-nates. You could also go with clover and when you turn it un-der, the soil will get the benefit of its high nitrogen content. The downside to walking in clover is that with such a high chlorophyll content, anybody wearing white shoes, including the bride, will end up with green ones. Having said that, starting your life off to-gether "in clover" has sort of a nice ring to it... If the stains are going to be an issue, you could lay sod over the area early in the season to get it established and when the reception is finished, have someone come in with a sod cutter and remove it again. You can then use that sod elsewhere. Another alternative would be to install the tent with a floor. When the tent is removed your garden plot will still be there. Depending on the size of the area, you could also position the tent so that the garden bed surrounds it with walkways through to the entrances. You could plant flowers into those beds to get any kind of show you want. Obviously, if you are only planting flowers for the one year, you will want to look at a mixture of annuals in there. Foliage-wise, try something like cannas or castor beans. You could purchase some larger plants that would take up lots of space in the bed and that would give you some striking foliage. In terms of cut flowers, do a mix of what is available in the annuals. Marigolds would be nice and zinnias are always a good show. Daisy and Black-eyed Susan do well as cut flowers and have a simple elegance. The fact that you only want this effect for one season doesn't preclude you putting in some shrubbery. You can even leave them in their nursery pots when you plant them. When the event is over, you can transplant the shrubs to another loca-

tion and reclaim your vegetable plot. If you decide to go with shrubs, you want something that will stand out but look fairly cool and colorful at the same time. The Silverleaf Dogwood, for example, would give you the effect of the foliage and would work as a very nice foil or backdrop to the colours in the annual material you choose. Sounds like a wonderful venue!

Appropriate Trellis for Wisteria Vines

There is a large wooden arbour over our patio and we would like to plant a climbing vine to grow up and over it. We really love wisteria but we understand they can be very heavy. Are they really so much heavier than the other vines that they might bring down our arbour? Also, would wisteria bloom as well on a horizontal structure like an arbour or would it do better on a vertical trellis?

Whether your arbour can hold a mature wisteria depends on whether it is made from flimsy material or constructed from heavier, larger-dimension lumber with strong support posts and cross members. If it is the latter, there is no need to be concerned. In the long run, wisteria vines, both the Japanese and

Chinese varieties, can get quite voluminous and heavy, but this would only be with older, well-established specimens. If you have a well-constructed structure and the patience to wait up to 12 years for a wisteria to flower, the rewards are well worth it. When it is established, cutting new shoots back to about 6 inches long at the end of the summer will encourage flower bud formation. First thing the following spring, trim the shoots back to 2 or 3 buds and that will also encourage maximum flower cluster size.

Cure for Canker

The five large Blue Spruce that surround our house are each about 25 feet high and some years back one of them developed some sort of a fungal type growth. We have a gardening reference book that helped us diagnose the problem as Cytospora canker. The one Blue Spruce that was affected started out with a kind of white exudate on the lower branches on the trunk so we began spraying them all over the last couple of years with a Bordeaux mix of copper sulfate and hydrated lime. We pruned away some of the branches that died completely and used bleach on the pruning shears so we wouldn't carry that fungus around. We have also been using fertilizer 2 or 3 times a year and

have a root feeder to give them water. I don't like to see them die and I am noticing now that this canker is starting to show up in the other four. Is there anything beyond this that we could be doing or is this disease just in the soil?

No, I think what you are looking at here is trying to keep these trees vigorous enough to resist further infection. They certainly have more than enough fertilizer, especially if you are applying it more than once a year, so don't add any more. You could get into a problem of producing susceptible plants, in that they are growing too lush and not hardening off sufficiently well in the fall. The lush growth also tends to be more susceptible to disease and pests during the growing season. The deep root watering is essential. There is a lot of moisture in the soil in the spring but as soon as things start to show any signs of drying out, make sure to give those trees lots of water. What has probably helped most in preventing the spruce from passing on the canker further than it has is your deep root watering, even more so than the Bordeaux mixture, but do continue with that on the affected tree. Spray it right down into the canker. If you can get to the inside, try and get that penetration. It is most effective if

applied right to the cankers themselves so that is really where you
want to concentrate your efforts.
Spraying once a season should be
sufficient. The disease is spread
by airbourne spores so your best
defense is to keep those trees
healthy and vigorous and they
should be able to withstand any
further exposure.

Grub Grief

*I'd be grateful if you could out-
line the procedure for an envi-
ronment-friendly treatment for an
extensive infestation of grubs.
How can I get rid of them without
resorting to chemicals? Would an
application of nematodes work?*

The best way to start getting
control of the grubs is to let
the starlings or the crows have a
go at them. In the spring, when
the soil is warmed up enough, the
grubs start to become active and
the almost imperceptible sound of
that activity is like a dinner bell
for all of their natural predators.
All those starlings, crows and crit-
ters you see tearing up your lawn
are really cleaning the problem
up for you. Unfortunately they do
chew up a lot of the grass while
they are at it and that can leave
quite a mess behind. This, however, is a lesser problem. Rake up
what is left and fling it into the
compost. Once that's done, you
can apply a top-dressing to the
area and over-seed. That will take
care of the damage. The seeds
will sit there until there is enough
warmth in the soil for them to
germinate. By the time the birds
are finished, the seeds will be
ready to take over for you and
everything should be nicely taken
care of. Do keep that seeded area
moist. Now if you really feel that
the crows and other predators are
not going to do the job completely, you could try using nematodes. Again, these are natural
predators. The trick with them,
however, is that they have to be
active in order to work. This
means the soil must be warm and
have the right amount of moisture. The instructions that come
with them will give you an idea of
the soil temperature, but it is usually well after the end of May
before it warms up enough for
them to be effective. The moisture
level in the soil will also have to
be monitored and maintained.
Unfortunately this is where the
problem comes for most people.
The nematodes have to remain
alive for quite a period of time in
order to eliminate the various
generations of grubs that will
come along over the course of the
season. If you go away in the
summer for a couple of weeks or
simply forget to water and the soil
dries out, that's the end of your

nematodes. Certainly applying them can be helpful, but encouraging as much natural predation from the birds as possible, nourishing the soil with compost and keeping the grass watered and healthy is going to do as much or more to get this problem under control for you. If you can get these three things happening, the grub problem should take care of itself. •

Transplant Tomato Shock

I received some heritage tomato seeds and got carried away starting them indoors at the beginning of March. I've just put them out last week in 5-inch peat pots. They were doing great, standing about 3 feet tall, but now the leaves have turned almost white and I am wondering what might have happened?

This is a case of shock. With a 3-5 inch peat pot, there is a heck of a shock when you finally plant them. There may be some sunburn happening there as well. Ideally what you would do with that size of plant is to dig a hole about a foot deep and then continue the hole on an angle off to one side so that you have a gradual incline or ramp angling up for another 1-2 feet to ground level. Split the peat pot and loosen the soil up around the roots. Then lay the plant along that angle with the root in the main hole and the

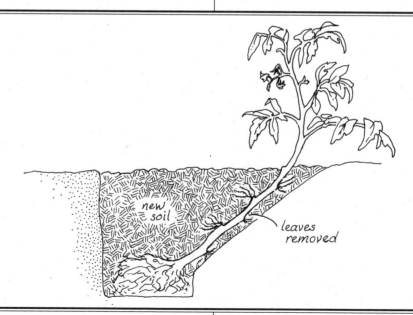

new soil

leaves removed

stem following up the ramp. Remove any leaves from the stem that will be covered with soil. Then just cover it up so only the top 6 inches or so of the plant is above ground. Tomatoes are great for this because they put out adventitious roots along their stems. You get the whole length of the stem rooting up and end up with a massive feeding system for the plant. This will also protect the plants from getting so much sun scorch because with such a proportionally larger root system established, the drought tolerance of the plant is also greatly increased. It is a good idea to shade them for the first week or so when they go out to help them to adapt to the much higher light conditions outdoors and prevent any problem with sunburn. Once those roots take off, so do your tomatoes, and you will be amazed at the results.

Reclaiming Peony Bushes

I am attempting to reclaim an old garden and my husband tells me these peony bushes are somewhere in the vicinity of 50 or 60 years old. I am attempting to move them but they have so much grass embedded in their root structure, I think they are probably not as healthy as they could be. Am I doing the wrong thing, first of all, in moving them, and if not, how should I prepare the soil, which is acidic and very clay-like?

Incorporating compost or organic matter, even old straw that can be worked in and break down over time, will be essential to lightening up and loosening that clay soil. The last thing peonies want is to have their feet constantly soaking wet so you do have to have reasonable drainage around them. To help with that you might also try to build a bit of a slope into the bed so any excess water that might pool on top of the bed can drain down and away. In terms of dividing the plants, they are going to be much happier if you can do that first thing in the spring. Get a good 12-16 inches of that compost and soil worked up and well mixed in where they are going to be replanted. I know it can be quite difficult to get that much depth, so try working just the pockets where the peonies are going to be planted to about 12 inches deep and then raise up the soil level for the whole bed by adding 4-6 inches of sandy loam on top and mixing it in thoroughly with the soil below. You'll likely have to do that work the season before so the bed will be ready for the transplanting first thing in the spring. When you lift the peonies, take a hose to the root system. Flush everything possible off so you can see clearly what is there and where there are viable eyes or sprouts on the individual root sections. I suspect you are going to find a lot of woody material throughout the crown and are not likely to see distinct individual tubers in clumps of peonies that are this old. At that age however, they have a hardiness that has been proven, so they are all well worth trying to save. Use a good sharp knife to split up the root system and divide them into clumps large enough to readily re-establish themselves. Add some bone meal, rock phosphate or a super phosphate type fertilizer to the soil and work that in well to stimulate root development in the new location and then add about a handful of horticultural or agricultural-grade crushed limestone. That will help counteract the acidity in the soil and give them a more neutral pH. Plant them in, making sure that there is only 1 inch of soil or less over the crown or they won't flower successfully. Water them well to eliminate any air pockets around the roots, keep them moist but not soaking wet throughout that first growing season and they should prosper in their new location.

Deterring Squirrels, Skunks, and Raccoons

We just laid some sod in our backyard and every morning there seems to be evidence of squirrels or raccoons digging in it. It's the same with the planters on our deck. I have tried Critter-Ridder but it just seems to have encouraged more of a disturbance. What can I do to stop them?

There are some other repellents that will give you a modicum of control, but these certainly can be pests. If what you are finding are small, neatly dug holes, it could be squirrels thinking there are some nuts buried there. If there are grubs in the lawn, it is likely skunks or raccoons. An application of blood meal will work and is safe to use if there are children or domestic pets around. The smell of blood meal is not appealing to any of the likely culprits. It will be a short-term deterrent and they may come back in time, but it's worth a try. On the other hand, if the problem is a grub infestation in your new sod, those skunks are probably doing you a favour by eliminating that problem for you. They can make a terrible mess in the process, but it is best to let them finish the job and then repair the divots and damage by filling in with compost, levelling things off and over-seeding with a bit of grass seed.

Nuisance Fruit

Three years ago I bought a house with a beautiful huge cherry tree in the backyard. Now it's great for shade, but it makes a huge mess in my yard and I want nothing to do with eating the cherries. Is there some way I can at least slow down the fruit or even stop it without killing the tree. Is it possible if I applied the wrong fertilizer or something, that I could stop it from producing so much fruit?

If you were to give your cherry tree a fertilizer that had an awful lot of nitrogen in it, you would get a lot more vegetative growth at the expense of some of that flowering and therefore limit the fruit production, but unfortunately that new foliage would be weak growth, so this isn't really a viable solution. If you don't prune at all, the amount of flower and the amount of fruit produced will also be reduced on the cherry. However, you do want to avoid having a very thick crown and limited light penetration or air circulation because that promotes some of the disease problems. If you do your pruning right after the flowering, you will have reduced the fruit production on the

tree. Or if you do your pruning as the leaves are coming out early in the spring, again you are going to be eliminating some of the flower buds and reducing fruit production. Normally we avoid pruning at that time because you want to maximize the amount of flower and fruit produced. If that is not what you want, prune at that point and you'll eliminate a lot of it. Be considerate in your pruning though. Make sure you are thinning that crown out a little bit to get good light penetration and air circulation – but no more than 25% of the tree should be taken off in any given year. Composting around the tree will keep it in good health without over-stimulating either foliage or flower production.

Weed Control

We are desperate to control the weeds in our vegetable garden this summer. We are going to be away for six weeks and I thought I heard you say something about layers of newspaper. Is there any way to keep the weeds from taking over completely while we are gone?

Once you have planted up the rows of vegetables, you will want to get a heavy layer of mulch down between those rows. If you put down newspaper, fold it so you have a thickness equivalent to between 5-10 sheets and then cover that with mulch to hold it in place. The easiest way is to do this one row at a time. Soak the newspaper thoroughly so that it sticks on the ground, then cover it with the mulch quickly so the wind doesn't pick it up. The mulch over top of the newspaper will give the effect of a total blackout. If you can use a straw mulch, it has the added benefit of reflecting the light up and around the other plants. It will also help to keep the soil moist which means you can pull out any weeds that do come up along the edges quite easily when you get back.

Rose Bush Transition

I am redoing my front yard this year and I have about eight rose bushes to move. Six are quite small, I only planted them last year, and two are in their fourth year and over 7 feet tall. Is there any problem with moving them?

You should be able to make that move without any problem, but I'm afraid you have left it too late for this year. Ideally you should begin first thing in the spring, as soon as the soil is workable and while the roses are still in their dormancy. That would be the time to dig them up and move them into the new location, preferably with a good quantity of organic matter worked into the soil. Throw some rock phosphate or bone meal in as well to stimulate root development and then have them come out of dormancy in the new location. Obviously the two older ones that are getting to be 7 feet tall are going to be harder to move. Trim them back so you get them to a comfortable size to work with and tie them up so that you don't scratch yourself. Move them all with as much of the root system intact as possible. Add some compost to the soil, water them in well, mulch over the top to help retain the moisture and they should come through the transition nicely.

Headless Tulips

My tulips seem to be all leaf and no flower this year. Is there anything that can be done to rejuvenate them?

The best thing you can do for tulips is make sure they don't dry out. A feeding of soluble fertilizer would also be well worthwhile. I say "soluble" because you want to get that nutrient right down to them while they are in active growth so they are picking it up and using and storing it. It is also critical that the foliage stay on the plant as long as possible and that it be allowed to die back on its own. Generally speaking, a mature tulip bulb that has heat in the soil will want to reproduce. In some cases, it will produce a multitude of new bulbs very quickly and the parent bulb just disappears. What you end up with is a cluster of smaller bulbs that are going to have to mature. If you find 4, 5 or 6 stems coming up where you had one large tulip, you are better off to lift those out in the spring, divide them and immediately replant them into their own space so they are not competing with each other. Plant them out 3 or 4 inches apart and soak them in thoroughly with a light feeding to encourage them on. Within a year or two, they should be flowering and you will have a very large productive display.

Encouraging Holly Berries

The holly bushes are taking over my front flowerbed but they are not producing any berries. When should I prune them back and what do I need to get them to produce berries?

It is possible that they are not holly bushes. They may be Mahonia or Oregon Grape, which has a holly-like leaf and a purplish colour in the fall, as opposed to the brilliant, bright, lustrous green of holly. For berry production in a holly you need to have a male and a female plant. If they did fruit and flower successfully in the past and have stopped, then it is probably a matter of too much nitrogen being available from the soil. That will cause a very lush, luscious growth at the expense of flowering. And if the plants do not flower, they can't get pollinated and therefore won't move on to that next stage, which is to produce berries. If you suspect that an excess of nitrogen is the problem, do not add any more compost or fertilizer to the plants, although you can continue to mulch to maintain the moisture. If the hollies are on the edge of a lawn that is getting fertilized – lawn fertilizer typically has a very high nitrogen content – be sure you shield that bed when the fertilizer is being applied. Don't rely on your ability to judge how far that fertilizer is being spread. Place a wide plank or piece of cardboard supported upright between the turf and the plants to ensure no fertilizer goes on to the holly. That should limit any unwanted exposure.

Blackberry Blues

My raspberries and strawberries have done quite well in my city garden and I would like to grow blackberries. Only one small corner in my garden has full sun. I planted a blackberry there last year with the understanding that they are quite rambling. I assumed it would grow about 5 feet in each direction along a trellis – but in one season it completely took over the garden so I removed it. Are there upright blackberry bushes rather than vine-type varieties? Or can I bend the canes around a three-dimensional support?

To bend the canes you must work them early and regularly to encourage them to grow onto a support or trellis. What happens with blackberries is that as the growth gets older, its production value slows down, much in the same way as you see with raspberries, and you have to keep rejuvenating them. In rich soil they do take off and once they get established, they will start climbing and running everywhere. The possibility of growing them behind your other plants on a trellis or fence is a good one, but they do need high light and constant attention. Blackberries flower and fruit earlier than raspberries so they will tolerate some of the late season frost more successfully and still produce fruit; however, if you have restricted space, the productivity with raspberries will generally be higher and more worth your effort. There has been more work done with them genetically so the cultivated raspberry vari-

eties now produce quite strongly. Certainly the ever-bearing or double crop variety will give you a higher production. If the blackberry plant is going to be a problem, it may be one you want to eliminate. You can try it on a three dimensional framework, but it will mean almost continuous work to have it stay there and give you the production you would likely be looking for. Blackberries flower on new shoots that are produced on second-year and other older canes, so don't cut everything down to the ground in the fall or there will be no fruit.

Recommended Shade Trees for Patio

We have a small patio in full sun and we are looking for a small deciduous shade tree, something that would grow to 15-20 feet. The soil is sandy and it gets full sun. Is there anything you could recommend?

You can grow all kinds of things in those conditions. Any of the crabapples can be maintained to the height you want: There are a number of producing apple trees that are columnar or dwarfing as well, so they would top off at 8-10 feet and do quite nicely. If you are looking for something to give you more shade and still stay in that height range, I would suggest the Japanese Tree Lilac. The "Ivory Silk" variety is excellent. They are quite beautiful and grow fairly quickly, but not so fast that you can't control them. They are also easy to prune and maintain. Similarly you might want to look at something like Gleditsia, the Honey Locust, either the "Glenleven" or the "Sunburst", which has a yellow tint to the foliage. It casts a lighter shade because of its shape and the size and shape of the leaflets. The open branch structure of a Honey Locust would certainly add a greater degree of interest to the landscape just because of the form. Having said that, any of these trees would be an excellent choice.

The Wonders of Sheep Manure

I am caring for our church gardens and we have access to some well-composted sheep manure. We have put a lot of topsoil on these beds in the past, however it is time to renew some of the nutrients in the soil again. There is sandy soil on one side of the church and good soil out in front. Is the sheep manure a good option for dressing the beds?

The sheep manure is an excellent option. Side dress around any perennials or plant material and mix it into the top few inches of soil. If you have enough to put a full 1 or 2 inches over the whole bed and work it down into an equivalent depth of soil – that is to say, an inch or 2 down – that would be ideal. The sheep manure should be well composted and have stood for at least a year. If there is a question as to how old the manure is, once you have incorporated it into your beds, soak them thoroughly to leach out any ammonia or heavy nitrogen content. That will help to prevent any burning of your plant material if, in fact, the manure was still a bit too fresh. If you have a large quantity of this available it is great for top-dressing the lawn as well. Raking a 1/2 inch over the entire surface would be very beneficial. Any weed seeds that were in the fresh manure when it was collected will have broken down as long as that manure has stood for that minimum one year period. Again, if you are unsure about its age go ahead and apply it. As long as it is going into a healthy, thick lawn, the weeds will not have an opportunity to germinate and the nutrient benefit will far outweigh any potential problems. In the garden beds, you may have to mulch over the top if you find there are too many weeds coming up but again, don't hesitate to use it. That sheep manure is pure black gold.

What to Plant Over a Shaded Septic Field

What can I plant over the septic bed on the north side of the house? I have put in hostas and now I am wondering if the roots are going to be a problem. Can you suggest some plants or shrubs that would be shade toler-ant but not interfere with the sep-tic system?

Your hostas should not be a problem at all. The roots will grow down a bit but there should-n't be any problem in terms of in-vasiveness. Any shallow-rooted plants would do nicely here. Jap-anese Yew would stand up beau-tifully and wouldn't be a big prob-lem in terms of the septic tile drainage system. The challenge there would be in the winter be-cause they are not really winter hardy. A better bet might be some of the dogwoods. You are not go-ing to get heavy flowering from them but they will stand up to lower light conditions, so that's a plus there. If you go with a Red Osier or a Silverleaf Dogwood, you will get the red bark through the winter months and that will create some interest to your win-ter garden as well. The Yellow-twig Dogwood would also stand up fairly well in those conditions, as would the Nannyberry.

Establishing Wild Sumac

We live on a couple of acres in an area where rainfall is usually plentiful and the soil is pure sand. There's a 12-foot gully with a southern exposure that runs through our land and currently has ferns, blackberry bushes and a few poplar and birch trees growing in it. I love sumac trees and would like to plant some on this slope. I've tried putting cut-tings in water to root up but have had no luck. I've also stored some fruit pods over winter hoping that the seeds would dry out but they stayed moist and waxy. Can you give me some guidelines on starting and planting sumac? I would like to have them become established and gradually take over the southern slope.

Sumac is an ideal choice here and will certainly help stabilize the sides of that gully. Replicating the natural method of reproduc-

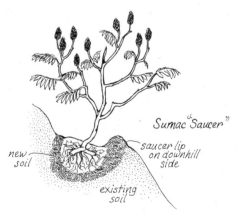

Sumac "Saucer"

new soil

saucer lip on downhill side

existing soil

tion for sumac using root shoots is the most effective way to get them established. They will spread out quite effectively on their own and eventually form the large colonies of plants that we often see. Once the soil is workable in the spring, take a shovel and dig up sections of the sumac root from an area just beyond the drip line of the parent. Amend your sandy soil with organic matter and add in some bone meal or rock phosphate to help stimulate root development. Bury the sections of root into the soil at about the same depth you found them, water well and mulch over top to help retain moisture. You can also create "saucers" to help catch extra rainwater on the hillside by mounding soil up on the lower edge of the planting hole. Water them as often as possible during that first year to help get the plants well established. Once they start to develop nature will take over. Sumac is naturally invasive and you should eventually see the plant start to spread and take over that slope.

Fertilizing Near Water

What type of fertilizer would you recommend for use on a waterfront property so that the nutrients don't leach into the water? We have bears near our home, so we are a bit reluctant to use any-thing that might attract them. Have you any suggestions?

Your own compost would be ideal. Put it on in moderation and stay back a minimum of 10, but preferably 25 feet from the water's edge. There will be a slope to the water's edge so there will be some moisture movement within the soil and over the surface that will pick up a small amount of the compost and take it further down, so do stay back from the water's edge. Because of the bears it is essential that you use well-rotted compost, but as long as it is well broken down it should not provide any attraction. Manure would also work well here but it should be at least one, and preferably several years old. If it is not already combined with straw you can mix the straight manure with some other green organic material like leaves or grass clippings in a 50-50 ratio and that would work quite nicely here as well.

Tilting Tamarisk

This is a cosmetic problem that's been caused by the Summer Glow Tamarisk in my front garden. It has sort of feathery branches and goes pinkish in the summertime. This will be its third summer coming up, but it is growing crooked and it is smothering my other plants. What can I do to prevent this?

You will want to tie a stake on to the back side of that tamarisk, that is to say, the side that is leaning away from the perpendicular. The stake should be at least 2/3 thirds of the height of the plant and you are going to have to support it for at least a year or two. Once it gets the hint, then you will be able to take the support away. You could also dig down into the soil from about the drip line, lift the tree up from underneath and tip the root ball slightly forward in the appropriate direction. Pack some more soil in to keep the plant leaning in the right direction and be sure to adjust the stake to provide the necessary support. If you end up with a couple of branches going the wrong way after all this, just remove them so they won't be throwing shade over your other plants. Once you get it straightened up, if you find there is still an awful lot of the tree leaning in the wrong direction or if it has started growing in the wrong direction, just trim it back, making sure that you limit the amount of pruning to less than 25% of the

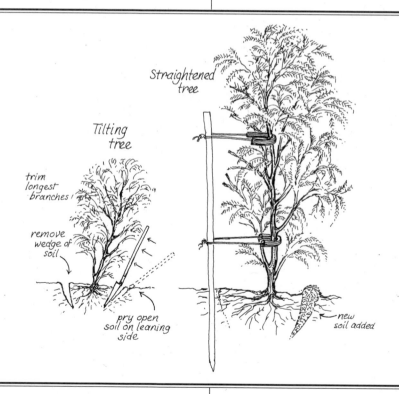

Straightened tree

Tilting tree

trim longest branches

remove wedge of soil

pry open soil on leaning side

new soil added

entire plant. If you have trimmed it back by a quarter and it is still in need of more, wait until next year and remove up to another 25%. If you need to completely remove branches, take them right back to the collar where the branch starts coming from the trunk. After a year or two your tamarisk should be coming along the way you want it.

Green Worms in the Evergreens

Some of the evergreens on our property have developed tiny green worms that spread out and eat all the new growth. Is there something I can spray to get rid of them or prevent them from coming?

Unfortunately, you cannot use dormant oil on evergreens so you will need to treat the worms when they show up. Soap and water will give you an effective measure of control but you have to apply it when the caterpillars are just starting to develop. If you can make contact with them and knock them down, you will probably get an effective kill early in the season with the soap and water concentration. That solution is 40-parts water and 1-part soap. I have also found pyrethrum sprays quite good for small infestations. Pyrethrum is a short-term contact insecticide obtained from a species of chrysanthemum grown in Central Africa and Ecuador. As a natural, botanical substance, it breaks down quickly once it is sprayed and has a very low toxicity for humans or pets. These sprays are generally sold in pressurized cans for household and garden insect control but be sure to check the label to ensure you have the right insecticide. And be careful when applying it because the propellant used in these sprays can cause local freezing, and therefore burning, of the foliage. Hold the spray can at least 6-12 inches away from the plant foliage to avoid this problem – and be careful not to inhale that mist yourself.

Waxy Growth on Spruce

This spring I discovered a waxy sort of growth that is about 2 inches in diameter on the trunk of my 40-year-old spruce. It sticks out about 2 inches and almost looks like it has been dripping – sort of like how a candle would have dripped and then hardened – and it is pliable. I haven't removed it because I would like to first know what it is before I do anything.

You don't have to do anything with that sort of a growth, including removing it. It may have been an injury. It may have been a resin pocket that developed and split. If it has accumulated more resin in one spot than the expansion of the bark around it can contain, you get a bit of a bubble. It would not be uncommon, if it were Black Spruce, to see very resinous bubbles on the bark. If there has been a perforation of the outer surface or cambium layer, the tree will naturally ooze and seal itself up, effectively shellacking itself closed, and that is what you are seeing there as the wax-like drips. The insects cannot get through it, which is a plus. Generally speaking, it is going to be fine. It is healing itself and won't need further treatment.

Grub Legacy

Last year the grubs destroyed my front lawn and now the skunks and squirrels are coming in and are making it look like a war zone. What do I face in the future?

What you face in the future is a low population, or possibly no population, of white grubs because the squirrels, skunks and starlings have come in and removed them. In fact, a war zone is exactly what it was. Once the grub predators have finished plowing up or turning back the sod and as soon as you can walk

on the lawn without leaving footprints, fill in the divots, replace the turf, top-dress over the affected areas and re-seed. You lawn should be fine.

Poison Ivy Tangled Up in Cedars

My son and his wife got a really bad dose of poison ivy last year while they were cleaning out the cedar hedge that separates them from their neighbours. What can we do to get rid of the poison ivy without destroying the cedar hedge?

Clearing out that poison ivy and saving the cedars is certainly possible. What would be helpful is if early the next season, they could prune back the branches under the edge of the trees to allow better access and then rake out some of that old material. If that's not possible, not to worry. What you want to establish are essentially black out conditions around the base of those trees. If they have compost, that goes down first, and after that they should put a 4 to 6 inch layer of either clean straw or any organic material like wood chips or leaves down as mulch. The cedars are going to love the mulch and the poison ivy can't grow without light. If you can get the light blocked out by putting the heavy mulch down there you will get rid of the poison ivy. In the meantime, try not to come into contact with the hedge. Poison ivy doesn't always behave the same way every year and it may start climbing and running up through the hedge. If there is some already in there you can get a reaction if you come into contact with it. Some people react more on hot days because the heat brings out the volatile oils in the poison ivy or if they have a particular sensitivity to it. I know of people who have picked it up from the smoke from burning material with poison ivy in it. If a cat or dog has gone through the hedge, it's the same sort of thing. They pick the oil up on their fur and you can react simply by petting the animal. It won't have penetrated through to the animal's skin but you can certainly pick it up on yours.

Spring Infestation

I have a big problem every year about the middle of June. Just when the leaves on my flowers and shrubs have come out, a huge swarm of flying insects with long spindly legs arrive. They sort of climb on top of one another and then they lace up all the leaves. You can squish them easily but if you don't get them all, by next morning the tree will be covered. They eat all of my hydrangea and the peonies. What are they and how do I get rid of them?

The stink bug is certainly one possibility. I am sure you would know them because of their foul smell and they do come in groups like that. More likely however, these are Japanese beetles, although yours sound like they are arriving a little early. You would be able to identify these by

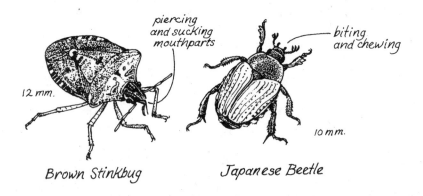

piercing and sucking mouthparts

biting and chewing

12 mm.

10 mm.

Brown Stinkbug   Japanese Beetle

their metallic green colour and they swarm in the manner you've described as well. The pheromone that the females give off is very strong and attracts a huge quantity of males into an area and their climbing on top of each other is all about the next stage, which is the laying of lots of eggs. In the interim, they feed heavily on whatever they land on. Now the fact that they land on your hydrangeas leads me to think they are stink bugs. You are not going to deter them from coming if they are already in the area. What you can do – as soon as they show up – is apply the soap and water spray: 40-parts water to 1-part soap. Alternatively, they are quite easy to pick off. If you do opt to pick them off, make sure you have a bucket of soapy water with you to drown them. To gain any measure of control you will need to pick them off a couple of times a day for several days. That frequency is essential to gaining the upper hand here. By reducing their population you put a dent in the number of eggs being laid and the successful laying of eggs is what is bringing them back year after year. In fact, if you look around the shrubs when these insects start showing up in June, you will probably find they are actually hatching right up from out of the soil rather than flying in

from elsewhere. If you do find them in the soil, you can get at them with a soap and water spray and kill them right off as they start to hatch, before any of your plants are affected.

False Bamboo

There is an invasive plant coming up on my property that I think might be bamboo. It grows about 10 feet high and has a large heart-shaped leaf. We did some work pulling it out last year but we just seem to have encouraged it. How can I get it out?

What you have is not a bamboo but looks very much like one. It is likely a knotweed. We have prostrate knotweed that is native to Canada and is in the same family as the one you've got but is a much smaller plant. This one that you are describing is Polygonum *cuspidatum*, more commonly known as Chinese or Mexican Bamboo, or bamboo-weed, that has been introduced to this country. And does it ever like to take over! One of its problems is that it spreads by rhizomes. If you chop up the rhizomes when you are trying to get rid of it, they will simply put out new roots and new shoots and start coming back up again. A better approach would be to surface cut anything that is showing up right now. Once that's done, cover the whole area with black plastic and leave it on there for a couple of months to bake what's underneath. Once that's done, lift up the plastic and replant in the area. Be sure to mulch heavily between the new plants to make sure that no light will get through and stimulate any of the rhizomes that have managed to survive the baking.

Ant Eliminator

I used your ant potion outdoors last year and it worked beautifully. I am wondering if I can use it indoors. I have a very woodsy place and the ants are both inside and outside the front and back doors. We put containers of boric acid out again this year but so far it hasn't made a difference.

You can certainly use this ant potion inside as well as outdoors. What you want to do is add 6 tablespoons of sugar to 2 cups of boiling water, mix it to dissolve the sugar and then add a teaspoon of boric acid. Boric acid can be easily found at most pharmacies. Take an old margarine tub or any pint-sized plastic container with a lid and cut small holes in the sides at intervals all around the edge at the bottom to allow the ants access inside. Dip a few cotton balls into the solution and place these in the bottom of the container. Seal the container so that the cotton balls don't dry out too quickly and to make sure nobody else gets in. Place the tub on a path that you know the ants take regularly. There is more than enough sugar in this solution to attract them when they find it, but they have to bump into it first, so the location of the tub is important. This solution takes a bit longer to work than using straight boric acid because of the lower concentration, but this is actually a benefit. What happens is that the worker ants take bites of the cotton ball and transport those small pieces back to the colony to feed the other ants. This way more ants are exposed to the toxic solution. The boric acid builds up and eventually proves fatal so you end up killing off a greater proportion or even all of the colony, although this may take a couple of weeks to accomplish. The plus is that the ants are less likely to come back because you have pretty well exterminated the entire population. Any leftover solution can be carefully labelled and stored in the fridge. Check the tub every few days to make sure the cotton balls are still wet and re-soak or replace them as necessary. Once you are sure the ants have been eliminated, you can remove the tub and discard any leftover solution.

Tents in the Bird House

I'm trying to control the insects in my large flower garden without using insecticide. I am also trying to attract birds. I have put up several nesting boxes but the tent caterpillars seem to be the ones coming and nesting in them. How can I stop the caterpillars?

If you were to look in your nesting boxes at the end of the summer, what you will probably find is a spongy substance that looks a bit like urea formaldehyde foam. That is the over-wintering egg mass of the caterpillars. Clean out your bird houses, which is just a matter of scraping that substance out and washing out the box. All birdhouses should be cleaned out at the end of the breeding season anyway. If you can scrape that mess clean, you will not have a new generation of caterpillars hatching from that location next spring. The birds will move in and the insects won't come back to lay their eggs once the birds are established. The birds would take care of any caterpillars that might arrive in any case. If the birds haven't nested by mid-summer, you may want to take those boxes down and try a new location. On the other hand, if you leave them there they will work as a trap where you can get to the over-wintering egg masses of the caterpillars. Then all you have to do is clean them out in the fall to prevent further infestations the next year.

Alternate Ground Cover Failure

I've had a bit of a ground cover disaster this year. Our front lawn is about 10 by 5 feet facing north and is on a bit of a slope. We have either a large cedar or a cypress, I'm not sure which it is, two little cedars, a Sand Cherry and a peony bush out there. The problem is that last spring all of our groundcover died because of winter-kill. We had ajuga and violets growing there but they were completely destroyed. Into the breach has leapt an amazing quantity of carpetweed. Do you have any suggestions on what I could do to get rid of that or should I just cover it all over with landscape fabric and bark it?

You could just cover it all up, however, the idea of violets in there is a marvelous one and gives you the benefit of some early spring colour. Your front yard is obviously fairly heavily shaded. The ajuga you had in there surprises me because normally it does not hold up in a shaded spot. Typically, it prefers a higher light location, so I wouldn't go with that again. You could plant periwinkle or pachisandra in there instead and add in some hostas or astilbes. All of these would do well in a shaded location and give you a bit more variety and coverage. You could also mix in some of the ephemerals, the spring flowering bulbs such as trilliums or Dog Tooth Violets, or a mix of daffodils and tulips. They will come up and give you a show early in the season and then the other ground cover will come along and fill in once they die back. In terms of the actual ground cover, the most successful would be the periwinkle or the pachisandra. Of course, any action should only be taken following a thorough weeding of the area. Mulch around any new plants as you introduce them and that should drastically reduce any future weeding requirements.

Black Spots on Leaves

Right from the time in the spring when the leaves unfurl on our oak trees, there are black marks on pretty well all of the leaves. The spots almost look like tar. It only appears on the oaks, not on the maples. Can you tell me what this is?

You've hit right on the name of that problem. Tar spot. The tar spot that shows up on an oak is a totally different beast than the tar spot that shows up on maples.

This one is quite host specific. It is actually a fungus. There are also bacterial spots that can affect trees and shrubs. In this case, if the conditions were right, it could spread. The dark spot comes from the fact that the small localized area on the leaf that is affected is not able to photosynthesize, but this is more of a cosmetic problem than anything else. It would have to be a really severe outbreak to actually cause the tree to suffer, in which case it would defoliate the tree early in the season. At the level you are describing, this should not a big problem – but what is going to help control it is to clean up all of the oak leaves in your garden in the fall and compost them. With oak leaves, they break down very slowly. Oaks are one of the link trees between deciduous and broad leaf evergreens. In fact in the south, there are actually oaks that are evergreens. Even in this climate, the oak leaves dry on to the tree, so the oaks tend to hold on to their leaves much longer than other deciduous trees. The thickness of the oak leaves means they break down much more slowly as well, so to accelerate that process, run a lawnmower over them before you throw them into the compost and mix them in well with whatever material is already in there. This type of leaf material is very, very good for your compost. And if you can throw your grass clippings in there as well, that would be an added plus because the nitrogen from grass is very useful in breaking down oak leaves.

Pruning a Saucer Magnolia

My 4-foot Saucer Magnolia has foliage all the way from the bottom up. There are four branches on it, of which two are the main branches. I assume it will grow into a 30-40 foot tree. Should I prune it to get a main stem?

Although you will see magnolias that grow to 30-40 feet in books and photographs, that will not happen in our climate. It can possibly grow to 20 or even 25 feet provided it is in a sheltered location. Winter hardiness will always be questionable with this tree and during a particularly severe winter you will probably get a fair amount of die back. It should be in a full sun location if possible, however it will take partial shade or mottled sun, especially if that gives it a more sheltered location. At 4 feet, the main thing is to get it well established. During the first couple of years any incorporation of compost into the soil will be worthwhile. Additionally, you should add rock phosphate or bone meal each

spring for the first 2 or 3 years as a minimum so that you are encouraging as much new root growth and development as possible. Once it is well established, it will withstand any of the other problems that might come along over time. If things get really out of shape, you may consider trimming some of the branches or tips of the branches back to maintain a controllable size and shape in your garden but you should not prune it to get a main stem. Let it keep growing along as it is. This is the normal branching structure of the Saucer Magnolia and is part of the appeal of this variety.

Dandelion Dilemma

I've heard about this environmentally friendly weedy seed stuff for dandelions. All the people around here are using it but I have a feeling it is not that benign. Is it harmful and if so, is there a non-chemical method I can use for getting rid of dandelions?

Elbow grease is probably the most effective method to get rid of dandelions. There are torches and such that can be used as well. Using a propane torch will create some greenhouse gases but it is certainly a more environmentally friendly approach than going with some of the heavy-duty chemical products on the market. If you are taking dandelions out by hand, certainly a weeder-type tool is very helpful because the further you can get down and the more root you can get out of there, the more success you are going to have in the long term. If you have a particularly large or concentrated patch, smothering them with newspaper and mulch can work, but only if you are able cover them for a long time. And if there are large tap roots on the weeds, even baking them like that in the soil might not be effective. If the tip of that root stays alive, the darn things tend to callus off and sprout again. As for the newer product alternatives, the jury is still out as to whether they are harmful, but certainly there is an environmental impact. Any herbicide will usually affect more than the weeds targeted – and that is where some of the problems come in. The kind of herbicide product that you are talking about works with a growth hormone and the plants essentially grow themselves to death. It causes all of this contortion in the plant so that they expend a lot of energy and eventually expire. It generally works best on broad leaf weeds in turf conditions. Many products claim to become inert on contact with the soil but the active ingredient doesn't just disappear –

some residue is left there. Prevention can alleviate a lot of the need to control weeds. Cut your grass a little longer and pop off the dandelion heads before they go to seed. Put down a light top-dressing of soil early in the season and over-seed with a good quality, drought-tolerant grass seed like Creeping Red Fescue. That will give you a lot of grass plants coming up and filling in the bare patches and the dandelions won't have a place to get established later in the season when the seeds start flying from far and wide.

Covering Exposed Roots

The roots of the huge 25-year-old Crimson King Maple tree in my backyard are all on top of the grass. Could I top those roots with about 8 inches of soil?

Adding 4 inches of top soil over the roots would be ideal, and don't go more than 6 inches. You don't want any top soil against the bark of the tree either, so taper the soil away from the base and outward. If you have to bring it up more than 4-6 inches around that spot, put a dry well around the tree extending a minimum of 2 feet away from the trunk and create a retaining wall. Even a ring of stones will hold the soil away from the tree base. Leave that interior area uncovered with new soil or with a minimum of soil cover so that it can breathe. The tree is used to that existing level of exposure, so good air circulation will be essential to prevent rot at the base of the trunk and keep this tree healthy.

Drought-resistant Grass

I am trying to re-seed my lawn because, between the grubs and skunks, it has been destroyed. I live in an area where I am on a well, so I can't really water the lawn. I have gone ahead and roto-tilled the lawn and I am wondering if there is a grass seed I can use that would not dry out so quickly?

Yes, if you would prefer something that is a bit more drought resistant and you are putting grass seed back down, fescue would work quite nicely. The name to look for is "Creeping Red Fescue". It is drought resistant and it will do quite fine in full sun. Now that you have roto-tilled, take a rake and level out your lawn. Once you have that done, take a half-filled lawn roller and flatten the soil down. That will show you if there are any dips or hills in the lawn that you want to fill in. Once you have gone over the whole area and have got the levels you want, do a light raking over the surface to scratch it up a

little and seed over top of that. Sow your seeds in perpendicular lines, so go east to west and then north to south. Seed it twice and then roll the whole thing again with a light roller. You want to ensure that the seed is in contact with the soil. As soon as the rain comes along it will dampen things down. Alternatively, you can do a light watering. You don't need to use a whole lot of water for this – just misting over that surface will make sure there is enough moisture for germination and that would be a plus. Once it gets established you can avoid the watering.

Spruce Bud Worm

The two spruce trees on our front lawn are both about 10-15 feet tall and about 4 feet wide, and we noticed yesterday that the new growth seems to be disappearing. Last night I went out and there were dozens and dozens of beetles around the tree and this morning when I had a closer look at the tree, it was just teaming with green caterpillars about 1½ centimetres long. I'm wondering if this is spruce budworm and if it is, what I can do?

It probably is the budworm. I'm not sure whether soap and water will be enough to get these under control but that would certainly be your first line of attack. Try spraying with a 40-to-1 solution of water-to-soap and check on the result. If this doesn't work, Rotenone certainly will. It is an organic solution, however it's deadly poisonous. Do not use it around water. If you have a pond with fish in it, for example, it will kill all the fish. It can be used on fruit within 24 hours of harvesting without a problem – however, it is deadly poisonous when it's mixed and applied. Take all the prescribed and necessary precautions when you're using it: gloves while you're mixing and a mask while you're spraying. Keep the gloves on there as well, to prevent any of it from getting on you. Be sure there are no children or pets anywhere around. You do have to make contact with the insect for it to work so try to concentrate it in the areas where you see the most activity. Budworms go in about a 10-year cycle so this could be an indication that we are coming up toward another peak.

Rusty Hawthorn

We planted a hawthorn tree about three years ago and it soon developed what I am pretty sure is rust. Now every year just after it blossoms it gets covered in rust again. Last year my rose bushes looked like they might have it too but it was a really wet summer so I thought it might just be the excess water. What I am wondering is whether the rust from the hawthorn is harmful to the neighbouring plants and if it is, is there a non-chemical way to treat it, and if not, should I just rip everything out?

Anything in the rose family is going to be susceptible to rust. Wetness would certainly be conducive to the spread. Early in the season, a sulphur dusting could be helpful if there is a fair amount of rust showing. More importantly, clean up thoroughly in the fall and remove any debris from the ground around the hawthorn, which is in the rose family, and around the rose bushes. The rust is going to be over-wintering on the ground in the leaves and in old branches, so if you can clean that up and open the area up to the air and light, you reduce the possibility of re-infection. Rust is a fungus however, and it is going to continue coming back even if your sanitation is perfect. They are airborne spores and always out there in the natural environment but if you can keep it under control in the immediate area with the sanitation, then you really shouldn't have a big problem.

Mole Mayhem

Last summer I had an in-ground pool put in and in the process my front lawn was totally decimated. The contractor came back and laid new sod and some time after I noticed hundreds of tiny tunnels made by moles. I had a pest person come in and he sprayed under the grass but whatever he used, it didn't kill them. They are all back again this year and they are so destructive. There are so many tunnels under the grass that it can't root up properly and the sod is just sort of laying there. I don't know what to do. Have you any advice?

If you can fill in the holes with soil, lay the sod back down, roll it and soak the daylights out of it to get it growing, that would be a start. With that many holes, it is definitely moles. One way to discourage them is to drop half a stick of Juicy Fruit gum, still in its wrapper, down into the holes throughout the entire maze and the smell of that should be enough to drive them out. If you see them coming back, mix up some castor oil about 50-50 with water and pour that in. They don't like the smell of the castor oil solution either and that should help to keep them away. Used kitty litter tossed down the holes will also work but it's usually easier to get the castor oil solution in there, so I would try that first. Once your lawn gets established and the moles have been discouraged

by the odours, you should see the problem disappear.

Cracking Quaking Aspen

The bark on our Quaking Aspens has turned a sort of darkish brown or even black colour at the point where the branches come out from the trunk. The bark is very brittle and some of the trees are actually breaking. The wood inside looks relatively soft. Any idea what's wrong with them?

This is not uncommon with the aspen. They are, generally speaking, a short-lived tree. In our climate they are considered one of the "settlement" or "pioneer" type of tree species in nature's plan of succession in that they settle in poor conditions and then through the next 15 or 20, maybe even up to 30 years, drop all kinds of leaves and twigs, go through their maximum growth and then rapidly into decline. But in the meantime, they do an awful lot to prepare and enrich the soil. Other species can then get established that need both a richer soil with more humus content and the shelter provided by the fully mature aspens. Aspens are generally less desirable as a landscape feature around most homes because they do not last very long and can get fairly messy. If the ones you have now break down, they will regenerate from the roots. They shoot up as readily as the ailianthus or Tree of Heaven and the stand will perpetuate itself for many years, so there is really no need for any treatment.

Watersprouts in the Viburnum

Our 6-foot viburnum tree has thousands of buds, but there are also watersprouts and they come right up through the graceful arches. It spoils the look of the shrub and I really want to prune them properly. Would this be all right to do?

The best thing to do is to take the watersprouts right back down to the stem they are coming from and if they are coming from the ground, take them down to ground level. Or if you like, let a few of them take over some of the other growth, but it is going to be a process that you will have to manage over the next few years. You can take a maximum of 25% out of the shrub in any given year. There may be more than 25% in water sprouts coming through your viburnum but usually that is the result of a very heavy pruning at some point in the past that has stimulated all that growth. So to keep it in balance don't trim too much and do it over a period of time. If you can do 25% this year

and then again the next year and the next year, you will have gotten it into a balance without regenerating a lot of sucker growth. Spring is a good time to do this and the plus of doing it then is that if you bring some of those cuttings inside, you may get them to break out into leaf and flower. Simply re-cut the stems just below a node and place them in water in a bright location. Not only do they bring a bit of early season colour indoors, they may even root up and provide you with new cuttings to replant outside.

Losing Battle with Violets

We are plagued by violets and all sorts of common weeds that started in the garden and have now spread into our lawn. We do not use weed killer, but rather pull up the violets and weeds by hand. It is seems like a losing battle. Is there any other non-toxic solution to rid ourselves of these invasive plants?

The most important thing here is to start early. As soon as you can walk on the grass in the spring without leaving a footprint, get out there and do a very thorough raking with a stiff fan rake. Give it a really good, vigorous raking. It's best to do this in a grid, going north to south over the entire area on the first pass.

Anything that pulls out will be something you don't want there, and can go right into the compost. Mix it in with the dry material already in there and it should reactivate things after the long winter. Then go over your lawn with a rake again, this time moving east to west. Once that is done, over-seed the lawn. Top dress first with a bit of compost if it needs it, but be sure to over-seed so that you have got something else growing in there that will compete with any of the violets that might come back. You can look at putting more clover into the lawn or if you want more turf grass, get the appropriate grass seed and over-seed heavily. When it starts growing, it will compete successfully with the weedy material you don't want there. You want to encourage the new plants and it will be at the expense of the other invaders. Raise your lawnmower up to 2½ inches and don't cut any lower. By increasing the length of the grass plants you shade the soil and block out the light that is essential for the violets and other weed seeds to germinate. Continue to pull out any violets that seem to be making a comeback as they appear, but you should find that with the raking and the new material in there, the problem will be much more manageable or eliminated completely.

Caring for Ginkgo Trees

Is it difficult to take care of the ginkgo tree?

The ginkgo is probably the easiest tree to take care of. There are no known diseases or insect pests that affect them and fossil records for the species go back something like 600 million years. They have that wonderful fan shaped leaf that turns a beautiful golden yellow in the fall and it is striking. You can source them readily through nurseries. Other than normal care to get them established and growing, there is really nothing to be concerned about. If you want a more upright or pyramidal tree, get a male. The female tree has a round crown. Another plus with the males is that they don't fruit. Ginkgo fruit actually smells pretty bad but it's supposed to be very good for your health. I never got past the smell myself.

Mauvey Mystery

A few years ago I bought a little plant that had a very pretty mauvey blue flower about 2 inches across, sort of trumpet shape like a Morning Glory with 5 overlapping petals. I looked through my books and I couldn't find a picture, only a written description that said it was a

Thunbergia grandflora, and it turned out to be a vine. I would like to know if this is correct and how I would propagate it because it is a very pretty flower.

It probably is a thunbergia. It does beautifully outside in the summer but you will have to bring it indoors later on. You can take cuttings from it quite easily. If you have an English Ivy that you can cut at the same time and root the two of them together in water, that would be ideal. The natural auxins produced by the English Ivy will be distributed in the water and picked up by the thunbergia as well, helping it root up fairly readily. If you don't have any ivy, you can still take a cutting about 4 inches long, cutting just below the node and slightly injuring the node of the stem of the thunbergia. Take a 1 inch cube of floral foam, and be sure not to use the instant floral foam but the standard kind, and soak the cube a couple of times. Once it is good and moist, stick the cutting about 3/4 of the way down into the cube with a bit of #1 rooting hormone on it. Then sit it in a saucer or tray and keep the water level about 1/2 of the way up the cube constantly until the roots grow out through the sides of the cube, which they should do readily. Once the roots are about an inch long, handle it by the foam and plant the whole thing up. Pinch the top 1/4 or 1/2 inch off the cube and make sure the top of the cube is down below the soil level so the foam does not wick moisture away from that new root system.

Best Time to Prune Flowering Trees

When is the best time to prune forsythia bushes and a Japanese Cherry tree?

The best time to prune both of these trees or any other flowering tree is right after they flower. Now if you don't get to them after they flower the best time to prune them is whenever you have the pruning sheers in your hand. However, if you want the best show of flower on the plant then you want to maximize the time between the pruning and

top of foam block removed and covered with soil

the development of the flowers. As soon as they finish flowering in the spring cut them back. That way all of the new spring growth from then on gets to develop and produce the flower buds that will over-winter and then bloom the following year. Likewise, pruning flowering trees and shrubs before they flower in the spring only reduces the amount of flower you get to enjoy on the plant.

Hemming a Mulberry

My Weeping Mulberry tree is overgrown and has spread out all over the grass. Should I cut it back?

You can lift the bottom of it up a bit. It is sort of like raising the hemline on a skirt. Cut it up to the level you are comfortable with. If you have turf below the tree you want enough space to get a lawnmower underneath it, but ideally, for the welfare of the tree and in terms of the penetra-tion of moisture and nutrients into the soil, you would be better off to remove the sod underneath it. Clear out a ring around the tree as far out as the drip line of the branches and then mulch the surface. Your tree will be much happier that way. In terms of the width or the size of the tree, if it is getting too wide, just follow the individual branches on the outside edge back up to their source in the crown and remove them completely. Often by taking off the outermost branches around the tree you will gain back 6-8 inches and if it is a very full mature plant that amount is certainly not going to hurt it at all. Look at 25% as the maximum removal you can take from the crown without there being any setback to the tree. More than 25% is too big a reduction in the photosynthesizing or food production capacity of the tree and also stimulates overproduction of sucker growth.

JULY

A. KARSTAD

Advice to Trumpet Vine "Thief"

Is there any way you can take a slice off of a Trumpet Vine? There is a good healthy one growing on a back lane in town and I have tried taking a slip off it and dipping it in hormone powder, but it never grows. I know crime doesn't pay, but is there any way I can improve my odds?

If there is enough of the vine growing close to the ground, getting a side shoot that is already rooted would be the ideal. Then just nurse it along. Alternatively, run one of the laterals out about a foot from the plant and cover about 3 or 4 inches of this stem with soil, then put a rock over top. Make sure the area stays nice and moist and check it once in a while. Probably after 3 or 4 weeks you will have roots developing at that point. Sever that piece from the main plant between the vine and the rock and then lift the section with the roots and soil intact.

Now you have a ground layered cutting that can be planted. If this vine is not in a public place, you may want to knock on the door of the owners and let them know what you are up to. They'd probably be relieved to know that the person lurking in the back lane is only propagating their plant.

Soil Contamination and Clematis Vines

My problem is with some 40-year-old clematis vines that are facing due south against the brick wall of my house. They start to develop in June and the flowers can get to be about 8 inches in diameter, but by then the bottom leaves have begun to turn black and fall off. I use a liquid fertilizer on the plants but I have also used a fungicide and although it didn't have much effect, I'm wondering if the soil might be contaminated?

Soil contamination is likely not the problem and on the plus side, the liquid fertilizer is where the 8 inch diameter blooms are coming from. However you want to be feeding the soil around them as well. Add compost, an inch or so over the surface, and mix it in gently. You can use your soluble fertilizer in conjunction with that but not too heavily. The lush vigorous growth, which often results from the available nitrogen in fertilizers, gives you a very soft tissue and a susceptibility to disease. With the vine facing due south, it is also going to be hot – so having something there to shade the roots and keep them a bit cooler would be worthwhile; a groundcover would be ideal. The top of the plant will toughen up nicely against hot weather as long as the roots are protected. If you put a few rocks over the surface to shade the soil that's another option, but a ground cover works just as well. Any material you want to put there will do, from annuals to perennials, as long as it is low and won't compete with your vines. Something that highlights the flower from your clematis could be quite interesting. Obviously, the growing conditions are pretty good, and there's probably enough soluble lime that is being carried with the moisture coming down from the brick siding into the soil when it rains to make sure things aren't too acidic. Generally the clematis are not going to have a problem that way, since they are comfortable with a soil pH anywhere between 6 ½ and 8, but if you think there may be a problem, try a handful or two of dolomitic limestone mixed into the surface of the soil before you put on the compost. Then remix the whole thing. It will be a long-term process breaking down the limestone but a few handfuls goes a long way and you wouldn't have to repeat the application for another couple of years. There are also a few fungal diseases which attack clematis but the only serious one is wilt, which causes the shoots to droop suddenly for no apparent reason. Cutting off the affected shoots is usually enough to solve the problem. Clematis must have a well-drained soil and I suspect yours may be getting too much water. That is why you are getting the dying and blackening on the lower leaves. Cut back on the water and remove any affected leaves and you should see a turnaround fairly shortly.

Raising Anemone

I made an impulse buy yesterday; I bought a package of anemone. They look like little corms or tubers. They are called Single Coronaria and my books have no useful information in terms of the planting or raising of these. What should I do with them?

This is commonly called "Florists Anemone" – those brightly coloured cut flowers that appear in the shops each spring. You want to get those corms planted in the fall at a depth that is about twice the thickness of the corm itself. So in they go and as soon as you get a decent hard frost, put about 4 inches of mulch on the surface of the soil. You

should be getting some root development by then. There will still be good warmth in the soil after the frost, but you don't want the cold to penetrate too quickly. So the mulch goes on right after the frost and it holds on to the heat in the soil for a little longer. As the soil is slowly cooling down, the root system will still develop and this is critical for spring flowering bulbs. Anemone are on the borderline for hardiness – when you get outside of Southern Ontario it is a bit touch and go as to whether they will make it – but a little more mulch over the top will make all the difference in the world. And one more thing: it seems that the squirrels will eat just about anything that is in the garden apart from your daffodil bulbs, including anemone corms. If you are worried at all about the squirrels, put some chicken wire over the surface of the soil to prevent them, literally and figuratively, from "digging in".

Mutant Iris

It's been about 5 years since I started growing irises and they have bloomed very well every year. The Samurai Warrior Iris I have is a maroon colour but this spring it mutated and turned dusty pink with an orange middle. I don't know why and I don't want my other irises to do that too. What can I do to prevent it?

That mutation would have to have been particular to this strain of iris. You can get a natural deviation or "sport" from other plant material. Before so much crossing or hybridizing of plants was done, it was usually these naturally occurring sports or mutations that were selected and propagated to develop new stock and varieties. In this case I would suggest you remove that one. Now in terms of the colour, going from a maroon to a dusty pink may have something to do with the type of compost you have incorporated into the soil. If you have a fireplace or woodstove, it might be worthwhile adding a little bit of the ash from there. Just sprinkle it over the surface of the soil around your iris early in the spring or when you put your compost down and make sure that it gets worked in. For a longer-term solution, you can incorporate a bit of dolomite limestone, either as a stone dust or horticultural-grade limestone, just to slightly raise the soil pH. I am thinking it might be getting a little acidic in there, which in some cases will give you a bit of a colour change – it may be that some of the blues are coming out, so the maroon is going to a pink.

The change in the beard of this iris from dark maroon to orange sounds like a reversion. This one would be interesting to lift. Take this one out and put it elsewhere. Do the same amending that you do for the rest of the "Samurai Warriors" left in the bed – it may be time to thin them out in any case – but put this one in a separate but similar location with the same treatment and see if the results change accordingly. If, in fact, you have got a sport, you may have come up with your own naturally selected new iris. With tulip bulbs for example, the sport is the greatest area of change. Even with all the hybridizing that goes on in the nurseries now, some of the most interesting bulbs still come from the sports of older bulbs that deviated naturally and were then propagated to increase their numbers to marketable quantities.

Rhubarb Leaves in the Compost

I've heard that you should not recycle rhubarb leaves in your compost. Is that correct?

The logic is that these are a poison. If you have a small quantity of rhubarb leaves mixed in with everything else, the leaves will break down but there will be a bit of residue. If some insects or other munching creatures come along to breakdown the compost for you, which is always a big plus, they will be poisoned. It is better not to take the chance. However, when you are cutting your rhubarb, if you can slice the stems off and leave the leaves intact you can stack the leaves around the base of the plants to act as a mulch. At the very least they will give some benefit by blocking the light and cutting down weeds, and as they break down they should introduce some nutrients into the soil as well. Rhubarb leaves can also be put to good use if you are looking to make some decorative stepping stones. Lay down the rhubarb leaves and then mix up some concrete with not too much slump, so a thick mix. Pour that mix over the veined, underside of the leaf and push the concrete mix out to the edges, trimming off any that spills over the edge of the leaf. The mix should be about 3 inches thick at the centre rounding down to about 2 inches at the edges. Let it sit to harden in place and when you turn the whole thing over and take the leaf off, the beautiful imprint of the veining of the leaf remains. It makes for some pretty impressive stones.

Orange Fungus on Evergreens

My Skyrocket Juniper is about 20 years old and about 20 feet high. Over the last 5 years it developed bright orange sticky looking growths on the lower branches from the base up to about 5 feet. There are no new needles growing on these areas and the existing needles fall off. The twigs also dry out and eventually fall off the main branches. I have given it evergreen spikes once every growing season for the last 4 years and this seems to have helped and gotten rid of the orange fungi, however there has been very little growth and I would like to encourage the shrub to produce more needles to cover the bottom area. Can you give me advice on how to improve the situation?

Your Skyrocket Juniper is suffering from a disease that is normally seen as more of a problem on apples, which is the other tree that it infects. Cedar-apple rust is caused by a fungus that infects the Eastern Red Cedar, which is actually a juniper, and apple trees, but both trees must be present in the same vicinity for it to complete its life cycle – that is to say, the disease cannot spread from juniper to juniper but alternates between the juniper and apple trees. This alternating

Jellylike
orange growth
on Red Cedar
Juniperus
virginiana

"Apple stage"
on underside of
Apple leaf

infection explains why the disease seems to have cleared up on your juniper. Usually before you see these orange jelly-like horns appear there are some less-noticeable symptoms. In the spring or early summer you'll see brownish-green swellings appear on the upper surface of the needles. They then form round spheres or galls that continue to get bigger until the fall when they can be as large as 2-5 centimetres in diameter. These galls turn chocolate brown in colour and are covered with small circular depressions a bit like a golf ball. During warmer, rainy weather the following spring these depressions swell and produce the odd orange jelly-like horns that can be up to 2 centimetres long. These orange "horns" release spores which are carried by the wind to infect apple trees. The galls eventually die but can remain attached to the tree for a year or so. The infected twigs usually die as well. Now you have an infected apple tree, but the disease appears on it by about mid-summer as orange spots on the upper surface of the leaves and on the fruit. If the infection is widespread the apple tree will lose a lot of its leaves. The fruit on infected trees is often small and deformed and may also drop prematurely. The spots on the leaves and fruit gradually enlarge over the summer and develop minute black dots. Very tiny cups develop on the undersides of the leaves in late summer which produce the spores and they in turn are blown back to the junipers to complete the cycle. For apple growers, junipers spell problems since the spores can be carried up to 5 kilometres. The same applies for juniper fanciers. One solution is not to plant the two types of trees within several hundred metres of each other – but that is no guarantee since the spores are airborne. Removing the galls on your juniper as soon as they appear in late summer can help break the cycle. Keeping your juniper growing vigorously is certainly another key to success. Feeding helps but water is even more essential since junipers are often part of foundation plantings and are placed under an overhang out of the rain. Water it well, mulch and that, in combination with pruning off the galls, should help give you some degree of control.

Lilac Won't Bloom

My sister has a 6-foot lilac bush that has never bloomed. It faces west with two maples beside it. What can we do?

The critical thing here is more light. One option might be to take away a few branches on the maples. Otherwise, it is worth moving the lilac forward to get more sunlight. It might also be getting too much nitrogen if fertilizer is being applied to the lawn. In that case, be sure to protect the area around it with a shield the next time fertilizer is spread so nitrogen exposure will be minimized. Those maples are heavy drinkers so remember to ensure plenty of water is available for everybody throughout the growing season.

Rotten Peonies

I have a single peony bush called Raspberry Queen that I moved from the country to our city home about 4 years ago. It has rotted at the base and I have cut those bits away but I would like to know what is going on. Could this be caused by the damp and the cold?

Quite possibly those conditions are partly to blame for the rot. Fluctuations in cold and heat could have been a factor but something else is likely going on down there as well. It may be that your plant is sitting in too wet an area. I think it would be worthwhile to lift the peony out and have a good look at that root system. Trim or pick off any dead or dying material you find on the root ball to help it to regenerate. If you see that the soil around the root is staying very wet, you can easily amend it with some sand and organic matter. You could also try to mound the soil up a little bit in the centre of the hole so that the plant sits slightly higher up and does not get as much of a build-up of water. A lot of clay underneath can act as an impermeable layer and trap too much moisture causing the sort of prob-

Battered and Buried Oak Roots

My daughter and her husband built up about 8-inches of soil against the trunk of a mature oak tree when they were leveling their backyard earlier this year. They also accidentally gouged it in a few places with cuts about 3/4 inch wide and 6 inches long. Is it possible to save the tree?

lems that are likely affecting your peony. A few simple amendments to those conditions will make all the difference.

Yes, but first and foremost, get the soil away from the trunk of that oak. If the leveling really has put 8 inches over top of all of the root system, that can be more of a problem than the damage. Start by digging out at least those 8 inches deep and a couple of feet back from the base of the tree so that there will be good air circulation all around the trunk. Don't let the soil come in contact with the bark. You might even need to build a small retaining wall to keep that soil back. A circle of stones placed in a ring around the perimeter so that the

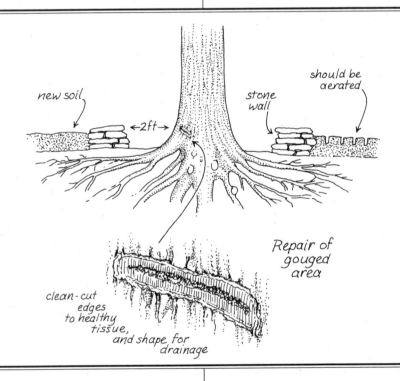

new soil

←2ft→

stone wall

should be aerated

Repair of gouged area

clean-cut edges to healthy tissue, and shape for drainage

soil doesn't fall back in on the base of the trunk would also work fine. The bigger problem now is getting the air, moisture and nutrients to the roots of that tree with this extra thick blanket of soil on top. Aerating over the soil, especially if it is a heavy soil, would be helpful in allowing a greater penetration of air through to the old soil level and down to the root system. Now, as for the gouges, you can trim the edges of those cuts or injuries with a sharp knife and cut back the bark around the edges, preferably in a teardrop shape. Just trace the injury and make a V-shape at the bottom so any moisture that does accumulate there can drain out quickly and easily – that is all that is required. It will heal on its own. It is just a matter of a clean cut and drainage at the base.

Overfed Pine

Our Pendulosa Pine is sort of a droopy looking thing with a twisted trunk. I have a feeling it has been over-fertilized. The tips of the needles seem to be burnt and a different colour than they were a few weeks ago. It's in the front yard so it probably got some lawn fertilizer on it and my wife decided she needed to help it out, so she put on more fertilizer. There is lots of new growth on it as well. If it has been over-fertilized, what can I do?

A thorough soaking will help leach some of that fertilizer out of the soil and away from the tree. Don't keep the ground waterlogged but if you haven't had rain and as it dries down again, another slow, thorough soaking will help. Spray off the foliage as well. That being done, it should recuperate and come back along. It's a good idea to put a screen or shield up in front of the nearby trees when the lawn is being fed so the fertilizer doesn't go there. And don't fertilize the tree again until it re-stabilizes. If you are going to fertilize, you would probably be further ahead to use a soluble fertilizer – pour it around the drip line at the base of the tree and then soak it in thoroughly with water. Make sure the soil is moist before you apply the soluble fertilizer, and I would try two applications at half the recommended rate, rather than one application.

Removing Vine Marks Off Brick Wall

The home I just moved into has brick walls on two sides and vines growing on both. I know that it is best to remove them before they affect the wall, but now that I've done this, I have these little black suction cups all over the side of the brick. Do you have any remedies?

I'm afraid the only remedy is a compromise between effort and patience. You can take a stiff nylon brush with a bit of soap and water and try scrubbing. That should clean things up a bit and provide enough abrasion to rip off some of the tendrils and suction cups left behind, but you are not going to be able to get everything off. Don't be too vigorous or you can damage the wall – and if done before winter it will expose the wall to a bit more weathering. Nature will eventually do the rest. You can touch it up again with another brushing in the spring. If you want to have vines up there again, it's best to put up a support system with strings and keep the plants away from the wall so you will not be faced with this problem again in the future.

Flea Beetles and other Grubs

My vegetable garden is full of flea beetles and I have these large black grubs about the size of my pinkie that nobody in the garden centres have been able to identify. I am hoping you can help me because they are clearing out my entire garden. The grubs look just like a Junebug larvae but they are larger and black and they can take down an entire pepper plant.

What you have are cutworms. Cutworms hide in the soil during the day and feed only at night. Some of them can climb stems and feed on leaves but generally they eat close to the ground. A single cutworm, which may be up to 2 inches long, can chew off a whole row of young plants in one night. Certainly digging them out from around the base of your plants and throwing them into a container of soapy water to drown will help give you a measure of control. Another quick solution is to pull the soil back from around the base of your plants and wrap the lower section of those stems with a strip of aluminum foil or a toilet paper roll, then put back the soil. That will create a physical barrier that the worms can't get through. You can usually find these culprits just below the surface of the soil. If you have a strong stomach, give a squeeze to any that you find. In terms of the flea beetles, a spray of the soap and water solution, 1-part soap to 40-parts water, should help. You'll also want to scratch up the surface of the soil so that it's drying out thoroughly. The flea beetles don't like hot, dry conditions and you can get rid of a good number of them by exposing the soil and drying things out. Soap and water will knock them back but general sanitation in the garden and a light cultivation of the soil should take care of them completely.

Villain in the Beans

We planted some green and yellow beans in a raised bed. Something is eating them but there are no footprints or other evidence. Some have no leaves left. I have never seen any bugs around them either. Have you any idea what it could be?

What you have to do is go out with a flashlight very early in the morning, ideally before sunrise, or just after dark, and have a look. What you will find is earwigs. They love bean plants and they are nocturnal. The other attraction here for them is that you have these plants in raised beds. There are probably cracks or spaces between whatever material you used to make the beds, so there are a lot of places for the earwigs to hide during the day. They are pretty easy to get rid of. Soap and water, 40-parts water to 1-part soap in spray form will kill them, but you need to make contact with their bodies. Try to take advantage of the fact that they love to get into dark confined spaces. Put a piece of old garden hose or pieces of bamboo stakes out in the beds so the earwigs can get in at one end. They will crawl

in as soon as the sun comes up and crawl out again to feed when the sun goes down. All you will need to do is to pick up the hose or bamboo each morning and shake all the earwigs out into a pail of soapy water so that they drown. You don't require the standard 40:1 mixture to drown earwigs in a pail of water – a tablespoon or 2 of soap per gallon will do nicely. Continue with this for a few days and pretty soon your problem will be gone.

Pruning Dead Branches

Ten years ago I lost half of my 20-year-old Scotch Pine, so I pruned it, tied the branches together and it came back beautifully. Until this year. The tree is approximately 20 feet high and all of last year's growth seems to have died. Should I prune it off now or wait until the fall when the sap is finished running?

If you can access the parts that have died off, I would take a sharp knife and give a scratch down through the bark. If there is any green underneath, any chance of anything coming back, leave it through to the next spring. If it is brown underneath and has died right back, cut it off now. The tree will seal itself off with pitch, the resinous sap of the pine, without too much trouble and it should come back again with new growth next year.

Thin Asparagus

We planted asparagus from seed about 6 years ago and about 3 years ago we started getting some production of very thin stalks. The last couple of years we have had a few larger stalks but really very few and the production has been much less than we expected. We haven't been able to find much information on growing asparagus. It's in a relatively shaded spot, very close to a cedar hedge, with only about 2-3 hours of sunlight a day; some morning light and some evening light. We have tried compost on it, as well as commercial fertilizer but it just doesn't seem to do a whole lot.

The fact that your asparagus has behaved this way isn't a bit surprising because its getting a fair amount of competition from the root system of the cedar hedge. The shade is a detrimental factor here as well. It would be much happier in full sun. It does want a reasonably well-drained soil and a good amount of organic matter – certainly the compost you have incorporated in there is ideal. If you could relocate it into an area that gets at least twice as much sun, it will pick up and probably start doubling produc-

tion within a year or two. There may be some transplant shock in moving it, but if you can do it now, go ahead and get it into a sunnier spot. That is the critical thing and you should see a significant improvement.

Resurrecting a Massacred Cherry

I had a tragedy on my pond. I have an island and a cherry tree that was standing about 3 metres high and in some overly aggressive brush clearing yesterday, it was hacked down. I have 24 apple trees I could graft the branches on to or is there any chance of putting it back onto the stump? The piece that's left is only about 8 inches high and 2 inches in diameter.

Remember the song "You Can't Grow Peaches on a Cherry Tree?" Well, I'm afraid you can't grow a cherry on an apple tree either. What you need to do is to take a hatchet and place the sharp edge of the blade upright across the top of the stump. Give it a tap so that it starts to split the stump down the middle and then turn it perpendicular so that you have a perfect cross and split it in the other direction. Now you have 4 splits on the sides. Take 4 of the best looking young branches from the parts that were cut off and give a wedge shape to the base of these. I am thinking with a 2 inch diameter stump, you probably want a piece of branch that is pencil thickness or just slightly larger. Make sure the cambium layer on the outside edge of both the branch and the stump are perfectly intact. Take another piece of wood to use as a wedge and insert it in the centre of the stump where you have the split and tap it down so that you open that cut a bit wider. Insert two of the cuttings, one on either side, making sure that the cambium layer on the cutting is perfectly aligned with the cambium layer of the trunk. Then remove the wedge and the stump will come back and squeeze the scions – which is the proper name for those cut branches now – into place. Turn the wedge 90 degrees and do the same thing with 2 more scions. Next, the top of that stump can't remain exposed, so you will need to get some grafting wax to smear over the top of the stump to seal the cracks and around the base of the cuttings that you have now inserted to keep them from drying out. Once that is done, cross your fingers. Hopefully more than one of them will take but a 25% success rate isn't bad with this kind of graft. If it's done fairly quickly

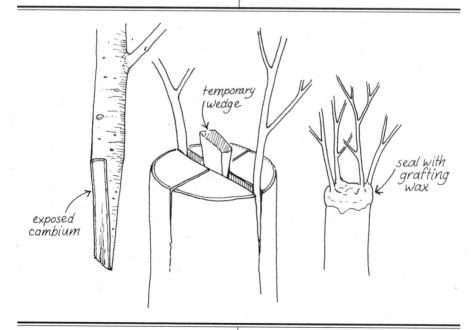

exposed cambium

temporary wedge

seal with grafting wax

after the branches were originally severed, it should take. You will probably also see that you get some shooting from the base. Don't take that off in the first year until the grafted material shows whether or not it is taking. Once you are certain the grafts have taken, you can take off any other shoots coming from the base to make sure that the energy is concentrated where you want it.

Getting Out the Gout

We bought a property in the country and discovered we had inherited a huge amount of goutweed as well. We are organic gardeners and we have the situation more or less under control but I find that we have a big problem under the peony bushes. I am wondering how to get at that. I am probably going to have to use a herbicide but I am wondering if there is one that I can just rub on the leaf and that won't be too damaging to the environment or dangerous to my young children.

I prefer not to recommend herbicides and there are definitely toxic-free methods you can use to eliminate the goutweed, but you are correct in suggesting that rubbing the herbicide on is one of the safest ways to apply it. It means you are using only the exact amount required. Certain of the glyphosates, like "Roundup" for example, do not require any mixing and come in "user strength" for home application. If you decide it is necessary to use it, get a very good rubber glove and test it by blowing into it to make sure it doesn't have any holes. If you find it is sound, put it on whichever hand you will use to apply the herbicide. Then get a cheap cotton glove and put it on over top of the rubber one. Dip your finger into the herbicide so the cotton glove absorbs the liquid and rub it over the goutweed leaves. The chemical will be translocated, meaning it is moved throughout the plant and transferred into the root system and other parts of the plant, so it is best to treat all of the leaves. The small stems and leaves of your peonies might die off as well, so be careful with it. And don't be breathing those fumes. On the other hand, if you want to avoid the chemicals, and this is especially advisable with young children around, there is another way to remove the goutweed from your peonies. Simply dig up the bushes, flush off the roots, and then disentangle and discard the goutweed plants. While you have the peonies out, you might as well divide them. Check the soil for any stray goutweed or roots and after adding compost and bone meal or rock phosphate to the soil, plant the peonies back into the bed and water them in well. That should be the end of your goutweed but keep an eye out for any that might come back from seeds left in your soil.

Plum Dried Out

Our plum tree gets beautiful blooms in the spring, then sets good fruit, but by the first of July, the plums start falling off. By the middle of July there are absolutely no plums left. We never get to eat any of the fruit. Have you any idea why this keeps happening?

Moisture stress is causing the tree to say to itself "cut your losses now". So it starts by dropping the fruit. That fruit takes up a lot of energy and moisture and if the tree is under stress and feels it can't spare either one, it will sacrifice the fruit to ensure its own health and survival. If you can water the tree as required it is going to hold that fruit. Mulching around the base would also help to retain moisture longer, but watering it is going to be the key.

Invasion of the Lily Beetles

I started out with a problem with beetles in my lilies. Now every plant has got them and I don't know what to do.

You want to be out there early in the season as soon as any lily shoots appear. Pick off the beetles, throw them into a bucket of soapy water and drown them. Just a few drops of liquid soap in the water are enough – it actually helps to make the water "wetter" by breaking down the surface tension so that the bugs drown more quickly and easily. I would recommend using gloves when you pick them off if you are at all squeamish. Make sure you stir that soap and water mixture well after you've finished picking and then leave it to sit for an hour or so. When that is done, the water can be thrown onto the compost. Just make sure that everybody in there has drowned before you throw it, otherwise they could escape from your compost and head back out to eat the lilies! I wouldn't bother spraying the plants with soap and water at this point because it is not likely going to knock them back. Neem soap however will give a measure of control and Neem oil does work as well. The spittle globs or slimy mass you see just at the base of the plants and up the stems is the egg mass and larval stage of the beetle. If you can get rid of those little masses early in the season either with the neem oil or by scraping them off, as well as picking off the first crop of adult beetles, you will have eliminated two, three or four generations, depending on how well they are established. It is just a matter of getting at them early in the season as soon as they show up, then doing regular spot checks on your lilies throughout the season to maintain control.

Haunted Tree

I seem to have a haunted tree in my garden. It's an ash tree, about 22 years old and maybe 16 inches around the base. I was standing beside it watering the flowers and I heard tapping. It came from inside the tree and it stops when the sun gets to it. Some of the branches have dried up and fallen away near the top of it and I'd hate to lose this tree. Have you any idea what this might be?

There are a couple of things that could explain it. The Mountain Ash is susceptible to fire blight but that would not account for the tapping. I have, at times, heard tapping from a Black Locust that we have at home, but this often turns out to be woodpeckers or nuthatches. What I have also heard is squirrels inside of hollow trees, and also raccoons, but these are obviously in much larger trees. Something smaller could be living inside yours. I think what you need is an arborist to come in and have a good look at the tree to see if there are some cavities or access holes where something has moved in. If the problem is a rodent and it is actually getting inside the tree, you could keep it out by putting hardware cloth or steel wool over a small hole or chicken wire over a larger one. If there is some rot going on in the centre of the tree, you will need a bit of cavity work or some drainage provided so that the rot doesn't continue and the tree can actually heal over and seal up that cavity. It would be worth having this tree looked at right away because what is happening is more of a symptom than a problem, and it tells you that something else is going on in there. Check in the yellow pages for arborists or with local landscaping companies who may be able to recommend someone to properly diagnose the problem.

Treatment for Slugs on Vegetables

Is it possible to use the same ammonia solution that you use to kill the slugs on your hostas on your vegetable garden without doing any harm?

No. With the hostas, you have to apply the 1:10 ammonia and water solution at the early stage before the leaves are unfurl-ing for it to be effective. It will give you a good measure of con-trol if slugs are present and will also be effective in controlling any eggs that might be in the soil. With a vegetable garden, the plants will already be well estab-lished by the time the slugs hit and the ammonia solution will probably be too strong to be go-ing onto them at that point. If you want to treat the soil on the sides of the rows, you may have some success and avoid burning the delicate leaves on your plants. The ammonia will break down fairly quickly in the soil and be-cause of the dilution, it would not be harmful for human consump-tion. You will also be providing a source of some nitrogen by intro-ducing that ammonia into the soil. But do avoid contact with the plants and use only a small appli-cation. The regular solution is 10-parts water to 1-part liquid house-hold ammonia – but you could try a slightly weaker solution of 15 or 20:1 and see whether that is effec-tive. It's best to err on the side of caution. In a large garden with a slug problem you can gain some success by cultivating the soil be-tween waterings so that the sur-face dries out immediately. Being slimy creatures, the slugs have a lot more trouble getting around on a dry, rough surface. It's also

worthwhile to sprinkle some sharp sand around your plants. If the slugs start scraping themselves against the sand, they will dehy-drate pretty quickly. You could al-so try putting out some dried crushed eggshells, or diatoma-ceous earth, which works on them the same way as the sand and has no toxic impact on your soil.

Infestation of Caterpillars

My problem is with an oak tree. It's about 6 feet high and I sus-pect tent caterpillars are getting at it in the spring. The problem is that they've moved on to the cher-ry trees. Now, I'm not one hun-dred per cent sure that is what is eating my oak, but this is the third year it's happened and I don't think it can take much more. I have tried taking the grass out from around the tree and aerating the soil. I've also put down sawdust for the last couple of years. I've tried that old 40:1 magic guru trick and rinsed it off but nothing seems to have an effect on whatever is eating it. What should I try next?

You may have tent caterpillars or it may be gypsy moth caterpillars are showing up there in the short term – a number of things like young oak leaves. I have the same problem at home. The spray will give you a bit of a knockdown of the problem, but the proper cultural conditions are what is essential here. Getting a really good start in early spring, cultivating the soil and getting sawdust down there as a mulch is certainly very helpful. If you have some compost to mix in there, that would be worthwhile. You have a very high carbon content with the sawdust and it tends to bind things up because there is not a lot of structure to it. It's all very uniform and that uniformity actually impedes the penetration of some of the moisture, nutrients and air, so if you could get some rougher mulch material in there with it, that combination would be more effective. Make sure the tree gets very thorough watering and that it isn't drying out. If it is in a healthy, vigorous condition, that is going to bring the tree through an infestation better than going to a chemical application on the foliage. If you see caterpillars or something else on there when inspecting the tree, just squash them. Breaking open the "tents" where the young caterpillars congregate in early morning or late evening works as well. Take a forked stick, insert it in the webbing and twist. The tent is then easily stepped on destroying the caterpillars inside. You may want to wear boots but this should get them under control in short order. Overcoming this infestation problem is mainly a mat-ter of getting the area around the base into good condition and keeping the tree healthy and growing vigorously. If you can achieve that, it should take care of any infestation problem.

Japanese Knotweed Invasion

We have an invasion of Japanese Knotweed. I'm afraid I'm not much of a gardener and my husband has a theory about how to get rid of it, but it is hard to tell if it's working. He figures if we pull it up constantly it won't have a chance to photosynthesize and will eventually die out. Is this true or is there some other method we can try?

It is true... but the thing with Polygonum *cuspidatum* or Japanese Knotweed, is that it's very invasive. Constantly pulling at it and breaking it, actually stimulates new growth. If you pull up some of the root and leave a little section, that section will root up beautifully and throw up new shoots, so this will be a constant battle. Eventually you will wear it out, but you can get very worn out yourself in the process. If you are going to go that route, I would suggest a good sharp hoe that you can run along just under the surface of the soil so you are severing the plants fairly cleanly, incurring less breakage of the roots and therefore encouraging less new root development. Just keep slicing off the tops. Leave those cuttings lying on the ground for a day or so before raking them up so they will dry out sufficiently. If you clear them away and throw them into the compost as soon as they're cut you'll run into problems with them rooting up in the compost bin. Alternatively, try cutting up all the knotweed with a tiller, chewing it up and leaving it to dry out. After a few days, rake through and take away as many bits as possible and then cover the entire area with a sheet of clear plastic and let it bake. As soon as you see any weeds start to grow again, pull the plastic off that section, chop them down, cover it again with the plastic and let it bake some more. You will eventually get things under control, at which point you need to mulch the daylights out of it. Take off the plastic and put a ten-sheet layer of newsprint over top of the soil with at least 2-3 inches of mulch over top of that to hold the newspaper in place. This will block out all the light and any last holdouts will be stifled. The odd one may still try to find its way up through that covering, so layer it as thickly as you possibly can. When you are ready to plant back into that area, pull the mulch back in the spot where you want to plant, slit the newspaper to insert the plant, backfill, water, and close the whole thing up again tight around the stem. Vigorous growers would be the first thing recommended to go in there – they can establish themselves quickly and compete with the knotweed if it were to try, despite everything, to come back up again.

Green Magnolia

I want to know why my magnolia tree won't blossom. It has been in my front lawn for 3 years and the first year that it was planted, it was covered in blossoms. The next year it had 5 blossoms and last year it had none. It sets buds so I cut one open and saw that there was an embryo blossom in there but it was all brown and sort of rotted inside. I don't know if there is something that I could be adding to the soil besides the fertilizer we use on our lawn, but I notice that everybody else in this town has magnolias that blossom and mine won't.

In this case, it is probably the fertilizer you are already putting on, rather than what you need to add, that is the problem. If you fertilize the lawn around the tree, chances are your tree is getting too much nitrogen. It will get into very active, lush growth but the bud development will stop and in a wet year, those flower embryos would probably start to rot. What I would suggest is that next spring you draw a circle around the drip line of your tree, or even 6-12 inches beyond the drip line, and remove the grass that is inside that area. Cover over the surface you have exposed with 1-1½ inch of compost, scratch it lightly into the surface of the soil and then put a couple of inches of mulch on top of that. When you go to feed the lawn, put up a shield around the mulched area so that the fertilizer doesn't go on to the area at the base of the tree at all. You can stand up a piece of plywood or cardboard, anything that will prevent the pellets from getting on to that space. The advantage of having the shield standing is that you can hear better when the pellets start to hit and know you have gone beyond the limit of where you should be spreading. If you can keep the lawn fertilizer outside of that circle, and get that compost and mulch into there, I would suspect your tree will come back into blossom the next year.

Pet-safe Herbicides

Is there anything on the market that can kill out Creeping Jenny and Creeping Charlie but is safe for pets?

There is, and it's called elbow grease. It's the only method of removal that is completely safe. You'll need to get out first thing next spring with a stiff metal fan rake. As long as the lawn is dry enough to walk on without leaving a footprint, it will be fine to do this. Rake from north to south across the lawn. Anything that pulls out quite easily at this point gets raked off and removed. The Creeping Jenny and Creeping Charlie will mostly be what is going to come up with a good stiff raking. Next, do an east-west rake across the lawn, so you are forming a grid pattern across the whole area, and that should get any loose ends you missed the first time over. Once you finish the raking, you can do a light topdressing with compost, about 1/4 - 1/2 inch maximum, and then over-seed with grass seed to fill in the spaces that the removal of the Creeping Jenny and Creeping Charlie have left behind. That will create some competition. The weeds will also have been significantly weakened by having a good portion of the plant taken away with the raking. Dutch White Clover added into the lawn will work quite nicely here, or try a combination of clover and grass seed. If it is a dry area, go with a fescue as opposed to a Kentucky Bluegrass, which requires a lot more moisture. If it is a shady area you can use a shade mix, and again, fescue will hold up better in shade than with Kentucky Bluegrass. Raise your lawnmower up to 2½ or 3 inches as a minimum. This will also favour the growth of your turf and the longer grass shades out these sun-loving weeds.

Slugs and Hostas

My hostas were doing great until a few weeks ago when I started seeing small holes in the leaves. I couldn't see any bugs eating them but one night I went out with a flashlight and I saw some slugs around. I'm not sure if these are the culprits but my hostas now look really awful. Is there an insecticide that is not too toxic I can use to get rid of them?

Yes, there is a pretty simple non-toxic treatment for slugs. Get some small saucers or aluminum tart tins and tuck a few of these underneath your hosta leaves. Push them down into the ground so that the lip of the container ends up flush with the soil surface and pour a bit of beer into the bottom. You will need a 1/2 -1 inch of beer, the idea being that when the slugs crawl in they will drown. Slugs are attracted to the smell of the beer and particularly the yeast in it. They crawl in; they can't crawl out; they drown. Next morning, empty the containers and put them back with some fresh beer. If you do this on a regular basis, you will drastically reduce the slug population. Laying down ground-up eggshells around the base of the plants will

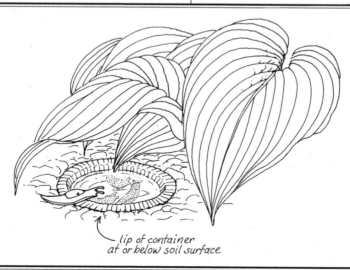

lip of container
at or below soil surface

also give you a measure of control, as will sharp sand or diatomaceous earth. These work by piercing the skin of the slugs as they move through it so that they dehydrate and eventually die. If I were a slug, I think I'd opt for the beer. First thing next spring, before the leaves unfurl and just as the pips or shoots are coming out of the ground, mix up a solution of 10-parts water to 1-part household ammonia and water that liberally over the plant and surrounding soil. The slugs only start becoming active just before the hostas do, so be careful not to do this treatment too early. If you time it right, that application will not only kill any overwintering or young slugs, but destroy any of the eggs as well. Any or all of these treatments will knock back the slug population significantly without a big environmental impact.

Eradicating Poison Ivy

What is the best way to kill off large areas of poison ivy that have appeared on our lawn?

Be sure to avoid any contact with these plants and your bare hands. To be on the safe side, wear long pants, socks, shoes and gloves when you are working with it. The easiest thing to do with poison ivy on a lawn is to mow it down with the blade of your mower as close to the ground as possible, making sure you are blowing the clippings away from anywhere you will come in contact with them. Once the poison ivy starts to come back, mow it closely again. Do that 2 or 3 times and once that's done, cover the whole area with newspaper, about 10-sheets thick, and mulch over top of that. What you want to do with this last step is to block the light out completely. The effect of this entire process is to weaken the plants, first by getting them to grow new sets of leaves 2 or 3 times over, then by cutting off light so they can no longer photosynthesize. Get at least 6 inches of mulch over that newspaper so it doesn't look like the devil or blow away in the first good breeze. Just about any kind of mulch will do, something like bark chips, pine needles or straw, but don't use hay. Old hay is full of seeds and you will get all kinds of stuff growing up there that you don't want. Keep the mulch moist, at least at first, so you don't get any light penetration at all – with no light, there's no growth. The newspaper is going to break down eventually but the mulch will stay much longer. If poison ivy turns up in areas other than your lawn, you can get rid of it there by tilling up the whole patch to weaken the roots and then do the same thing with the newspaper and mulch. The mulch should be left at least a year, and preferably two, before you take it up. When you do, rake the area over lightly and re-seed. Make sure, however, that all the poison ivy is dead. An alternative to returning that area to lawn – and one that can be accomplished right after you lay down the mulch – is to establish some perennial plants or shrubs in that area to create a garden. To do this, make a hole in the mulch right down to, but not through, the newspaper for each new plant. Add soil to whatever depth you require to cover the new roots or root ball of your selected plants and replace the mulch around each new stem. As the new plant establishes, the roots will penetrate through the newspaper. By the time the poison ivy is dead, you will have a new, well-established garden.

Parking Lot Invasion

We have a shared driveway that leads into a parking lot in the backyard and this year we have what looks like millions of maple shoots growing there. The lane looks like a green lawn, there are so many. Is there some kind of herbicide we can use that doesn't do too much damage to the environment or to the rest of our shrubs and flowers?

There really isn't any type of benign herbicide but in any case, the easiest thing to do with any seedlings that have invaded like this is to cultivate the whole area with a hoe. That will lift up the root system of the seedlings and they will dry up within a day. Alternatively, if the gravel is smooth and the surface is even you can raise the level of the blade on your lawnmower and just run it over the area to chop the leaves off. That will be the end of them. If you have any concerns about the safety of using the mower here, a weed whacker will have the same effect. You really do not need to use a herbicide at all.

Spider Mites in the Marigolds

There are two large beds of marigolds on each side of my house. On one side, webs have started to appear and I suspect spider mites. I pulled out the affected plants but now they seem to be invading the whole garden on that side of my house. Is there anything I can do?

I'd guess the right side of your house gets more sun than the left side and that it is particularly hot and dry there. Spider mites adore the heat and they multiply rapidly in those dry conditions. Any plants you have there would be susceptible. spider mites travel on other plant material so yours may well have come from one pregnant spider mite or from the nursery where you bought the marigolds. Once they take up residence, they start multiplying. You can try putting a fine spray of water from the hose over all of the plants. That will break the webbing, flush everything down and cool the plants off. You will probably see a turn-around right away. A soap and water spray would knock them down as well. If you use the soap and water, spray thoroughly from the bottom of the plants up and try to get to the underside of all the leaves, which is a bit hard to do in a full bed of plants. Use 40-parts water to 1-part soap, or if it is one of the commercially available insecticidal soaps, follow the application directions. Leave the spray on the plants for 5 - 10 minutes maximum and then thoroughly flush the whole thing off again with clear water. If the weather continues to stay hot and dry, a daily spraying of cool water might be required. The higher humidity and cooler temperatures you create are conditions the spider mites do not like and this will discourage them from multiplying as

quickly and coming back in great numbers.

Powdery Mildew

There is powdery mildew on my maple tree. How can I prevent it or treat it?

When moisture levels are up, you will see some spread of this mildew. Cleaning things up around the area will be helpful. Remove the leaves as they fall so that you get good air circulation and a thorough drying out of the soil at the base. This will also remove any concentration of the powdery mildew on the foliage that has fallen. It is not necessary to treat the tree, simply ensure there is good air circulation and that it is not stressed to start with. The leaves can go into a good, active compost – otherwise bag the leaves into black or green plastic garbage bags, add a gallon or two of water and leave these in a good sunny location all winter where they can bake; then the contents can be incorporated back into your beds next spring. The essential thing with the maples is to ensure that moisture stress is avoided. In rainy, humid conditions, there is more of a spread of the powdery mildew but ironically, it actually starts up in hot and dry conditions. Having the crown thinned out a little to get good light and air penetration through the branches will also be a good prophylactic in terms of avoiding the conditions favourable for the powdery mildew to start up.

Ants Put New Homeowner Over the Hill

I moved last year and inherited some lawns that really need help. The backyard has a lot of moss in it, but I can live with that. The front yard and backyard have Creeping Charlie, but that's also green, so if I have to, I can live with that too. The front yard however, has ants and they must have delusions of grandeur because they have the most enormous ant hills. These I would really prefer not to live with. Is there any way to get rid of them?

Let's deal with the two problems that you can live with first. If you can get out first thing in the spring, as soon as the ground is dry enough that you don't leave a footprint, take a good stiff rake and give the lawn a good going over in one direction, and then do it again working perpendicular to the direction of the first raking. You will pick up most of the moss and Creeping Charlie with that raking alone and this will solve a big part of the problem right there. The appear-

ance of moss is generally a sign you have poor soil and that things are pretty hungry and need some fertilizing. To help address this I would suggest that after you have gone through the mossy area with a stiff rake, go over the whole area with a plug-pulling aerator to alleviate any compaction problems and ensure there is good air, moisture and nutrient penetration into that soil. Top-dressing with some compost or some composted cattle manure will add a bit of nutrient to feed the soil under that lawn and help sustain growth as the spring progresses. Then over-seed, either with grass seed or a mixture of grass seed and clover. Since you said you can live with the lawn not being uniformly grass, I would incorporate some Dutch White Clover in there as well. It does an excellent job of filling in and also fixes nitrogen into the soil. As little as 20% of your lawn given over to clover will fix enough nitrogen from the air into the soil to feed it all season. That means you don't have to do any supplementary feeding once the lawn is established. In terms of the ant problem, they are always going to be there and likely they'll keep coming back since it's obviously an ideal site. I'd wager that it is south or west facing. Certainly putting out a little borax mixture is helpful. You can set up some ant traps by mixing boric acid with sugar at a rate of a teaspoon of boric acid to 6 tablespoons of sugar in 2 cups of boiling water. You should find boric acid at any pharmacy. Mix that up thoroughly, soak a piece of cotton batting in the mixture and place it inside a plastic tub or container. Cut holes around the bottom edge of the container and put the lid back on so that the ants are forced to go in and out through the holes at the bottom edge. With a weak concentration like this the ants won't die immediately. They will take that sugar/borax/cotton mix back to the colony with them and all the ants will feed on it for a while and eventually it will eliminate all or at least a large proportion of the colony. Don't be surprised however, if they move back in. You obviously have a nice sunny location and a friable soil that they can work through easily and ants will likely keep coming back because the habitat is inviting. The best defense is to maintain a healthy ground cover to fill that soil with roots, which ants don't like as well, and also shades and therefore cools the site. That should certainly discourage them from re-establishing and minimize the problem you're having.

Mouldy Delphiniums

For several years now we've had this greyish white mould on our delphiniums. They seem to grow well in the spring but this mould appears once they start developing further. This year it also went on to the climbing honeysuckle. What can I do to get rid of this or at the very least, prevent it from spreading any further?

Lifting and splitting some of the delphiniums would be a good start. By thinning the clump out a little you'd allow more air circulation among the plants. In the fall, you will need to clean out all the debris accumulated there – then repeat that cleanup again first thing next spring. Just go through the patch to pick out the leaf litter or broken stem pieces and take them completely away from the bed into the compost so they can decompose in there. Compost that is active and hot enough should be sufficient to break it down. It is not guaranteed that you will get rid of the powdery mildew, but it will certainly help to control it. Unfortunately, this type of mildew is in the air and travels very easily, so eliminating it completely is very difficult. It generally likes hot, dry conditions to start, but then needs cooler, damp conditions to spread. In spring, when things are usually cool and damp for a longer period of time it has trouble getting a foothold, so you rarely see it early in the season. Further on, when the weather turns hot and dry, it starts up and a good rainfall is all it needs to spread like wildfire. That's how it moved on to your honeysuckle vine. If you cleanup each spring and fall and encourage a reasonable amount of air circulation around the plants, it should make all the difference. Avoiding watering over the foliage – especially around or on the infected plants – will also help to minimize the spread.

Mesh Dilemma

I live along a river and at some point in the past the local parks department clad most of the trees next to the river in chicken wire mesh to deter the beavers. These trees have since grown and the trunks are now straining against the mesh. I don't know whether that is a concern, whether the tree can just grow through it without much injury, or whether I should let someone know so they can have the wire mesh removed.

I would be calling the parks department and reminding them of it, and yes, restrictive material like that can be a problem for the trees. Many of them will grow right through it and it will slow them down for a couple of years while the cambium works through that foreign material. In the future, if something happens to the trees and somebody comes along to cut them down, guess what the chain saw runs into? It can be a major danger, so do remind them of it. It is certainly best if it is loosened off. The parks department may feel there is still a need for some protection if there is a beaver problem in the area, but they are going to want to loosen the wire mesh and move it back out of contact with the trunks. Unfortunately, beaver will take on larger trees. Generally, they prefer smaller ones and soft wood, but I have seen situations where they have taken down beautiful oaks that were standing right beside poplars. There is really no absolute predictability there.

Crabby Over Crabgrass

Last year we took out an old Black Willow that had a very large root system and the end result was I imported a huge number of yards of top soil from a reputable dealer and spread it all over the lawn. I now have a horrific amount of crabgrass. I am told I can do nothing until next spring when we can apply a crabgrass seed preventor. Is there nothing else I can do to help get rid of this crabgrass before then?

Crabgrass is a smart little devil. When it goes to seed, the seeds remain very close to the surface and are not easily cut down or destroyed. The best approach is to go over the crabgrass a couple of times with the bagger on the mower. The plus of doing this is that you are going to suck up a good quantity of that seed and stop it from getting spread about. Crabgrass is an annual and can only grow from seed, so to contain or eliminate it you have to look at a way to prevent the germination of those seeds, which is what your chemical crabgrass products will do. However, you can get the same effect without the chemicals simply by applying cornmeal gluten to your lawn. It's been shown to be equally effective and can be found quite readily at garden centres in the spring. In addition to inhibiting the germination of the crabgrass seed, using the cornmeal gluten also has the benefit of adding some organic matter to your soil. All that being said, it becomes a bit of a problem to over-seed after the cornmeal gluten is applied because it will have a similar inhibiting effect on the germination of other types of grass seeds. A way to get around this problem is to tear up some of the crabgrass in the fall, get rid of it and get some grass seed down and germinating before winter sets in. Grass plants are perennial and those new plants will come back up again the next spring and compete successfully for light and moisture with the crabgrass. Crabgrass seed needs light to germinate and it can't do that unless there is an open space for it in the existing turf. That's a first line of attack. Then apply your cornmeal gluten. Your new grass will already have become established and the cornmeal gluten won't affect the young plants. The combination of the competition from the new grass and the inhibiting effect of the gluten should take care of the crabgrass. Once your new lawn is well established, a light top-dressing with compost annually and watering as required should prevent any further problems.

Out of Control Birches

My birch trees are hugely overgrown. Last fall I took about 10 feet off the top branches of a 25 footer in the backyard and, of course, this spring we got about 4 feet back of second growth. How can I get these things under control?

The best time for pruning birches is very early in the

spring before they come out of dormancy, or if you miss that window, when they are fully out in leaf in the summer. Do not, under any circumstances, trim that birch in the spring or anytime closer than 6 weeks before spring thaw. If you do, it won't have enough time to heal or seal itself off and the sap will run like a tap and drain a lot of energy out of the tree. Now before tackling one that is the size of yours and just taking the top off, it would be preferable to look at some of the strategic branches in the structure of the tree. Which ones could you reduce to have a reasonable shape left in the crown of the tree? That may mean reducing some branches or parts of branches right from where they start at the trunk. If, for example, you have a birch that is 30 feet high in the centre, that centre leader could comfortably come back 10 feet, and the branches around it could all come back 3-5 feet. If you did that you will have reduced the size of the crown and height of the tree, but you would not be taking more than 25% of the tree off in that pruning. If you take more than that, you are going to get so much sucker growth stimulated you will end up with something that looks like a witch's broom. It won't grow back with the nice structure and form

that you want, which defeats the purpose of the pruning. So take 25% off strategically as a maximum, let it redevelop next year and then repeat the process. With that schedule of repeated pruning, you gradually encourage the tree to grow out to the ideal shape and height you want. That birch really wants to be 60 feet high, but you have other ideas, so this is where the strategy comes in. The essence of gardening is control!

Encouraging Reluctant Raspberries

My raspberry plants are not producing any fruit. I have had them for 2 or 3 years now and have been feeding them religiously with compost and watering every 2 or 3 days. They are pretty much always in the sun so light shouldn't be the problem. Is there anything I can do with them to encourage them to fruit?

It may be that your compost is a bit on the rich side for them. What I would suggest is to thin things out a bit by going through the patch and taking out the oldest canes. Take no more than 25% of the oldest ones and make sure you're not taking out any second year growth because those are the canes that they bear on. Thinning will ensure you have good light penetration. If you find the canes are too long and unruly, reduce them back to a metre and a half as an absolute maximum. That should cause a bit more branching. No more compost this year. Water as required and as the temperature picks up in the spring you should see some flower production. If not, don't compost again until you get some flowers. I suspect that the soil has been too rich for them. There can also be a problem with raspberries if they are allowed to dry out early in the season. Moisture stress is difficult on them and the first thing to go is the flowers. It's nature's way of ensuring that the plant is not wasting any excess energy trying to sustain something as delicate and moisture laden as flowers and fruit. Now if you have been watering them regularly and they are constantly wet, that can also be a problem. Give them enough time to dry out between waterings. A thorough watering is good when you do water, but with that much compost they are not likely running out of moisture. Once a week, or even 10 days to 2 weeks would probably be fine. So thin them out, no more compost for the moment, water only as required and you should see some fruit coming along very soon.

Transplanting Larger Trees

There are a large number of trees on my lot and I have thinned some of them out but some are still growing too closely together. I need advice on how to transplant them to a more open space. One is a Blue Spruce about 10 feet tall and the other is a 15-foot deciduous maple.

Wow! I think what you would need to do is have somebody with proper equipment, like a tree spade, come and dig those out for you. You could call around to a couple of firms to see who has the equipment and get some prices. The larger the root ball they can take with them, the better the trees are going to do after transplanting. It would be worthwhile to make that investment because both trees are probably very good trees and certainly the Blue Spruce is worth a lot both in terms of money and as an asset to the landscape. If it is overgrown or doesn't suit the location where it is standing now, it's not going to be worth very much. I would look for some professional help here. The advantage of the tree spade is that it can dig the new hole to the required shape and size first, and then when the tree gets lifted out and placed it fits almost perfectly into the new hole – which does benefit the tree. There will be a combination of factors as to when they can best do it and you will want to get their professional advice on that.

Elm Ailments

I planted a Camperdown Elm 7 years ago that was about 2-3 inches in diameter at the time and it has grown considerably. After the first year the leaves lost their green and turned brown and papery but then the tree came back. Each year I try something different like dormant oil or malathion or some other pesticide because I'm worried about an infestation of bugs. I've made sure that underneath the tree was clear; I sprayed the ground; I didn't spray the ground; I've tried everything. What should I be doing?

One thing that all elms are susceptible to if they undergo any heat or moisture stress over the summer is showing early fall colour and drying out. To avoid this, when you do the watering ensure that it is long and slow, a few hours or overnight, so that you get a good deep penetration of the moisture. Any infestation you might experience is likely to be beetles but that is only part of the problem, not the whole problem. The problem is wilt. Dutch Elm Disease is a fungal growth that plugs up the pores, or conducting tissues, in the plant. The insect is the vector so it carries the fungus and infects the plant as it burrows into the tree. The fungus then starts to grow in the xylem, phloem and the conducting tissues of the trees. Camperdowns have shown some resistance to Dutch Elm Disease but they are not immune to it. If the tree keeps coming back however, I would say that you do not have Dutch Elm Disease and the problem is probably moisture stress and poor soil. There should be nothing growing under the tree. Mulch the soil with approximately 4 inches of mulch around the base but be careful not to pile the mulch up against the trunk of the tree. With enough nutrient and moisture your tree should be able to fend off any infestations without resorting to sprays of any kind.

Disappointing Crab

Last year all the blossoms fell off the two large flowering crabs in our front yard and there were only a few apples that fall. Then the leaves started to fall off. My husband was told to spray the trees with dormant oil very early in the spring, which he did, and we had beautiful blossoms again but they didn't last. There are no apples this year and the leaves are falling off again. Have you any idea what is wrong?

Moisture stress is always a factor, especially if you consider that those thousands of blossoms are doing a lot of transpiring and therefore losing a lot of moisture. A great deal of energy is used up to put on that magnificent show and so it is easy for the tree to run short of moisture. If enough water is not available, the fruit will just abort rather than stressing the tree further – while we might like the show, the prime objective of the tree is self preservation. Making sure there is enough moisture in the spring is going to be critical. In a cool spring, with few insects, you are going to get very sporadic, if any, pollination because the insects are not there to do their job spreading the pollen around. That will result in little or no fruit showing up on the tree. The fact that the leaves were also showing stress and dropping is probably the result of either heat or drought. The dormant oil will be helpful. If you could loosen up the soil around the root system, that would also be helpful. If they are growing in an area with grass right up to the trunk, you could remove at least a 3-4 foot diameter of sod from around the base and mulch over that area. That would help relieve a lot of stress on the tree. It would

also ensure you don't get close to the trunk with the lawn mower and the bark will never get accidentally bumped or damaged. You can plant flowers under there if you like – they will not be as draining as sod. If you were to put an inch or so of compost over the surface of the soil and then another mulching material on top of that, with or without the flowers, this would add that much more nutrient into the soil and the trees will love you for it.

Absence of Currants

I have a question about my Black Currant bushes. I have got lots of growth but no berries. The bushes are located on the south side of the house in a sandy soil and I have put down landscape cloth and straw mulch but have yet to get any fruit. Why would this be?

Currants do need a lot of sun so a southern exposure is ideal. Having said that, the full sun location will also lead to a higher moisture loss so you'll want to incorporate some compost in with that sandy soil. Black Currants, more than Red and White Currants or any of the gooseberries which are their first cousins, are much more susceptible to blossom drop or fruit abortion early in the season if they get at all dry. They just drop their flowers, and with it the potential for any fruit later on in the season, or abort the young fruit if there is any moisture stress at all, so mulch is critical in holding the moisture there. Early in the season, make sure they are getting all the water they need and that will guarantee your production. The only other thing you have to worry about is making sure you get enough pollinators around your bushes early in the season. A few early-flowering shrubs will make all the difference. If you were to put in a lilac or two, or forsythia, or any plants that will give you a succession of early season flowers, this will attract and keep some of the pollinating insects in or around the plants. With that attraction and adequate moisture, you should see currants coming along very soon.

AUGUST

A. KARSTAD.

Eliminating Smut

My question is about corn. This year I planted Harmony and it has the most ghastly looking eggs on it. Where did they come from? Were they in the seed? How do I get rid of them? Can I bury this? Do I burn it? Should I use it as mulch?

Do not use it as mulch. The best thing you can do is to chop it down and put it into your compost. Corn works extremely well in compost piles. Stack it ver-

tically in the centre of the pile to create a bit of an air column and build the rest of your compost around it. The heat will take care of anything worrisome and you will recuperate all the energy that is still in the stalks and all of that nutrient. Not only that, having a large mass of fibrous material in the pile can make a big difference to the air circulation in there. Oxygen is essential for the successful breakdown of compost because it supports the beneficial bacteria and microbes in there. In terms of the eggs, I suspect the cause is most likely an airborne source. You say the eggs are "most ghastly looking" – that suggests to me what you are seeing are probably not eggs at all but rather deformed and discoloured kernels. In that case, what you have is very likely corn smut, a fungus called Ustilago *maydis*, which lives in the soil and spreads by spores blowing in the wind. Corn affected by this disease will have tassels, stalks and other above-ground parts that show smutty boils, but the damage is most conspicuous in the ears. The kernels become monstrous grey and black blobs. The galls form only where a spore lands and only if there are favourable heat conditions in the 27-32° celsius range in mid summer. The spores in the soil can remain viable for several years. When conditions are right for the fungus to grow, small galls develop on the young corn plants – usually too small to be noticed by most people at this point. These galls are filled with black powdery spores which are released a few weeks later and blow on to the corn silks. The fungus then migrates down into the ears or enters the cobs via holes in the husks made by insects or birds. Resistance to disease is usually assumed when plants are vigorous and healthy,

but unfortunately, the health of the plant makes no difference with corn smut. Likewise, dry weather early in the season followed by moderate to heavy rainfall is ideal for the corn plants but unfortunately, also perfect for the fungus. In terms of prevention, it is best to avoid using cow or horse manure as fertilizer around corn since this fungus can pass intact through the digestive system of these animals. Crop rotation and excellent sanitation in your garden will reduce the recurrence so be sure to gather and destroy every smutty stalk, leaf or ear by removing them and burying them in your compost as soon as you see them. There are other pests that affect corn, the most serious being the corn earworm. It feeds on the tips of the ears just inside the husks and the parent moth lays its single yellow eggs under the leaves and on the corn silks. I'm sure however, that this is not your problem. In all likelihood, what you have is smut.

Fed Up Watering

I am sick and tired of watering! All summer long I feel like I've grown an extra appendage: the hose. It breaks my heart to see my garden wilt and yet I'd like to be able to get away for a few weeks in the summer without feeling guilty about leaving it to dry out or bothering someone else to take over while I'm gone. I've heard of something called xeriscape gardening that uses very little water. This may be the answer to my prayers. Do you know anything about it?

Xeriscape gardening could well answer your prayers. The aim of xeriscaping is to cut down the need for supplemental watering in gardens and landscapes and thereby lessen the strain on water supplies – and gardeners. Xeriscaping essentially means establishing plants that can withstand drought conditions. It also means creating the kind of environment necessary to support and encourage the growth and development of these plants. That usually means installing windbreaks to cut the effect of drying winds, mulching to reduce the amount of moisture loss from the soil and grouping plants together that have similar moisture needs to increase the efficiency of any watering that is needed. If you plan to do this, first you have to take a survey of what elements you already have to work with, for example, any existing driveways, fences or walkways, the type of soil you have, whether the land slopes at any point and what trees and shrubs already exist. Decide what activities will take place in each area, whether you need a playground, a deck or a patio, and where these areas would best be located: close to a door or in the shade, for example. Hard surfaces never need water but you may need to plant trees to provide a windbreak or privacy screen. The next vital step would be to make sure that your soil is suitably fertile and able to retain moisture. The easiest way to do this is by adding organic matter, such as compost or manure to the soil to help improve its absorption and retention of water and to feed the micro-organisms and worms that help break that material down and convert it to usable nutrients for your plants. If a lawn area is essential for you, choose drought tolerant grasses, such as fescues, rather than something like Kentucky Bluegrass that will turn brown and go dormant in hot, dry conditions. Dutch White Clover, thyme, bugleweed and Creeping Juniper are all suitable low-water, groundcover alternatives to turf. In terms of what plants to put in there, your local garden centre would likely have lists of drought-tolerant plants that would be best suited to your region. These would include things such as beebalm, Black-eyed Susans, Shasta Daisies, echinacea and sedums. It takes a fair bit of planning and effort to set up a drought-resistant garden, but once you have it established you should be able to cut back significantly on the time you have to spend watering and leave for a period in the summer without the worry of coming back to some very unhappy plants.

Aliens in the Junipers

Something very strange started happening to my junipers. Near the end on many of the branches little brown balls have developed about the size of a marble with multiple little dimples or dots on them. These were there for years and I never paid much attention to them until about a year ago. We had a very rainy day and I looked out the next morning to find all the bushes looking as though they were decorated like Christmas trees. They were covered in brilliant orange pompoms where the little brown knobs had been and each had tentacles about an inch long and roughly 1/8 inch in diameter. They looked like some sort of alien creatures — about 30 or 40 of these tentacles were coming out of each of the little brown knobs. They are soft and wet and look and smell like fungus. Driving into work, all the trees down the side roads were just covered in these things. It lasted one day and the next day the sun came out and all the tentacles shriveled up into little black threads. Then a few days later we got another rain storm and they all reappeared. This happened 3 times last spring and interestingly, it happened again today. This is our first rain of the spring and all my junipers look like Christmas.

Amazing sight isn't it! You must have apple trees around. For this to happen, that combination

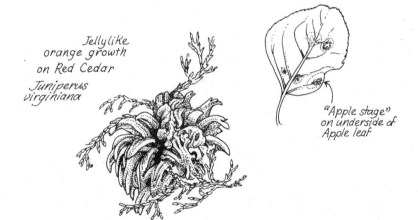

Jellylike orange growth on Red Cedar *Juniperus virginiana*

"Apple stage" on underside of Apple leaf

of cedar and apple is required and guess what it is called: cedar-apple rust. The apple trees and cedars are alternate hosts and the fungus goes back and forth between the two. All those little tentacles you are seeing are the fruiting bodies. When the conditions are right it's like a mushroom bloom in the fall after a heavy rain. Out they come and off go the spore and they just keep spreading around. To control it, trim your trees, take all of those knobs off and destroy them. But if you've got these native hosts with the pathogen present all over the area, and with it being an airborne spore, it will likely keep coming back. Most times you just have to learn to live with it. Generally it is a problem of aesthetics. It is going to be a bit of a drain on the trees but it definitely won't kill them. It's really a perfect symbiotic relationship. The apples and the cedars grow fairly well in the same conditions so the rust goes back and forth between them. Every now and then, it puts on this spectacular show. It's just one phenomena of nature.

The Story of Cain and Abel

I have two cherry trees, a good one and a bad one. The good one is right behind my house and is quite large. I have managed to get about 18-20 quarts of dark red, very sweet cherries from it each year. The bad tree is in the middle of a perennial bed surrounded by Lily of the Valley and maybe 8 or 10 rose bushes. It is a little scrawnier than the other one, doesn't produce nearly as well and I am starting to see some die back in the middle. I am wondering if this may be because it is in the middle of another garden. I put a lot of compost around the bottom of it, particularly for the roses. Is there anything I can try to save that second tree?

You'll want to start by pruning out any of the dead or dying material. Anything that is damaged comes next, then any branches that are crossing or rubbing. After that, take out any branches that are coming straight up through the middle like the water sprouts that you would more typically see on apple trees. These will show up on cherry trees as well and are among the first things that should go. Anything that is dangerous should be taken away, so if there is growth sticking out over a walkway or branches that are in the way when you are working in the rest of the garden, these should be taken out as well. Then you should start pruning for shape, working back from the tips to make the tree a little more compact. It will be a little easier to harvest when the trees are more compact as well. The maximum that should be pruned out in any given year is 25% of the tree, with any dead material you take out counting towards that 25%. The best time of year to do this would be February. If you are not sure about which are the dead branches, leave a little pruning for the spring and as the tree starts to flush out you can see where any dead bits are and trim them off then. A thorough pruning is going to be helpful to open up the crown and allow a deeper penetration of light. The critical factor here is that the tree is in the garden and needs to compete for moisture and nutrients far more than the other one. The Lily of the Valley in that bed, in particular, is going to form a mat across the surface which will impede any deep penetration of nutrients, even with the addition of your compost on the surface. If you are not too attached to it, remove the Lily of the Valley completely, or at the very least, thin it out every year for the sake of the tree. It is not allowing water to penetrate down deeply enough to reach the tree's roots. Make sure you get enough water onto the surface of the soil to supersaturate it and allow a really good soaking down deep into the bed to the root system of that cherry tree. Some deep root watering may be help-

ful here as well. Punch a few holes, 12-24 inches deep, and water right into each hole so that the water penetrates down deep into that soil. With more light and enough moisture available, you should see things start to pick up within a season.

Inundated Ajuga

My ajuga are curling up. I water them twice a day and I use a good soil with lots of compost but they don't seem to respond. Have you any idea what I might be doing wrong?

They are drowning. They simply do not require that much water. Let them dry right down and then give them a thorough soaking that is long, slow, deep and penetrating. If you are concerned because they are in a very sandy soil, don't worry. The root system will grow down to where the moisture is available and as the leaves uncurl over the surface of the soil, they are going to stop some of the evaporation. Ajuga can actually tolerate drier conditions and as long as they have lots of sun, they will get the moisture they need to establish themselves. Once they dry down again you may want to give them a light top-dressing or side-dressing with your own compost and another thorough soaking. A light application of bone meal, rock phosphate or super phosphate would also stimulate root development. You should see them turn around within a few weeks.

Ant Invasion

I've got a simple vegetable garden and I'm having a problem with ants. I was wondering what is the best non-chemical way to deal with these.

If you feel the ants are a major problem you may want to deal with them, but generally they are not going to be an issue. With the aeration they are providing in the soil and their ability to work organic matter down into it, they can be well worth having around. You will probably find that they are not attacking the plants at all. Where they can become a little disruptive, especially if you have a south facing exposure, is when they start nesting and you get a lot of disruption of the soil around the plants. The nesting creates a lot of air space around the root system and the plants start to dry out. If you soak those areas thoroughly, the ants get upset and they'll often move out. If nothing else, you are getting water down into the root zone around the plants and again, the plants will survive quite nicely. If it's really a situation where they are overrun-

ning your garden and you want them out, you could put out some plastic containers with some home-made ant killer inside and holes punched around the bottom edge so that the ants can get in and out easily. One formula that seems to work well is equal parts of baking soda and white sugar mixed thoroughly together. Put enough in each container to keep them going for a few days, put the lid back on, place it in the garden and let the ants eat it. As I understand it, this works because the ants can't get rid of gas and are slightly acidic, so when they take in the baking soda with the sugar, which is the attraction, they start to fizz, can't vent the gas and that is the end of them.

Regenerating Hollyhocks

My question is concerning hollyhocks. I have them growing at the side of the house, close to the basement wall, and they seem to do very well there. However when I try to harvest the seed pods they produce each year and plant those seeds elsewhere, nothing happens. What am I doing wrong?

Collect the seeds at the end of the summer and loosen up the soil where you want to establish them. Sprinkle the seeds over the loosened soil. Covering them up with a thin layer of soil is optional. Either way they should come along fine. If you want to ensure better success, collect some of the seeds and leave them in an unheated garage or an unheated area of the porch until about mid January or mid February. At that point you can germinate the seeds inside and start the plants up in individual pots. You want to encourage as much root system as possible – if they start to get root-bound you will have to move them into larger pots. Plant them out next spring and they should come along nicely.

Stumped

A neighbour of ours cut down a very tall Tree of Heaven and for two summers now we've had little saplings sprouting up all over our backyard. Is there anything our neighbour could do to the tree stump that would solve the problem?

If you cut these saplings back regularly they will eventually run out of steam. If the tree that was cut down was an old tree, 8-10 years at least, it would have developed quite an extensive root system. You may still see shoots coming up for a few years but if you cut them off as soon as they show up it will drain the energy

from them. If you want to get more aggressive in controlling them you can dig down where they are coming up and you will find some of the root of the ailianthus, or Tree of Heaven, and if you take out sections of that root it weakens it a bit more quickly. If it is re-shooting at the stump, you might be tempted to try a treatment of glyphosate or "Round-up," something that is absorbed and trans-located, but I am sure that the volume of foliage there and the absorption that would be possible through any of the foliage regenerating from the stump is probably not enough to get out to the full extent of the root system of the young trees and saplings. It is much easier and less of a risk to avoid the pesticide and just clip them back as they show up. Eventually the plant will run out of steam.

Rats in the Compost

My backyard composter had some really nice compost at the bottom, but then we got some really big rats that dug in underneath and fed off of it. Is there any way that I can have a composter without this problem?

Yes there is. Rat traps or rat bait will work but be sure not to put the bait out where anything else can get at it. If you have a cat, you don't want it feeding on the sick rats after they have eaten the bait. Traps will work quite effectively. Use fresh bacon, and torch it with a match to start it sizzling and let the rendered drippings spill around the trap. Ideally, you should raise your compost up off the ground a little so that the finished compost can fall through easily and you can get at it. This bit of space should also help discourage the rats from burrowing in.

Lightning Strike

Our 50-foot fir tree was hit by lightning and it is now split from top to bottom on one side with about a half inch gap. You can follow the line where it has slightly cracked all the way to the top. Do we have to cut it down?

You should consult two to three tree companies and have them give you an evaluation of the tree and an estimate for repair and removal. It sounds like it will have to be removed, however an on-site evaluation would be required to see if it is worth taking a chance on leaving it standing and encouraging it along. Often trees will heal. In natural forests you see lots of evergreens standing that have been subject to lightning strikes. They eventually deteriorate over a longer period of time but perhaps you can nurse this one along. Alternatively, it may be better to remove it, do a replant and watch the new one develop. That is what the experts can help you determine. The danger of having a weakened and deteriorating tree next to your house has to be weighed against the landscape value of the tree. Although the obvious damage to the tree appears relatively small, more extensive damage from the lightning strike may be present inside the trunk and this may have damaged the structural integrity of your tree. Only a professional assessment will be able to advise you on how extensive the damage is and what can be done about it.

Removing Moss from Walkways

Can you give me some advice on how to control moss on stone paving?

This is not an uncommon problem. Depending on the stone and the severity of staining or moss build-up, it is fairly easily cleaned up. For minor growth the cheapest and easiest solution is to apply full strength white vinegar directly to the moss. Some sweeping or brushing with a reasonably stiff push broom may be needed but if you allow the vinegar to sit for 10-15 minutes most of the problem should lift off easily and can be finished off with a hard spray from the garden hose. A thorough rinsing afterwards is required for any of these treatments. The stubborn sections may have to be re-treated with vinegar and brushed more vigorously. For more severe staining or build-up you may have to apply chlorine in the form of liquid household bleach or the flakes used for pools. Again, let the chlorine sit for 10-15 minutes to do its work before brushing and then flush thoroughly with water. There are some environmentally friendly commercial de-mossing products available which work well but they are more costly. If you have really severe staining you will likely have to resort to stronger acid products but I would advise that you talk with a masonry company first to find the exact product for the type of stone you will be treating. Of course a power sprayer, which can be rented, can often achieve the same results as all the suggestions I've made here with just a very strong jet of water.

Growing Grass Beneath Pine Trees

We live on a tiny piece of property in a subdivision but are lucky enough to have a row of pine trees at the back of our property. The problem is we have no grass where the pine needles fall. We are trying to sell the house and this area is a real eyesore. Is there anything that we can do to get grass growing there again?

Yes, you want to do a couple of things. First, rake up the needles and get them off this area, then top-dress over the whole surface with a horticultural or agricultural grade lime. The particles of lime are about the same size as commercial or chemical fertilizer so you can use a spreader to do this. Apply it across the whole area and follow that with a light top-dressing of soil or compost. Once this is done, over-seed, preferably with a shade mix. You will get a higher concentration of Creeping Red Fescue in a shade mix and it tends to stand up better to acidic conditions.

Problems with a Trumpet Vine

My Trumpet Vine is growing against a cellar wall with a southern exposure. The leaves are all curled up and it never flowered this year. What could be wrong?

That south wall would be a good hot spot for it. What has likely happened is you have red spider mites in there and they are piercing and sucking at the foliage. In the hot dry conditions offered by the southern wall, their population just explodes. I suspect the leaves aren't quite as green as they normally would be either. First, clean up all the foliage off the ground underneath the vine and get that debris into the compost. Once they are established it's usually well into the season, but I would try to give the plant a light application of dormant oil in the fall. Before you start spraying though, slide something between the vine and the wall to protect the cedar because unless it has been painted, the oil will stain. First thing next spring, cut off any winter-kill, spread some fresh compost at the base and just as the buds start swelling, but before they open, spray the whole thing again with dormant oil. After the leaves have opened, monitor the plant and watch for any signs of the mites. If you see leaves starting to crinkle, give it a thorough spraying from bottom to top and top back to bottom with a mixture of 40-parts water to one-part soap. Leave it for on for 10 minutes and then spray it again with clear water to clean everything off. Another thing you can do to relieve the stress on the plant is to raise the humidity and cool things down a bit when it starts getting very hot. If you can go out in the middle of the day and spray the whole plant with water, that will help reduce the population of spiders. The Trumpet Vine actually loves that southern location in terms of flowering, but unfortunately it's perfect for the spider mites as well. Be sure not to do your misting or spraying late in the day – wet foliage overnight can lead to problems with fungus or powdery mildew.

Gladiolas from Seed Pods

I removed the pods from my gladiolas after they flowered and I'm now wondering how I should store them and start them up again? What should I do with the glads that are still standing in the bed?

You should let the flowers continue growing until they have been frosted. After the first frost, lift everything, including the corms. Leave them out to dry on a very sunny day. If there is a danger of frost at night, bring them in. You should do this for a couple of days and then shake any excess soil off, although that is not essential, and remove the dried foliage. After they have dried, layer them in vermiculite or dry peat moss and put them in bags or trays. Ensure that you have 1-2 inches underneath the individual corms and keep a good distance between them and an inch or so around and over them. You can put a second layer on over the first but make sure you have a couple of inches between the corms in the first and second layer. Then seal them up – a large plastic bag here is ideal. Store the bags in a cool dark location. The moisture exchange that occurs will happen between any surplus moisture in the bulb or corm itself and the drier material of the vermiculite or peat moss. Any rot is usually confined to individual corms. As you go through them in the spring, you will be able to discard the rotted or diseased corms and it will not have affected the others. If you wanted to save some of the seed pods on the flowering stalk, which will potentially give you different coloured gladiolas because of the possible cross pollination, they can be stored quite successfully as long as they are kept in a clean dry container and in a dark, cool, but not freezing, location. In terms of germination, you would want to start those as you would any other seedling at about the end of February or early March. Put the seedlings out in the spring and let them grow on, although they rarely flower that first year. Lift them out after the first frost and treat them as you did the parent corms and you will be harvesting larger corms for next year's flower production.

Lemon Tree, Not Very Pretty

The leaves on our 4-foot lemon tree keep curling up and eventually drop off. The small lemons start to form and then they fall off too. We have the tree outside in a large pot, and it has recently been re-potted in topsoil with peat moss and vermiculite. Is there anything else we should be doing?

That soil mixture should be fine. Make sure it gets a thorough watering but also that it is drying down between the waterings; having said that, don't let it dry out completely. High light conditions are essential. You are getting flower formation so you've got enough light. You may very well have spider mites in there – I would check very closely on the underside of the leaves, at the base of the leaves, and at the joints between any small stems and larger stems or branches on the plant. Even if you don't think there are mites there, they are really very small and can cause an awful lot of trouble. Watering is going to be a critical factor for sure, but I would go ahead with a soap and water spray. Spray from the bottom up onto the undersides of the leaves, into all of the crotches, the trunk and fully up and down all of the branches. Mix 40-parts water to 1-part soap and give it a thorough spraying. Leave the solution on for 15-20 minutes and then spray the whole thing off with clear water. If you are on well water, let the water sit for a while to get the ambient air temperature to rise at least above 10° celsius, so you aren't shocking the daylights out of the plant. The spray will certainly set back the mite population but one application won't kill future generations or eggs. If you see a major change in the plant after that initial application, watch it carefully. If the problems show up again reapply the soap mixture. You would need to do it 3 times over a 10 day period to eliminate the population completely including any re-hatch.

Impact of More Light

Our Red Maple is about 8 years old. Just over a year ago the big oak beside it got ants and we had to have it cut down. After that the Red Maple grew up about 4 feet and this year the lower part of the tree has leafed out fine but that new upper section only has little tiny leaves. Should we cut the top off?

Typically Red Maples will sit in a forest as saplings and wait until the trees around them start dying out. When they get more light, that is their signal to go into accelerated growth and start filling out that space. This is what has happened here and the tree is responding to the increased light. If the oak was taken down late in the season, the maple may not have had enough time to harden off properly and has sustained some frost damage. It certainly would have had a more difficult winter than it has ever had before because of increased wind exposure with the oak gone. Give it a chance to fill out. If by the middle of the summer it is still struggling, you may want to do some thinning to concentrate the energy in specific areas of the crown but I wouldn't cut anything at this point.

Encouraging a Hydrangea to Flower

I have a beautiful green climbing hydrangea that is 3 years old and hasn't flowered yet. Could you give me some ideas on how I could promote flowering?

It sounds like your climbing hydrangea is growing well, but the "beautiful green" you describe could be a clue to the non-flowering. Bright, dark-green foliage is usually the result of a high nitrogen level in the soil and that discourages flowering. Don't fertilize your hydrangea this year at all and see if that makes a difference. If there is a chance that lawn fertilizer could inadvertently be spreading on to the base of the plant, shield the area around the hydrangea before you fertilize the lawn. Also, this is a plant that blooms on old wood so don't prune it back too hard if you want to encourage more flowers. Climbing hydrangea need full light to flower successfully but in zone 5 it is at its hardiness zone limit. Here it does best on an east-facing wall since the heat build-up on a south or west-facing wall during the winter causes heavy winter-kill and dieback.

Powdery Pine Needles

For the past few years our 40-year-old Mugo Pine has had this white stuff, almost like a fungus or a mold, on its needles and they are turning brown. It looks very sick. Have you any idea what it might be?

This may not be a fungus or a mold. That whiteness you see may be caused by a wooly aphid or a pine aphid. The sort of buff brown colour in the foliage is from the aphids feeding on the needles, sucking the chlorophyll out of them and browning them off. Both of these insects envelop themselves in a waxy secretion that can look very much like mold. It's there for their protection – birds don't like the taste of it, and moisture and chemicals cannot penetrate it successfully. However you can treat for them. A good jet of water will wash them off initially but they do tend to climb back up if they can. Combining some soap with the water is going to give you a better measure of control, but to really get through that waxy exterior you have to go with a spray of 40-parts water to 1-part liquid soap and add to that 8-parts of rubbing alcohol. That will give the sort of penetration you need. Now you can also imagine what that rubbing alcohol is going to do the resin or waxy coating on the needles themselves, so try and be fairly specific to the affected areas when you spray. Blast the aphid clusters as soon as they show up, wait ten minutes, then take clear water from the hose and flush the foliage again to get the residue off. You don't want that spray to dry there and remain on the needles. With a really widespread infestation that you are able to catch when it is still concentrated out at the tips of the branches, trim those tips off and try to eliminate the aphids that way. Don't leave any of the cuttings on the ground. Pack them all up into a large plastic bag or burn them. If you are putting them into plastic bags, seal the bags and sit them out somewhere in the sun where they will bake for a couple of weeks. That should take care of any problem.

Battling with Hawthorns

We just bought a small rural acreage and I am becoming very familiar with the hawthorns when trying to walk through our bush. I have been impaled several times and I am not sure by what type of hawthorn. I understand that there are quite a few varieties but these ones have huge needles on them and they are very sharp. We have sort of started a battle with these and I have dug out a large section, trying to get down into the roots as deep as I can get. I am wondering how they reproduce and if they are going to come back. Is this a battle that will be won?

If what you have got is hawthorn, then yes, they will shoot back up from the stubs that are left. Re-cutting those bits is going to be an awful lot easier the second or third time round though, and you can cut them very close to the ground. Just

keep cutting them back and eventually that will get rid of them. There are also other possibilities in terms of what these might be. One might be Prickly Ash, although it doesn't have as long a needle or spike and would be much shorter and more entangling. These respond very strongly to cutting back and will sucker up and shoot up all over the place. In that case, you would have to get a good heavy mulch down. However, it does sound like hawthorn with the long, heavy needle you describe. Don't attempt to eradicate everything unless you are planning to use the land for something else. As a native plant, they fill a very important role in our ecosystem. The heavy flowering in the spring is magnificent and feeds an awful lot of pollinators early in the season. In bloom they can be as attractive as apple trees or other flowering trees – sometimes even more so. The hawthorn berries, or "haws", that follow along are a great source of food for birds. Shrikes actually use the hawthorn in a different way for food. I imagine their nickname of the "Butcher Bird" comes from the fact that they don't have talons but do have quite a sharp beak, so they catch their prey, impale it on the hawthorns and leave it there. They seem to actually use the bushes as a storehouse. In fact, don't be surprised when working with the hawthorn to find the remains of a little field mouse or mole impaled there for future consumption. Much like the squirrel, shrikes tend to forget where some of their catch was warehoused and they get left behind in winter.

Melons in Compost

There are two mysterious cucumber-like plants that have come out of my compost. The fruit looks like mini Honeydew melon and are about the size of tennis balls. Yesterday I cut them open and there are seeds in the middle. I tasted them and although they have the texture of a cucumber, they have the sweetness of the Honeydew melon.

I think you grew a couple of Honeydew melons. Quite possibly the seeds came from a melon you discarded in your compost that didn't break down. The seeds germinated in that rich environment instead and there they are. Actually, the best place to grow your melons is on your compost, especially if it is a fairly active one. The extra effort you make in watering to keep the melons growing nicely also helps the compost break down and when you do finally use it, you will have a lot of mature bacteria and flora there that will make the mix that much better for your garden. That extra warmth provided by the active compost pile is always welcomed by heat-loving melons and the bonus is their foliage covering the top of the pile helps to inhibit any weed seeds from germinating.

Mitigating Acidic Conditions

I took out a large spruce tree about two months ago, spaded all the ground up and took out most of the roots. I put some peat moss into it and the grass came up well but now in the centre where the tree was, maybe 2-3 metres in diameter, there is quite a large yellow spot. I wondered if there was a fertilizer or something I could use without digging everything up again?

Yes. If it is a question of the soil being acidic, it's very simple to overcome that problem just by sprinkling wood ash over the area. That should certainly give you a temporary remedy but for the long term you will want to apply some agricultural or horticultural grade dolomitic limestone to the area as well. That will neutralize the acidic condition that is there. Acidity shouldn't normally be a big problem when removing a tree but in this case the spruce needles that were left probably got incorporated into the soil and with the addition of the peat moss, which is also slightly acidic, you may have tipped the balance. The yellowing could also be caused by a fair amount of organic matter being in there and that area drying out more quickly than the rest of the lawn, but the addition of the limestone is going to be a plus for the soil in any case.

Villain Identification

There has been some dispute among my family and friends as to whether a plant I reacted to was poison ivy or Deadly Nightshade. The plant has 3 leaves and berries that start out green and then turn red. I find

very little in any of the gardening books regarding poisonous plants and I'd like to know what it was that made me so itchy.

If it has the three leaves it is poison ivy. The Deadly Nightshade would have a single leaf with 3 lobes along the centre section and 2 lower lobes off the side. Some people do have allergic reactions to it because of the high solanin content. Three individual leaves is definitely poison ivy. The best way to get rid of it without getting into too heavy duty pesticides would be to mulch the daylights out of it. Cover it with about 10 sheets of newspaper and spread 6 inches of mulch on top of that to block out all the light. That should kill it off.

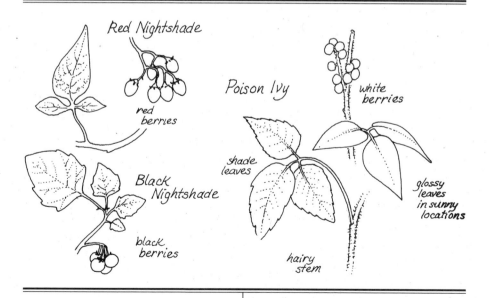

Tree Crack with Fungus

We live on a ravine and at the front of the house, facing south, we have a maple tree that started up from one of the seeds from that ravine, so it is kind of special. It is about the height of the house now and last year I noticed a split in the bark. This year there are more splits and some fungus. It looks perfectly healthy but I'm concerned that this is the start of something serious. Do you know what could be happening?

Even though that tree came up from the ravine and self-seeded, I suspect you have Norway Maple. They seed very heavily and they do fairly nicely on their own. However, they are from Norway not from Canada, so they have a great susceptibility to frost cracking. What happens when you have a very cold, bright winter day with the sun pounding down on the south or west side of a tree with nice dark-coloured bark is that the bark heats up readily and some of the sap underneath starts to liquefy. When the sun goes down and the temperature drops, the liquid freezes, expands and cracks the bark. When this happens year after year, you end up with what are often known as target cankers. The tree splits in winter and then begins to heal and callus over the

next season. The following winter, you get the same conditions occurring and it cracks again, so you get rim after rim of callus building up. The fungus is really a fruiting body and its presence is telling you that there is some deterioration going on underneath or that there is enough nutrient, moisture and organic material at that crack point for fungus to live on and it has become sufficiently well established to put out a fruit-

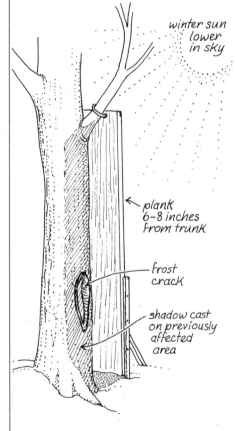

winter sun
lower
in sky

plank
6–8 inches
from trunk

frost
crack

shadow cast
on previously
affected
area

ing body. Removing the fruiting body isn't going make much difference. What you want to do is check inside where the fungus is located and see if the wood behind it is still solid. If it is, that's great. Make sure that the bark is trimmed back but you don't have to cut the cambium for this. Just loosen some of the bark around the edges, especially if it is rougher old bark. Smooth that out and get some good air circulation going, especially during the summer months. When you trim away the peeling or split bark, you will be able to clearly determine the state of the heartwood underneath. If the wood is not solid – that is to say, if it's split, mushy or punky – then allow it to dry out through the growing season. Now that the area is exposed, it should dry out readily. If after a season of drying the heartwood is still punky, remove the soft material with a chisel but be careful not to damage the callused tissue around the edges of the injured area. Make sure water is not accumulating at the bottom of that cavity. You can do this by cutting a channel downward toward the outer edge at the bottom of the hole to direct the moisture to the outside. Once all this is done, get a board about 1 foot wide by 6 feet high and place it about 6 inches away from the trunk on the south or south-west side so that the light hits the board instead of the tree trunk. This will be immensely helpful. Install the plank late in the fall after the first frost and remove it each spring. Horticulturally, this is done in other countries – for instance where there is great intensity from the heat of the sun in the summer months, they paint the trunks of some trees, like olive trees, white. The whitewash reflects more of the light so you don't get a build up of heat underneath. Water expands when it boils but it also expands when it freezes so you can get the cracking in both conditions. In your case, if you can stop the daytime heat build up in winter by placing a board on the sunny side, you should reduce or eliminate the problem.

Mushroom Mayhem

I'm having an incredible problem with mushrooms and seem to be the only one on the street that does. They have come up all over my lawn for years, but in the last two years they have been coming up through my driveway as well. I have at least three places where they have pushed right up through the asphalt. How can I get them out of my lawn and what can I do about the ones that are already under the asphalt?

There isn't much you can do about the ones under the asphalt without redoing the driveway. It is really quite amazing to realize just how much strength a fungus can have when you see them popping asphalt. I've actually seen instances where a mushroom has lifted an 8 foot wide by 8 foot long section of concrete on a sidewalk. Just that one mushroom coming up lifted that whole square, so you can imagine what kind of power is there. In terms of your lawn, the critical thing is to cut them off as soon as they pop up. If you get them right off at the start, the plus is that the spore doesn't have a chance to ripen and spread so you are reducing re-establishment or expansion of that colony of mycelium. There is obviously a good quantity of organic matter in that soil – probably some old rotting roots left down there are housing the real growing part of the mushroom, as opposed to the fruiting body that you see breaking the surface. They do tend to prefer woody, humid, acidic conditions, which is why you often find them on rotting trees in damp, shaded areas. Mushrooms are generally not a bad thing aside from the aesthetics, but in the case of a driveway they become more of a problem. You could try to alter the pH of your soil by applying some horticultural-quality lime over the entire surface of the lawn but if the old rotting roots are well down in the soil, it would take a great quantity of lime to alter the conditions enough to discourage the mycelium – especially when they are already established and growing so successfully. As far as the driveway goes, again, you're not going to have any great success in killing off the colony if the root or organic matter that is feeding it is at a fair depth. Try mixing up 4-5 tablespoons of baking soda in 4 litres of warm water. After you have removed the mushroom, pour that mix down the crack a bit at a time and let it penetrate down into the soil. You want to do this on a warm day – not any time close to freeze-up because if that water were to freeze and expand it could end up doing more damage to your asphalt. So pick a warm day and try that solution. It will act to create a more alkaline environment underneath the pavement and that should help to discourage the growth of the mushrooms.

White Spots on Maple

The canopy on my 20-year-old maple tree is looking very sick. There are huge bare spots and some branches have no leaves at all. There are also some white spots on the trunk that are oozing liquid. Do you know what the problem might be?

It's possible the white spots may be lichen, or something a bit more serious since it is all over the trunk. The problem you are seeing in the canopy may not be related to the problem on the bark. Start with the bark. Take a sharp knife and scrape at one of the spots. If the white spot comes off and there is healthy bark underneath, it is likely lichen and that's not a problem. If however you find that the problem goes deeper than that, take the knife and cut open around one of those white spots in a teardrop shape with a point at both ends. The first cut should be small, a half-inch wide at the centre and 1 inch long in total. Lift the bark out and see what is there. If, when you do this, you find it is green, healthy, and vigorous underneath, then leave it alone. What you probably have is a surface infection that is moist and mushy when you push on it but is just affecting the bark itself, as opposed to something that has attacked the bark and gone through the cambium and into the hardwood of the tree. If the problem seems superficial, leave it. However, if it is still mushy underneath, open the cut a little longer and a little wider until you get to healthy tissue and leave that area exposed to the air. What that air exposure is going to

do is dry the area out and it should heal itself back over. If, after doing the cuts, you find a couple of them are quite mushy through to the hardwood, you should call in an expert to evaluate the tree. With regard to the canopy, water stress may be the issue there and dead branches will have to be removed, but you may want to get an evaluation of the tree first before deciding to do the work on the top. If the tree is in such bad shape that even after doing the work on the top you are going to lose it in a couple years, perhaps now is the time to have it taken down and put in a new one. The money spent on an evaluation by a professional arborist is well worthwhile and may save unnecessary expenditure on major pruning.

Crisped Clover

There is an area at the back of my yard that is about 70 by 35 feet. It gets full sun and is flat and dry. This spring I planted clover there and it did well until about 3 weeks ago at which point it all turned brown and died. Now it looks dreadful. I am wondering if you could suggest something that will stay green throughout the summer and that I won't have to replant year after year. My problem is that I don't want to cut grass and I don't want to have to water it either. Is there anything that will work?

The clover is most likely going to come back. It takes pretty extreme conditions to beat it down completely but you may want to mix it with some other plants that can benefit from the clover by getting a bit of a larger leaf growing over the area. A couple of things could work well here. Ajuga, or bugleweed, would be one. There are a number of varieties that would stand up nicely but you are going to have to encourage it a little to start with. Once it is reasonably well established, it can fend for itself. Don't worry about the clover being dried off, just try to work the ajuga into the spaces. The two varieties of plant are going to end up duking it out a bit but it will be a good mix. You will have occasions when the clover comes on a little more strongly and there will be other times when the ajuga does, but that's fine. Any of the thymes would also do well here. Again, it is a matter of encouraging them until they get established, but once they start spreading, they will do quite nicely. Low spreading junipers are another alternative if you want to alter the colour and texture of the foliage and add a little bit of variety to the landscape.

Tree Canopy Killing Grass

There are several hemlock trees in my backyard that are probably close to 30 feet tall with the typical wide spread branching and the grass is dying out underneath them in quite wide and ever increasing patches. Is there anything I can do to treat the soil to encourage the grass to grow or is there another ground cover that is more suited to these conditions?

I would say start looking at alternative ground covers. Grass doesn't generally grow well in the shade and at 30 feet tall the amount of direct sunlight coming down through those branches would be pretty low. Even with a "shade mix" turf, it is going to be tough. Combine that with the competition from several hemlocks that are drawing as much moisture and nutrient from the ground as they can get and you have got a pretty good contest going on there. I would say your best bet would be to outline and open up some beds that extend from the trunks of these trees to the drip lines. Incorporate a couple of inches of well-rotted organic matter on top of the soil, mix it lightly into the surface and then plant something like Japanese spurge, pachisandra terminalis, or periwinkle, Vinca *minor*. Either of these would be a good choice for that location and would do very nicely once they get established, but you are going to have to be patient to start with. Keep things on the moist side and make sure to weed regularly at the beginning. It gets much harder to get the weeds out of there once these plants start filling in so be vigilant in the early stages. The other thing you might have a look at is Marjorie Harris' book, "Botanica North America", because the situation we are looking at here is very similar to conditions in a native evergreen forest. There are numerous ephemerals or spring flowering plants that can be incorporated into a garden like yours and that will come up through the Japanese Spurge or the periwinkle quite nicely. As they are dying down, their foliage is rapidly hidden by the foliage of the groundcover, so it doesn't look untidy. And if you want to add greater pockets of colour with that, you may want to include any of the tulips or daffodils. They would do very nicely in that setting as well. Try and get them into brighter spots around the edges where they get a little higher light for longer periods of time and lots of light early in the season.

Sumac Invasion

I just love the sumac trees that grow along the slope at the back edge of my lawn, especially in the fall when they are red. The problem I have with them is in the spring and the early part of the summer when they try and take over the whole lawn. It was the bane of my existence last summer. I even have little shoots 50 feet away from the main trees. I've been getting at them with the pruning sheers to cut them off as low as I can and then I put poison on the ends, but I notice the following week that there are more new shoots coming up. I don't know how to stop them. Part of my concern is that I have a septic system underneath there and I'm worried that they are going to cause some major damage. Is there any way to control sumac?

That invasiveness certainly tells you what a great root system those sumac have. On a sandy slope, can you imagine what a great job they do at holding the soil back! They are expansionist by nature and they throw up their shoots from nodes on the root system. However, if you mow them off, just by cutting the lawn, that is going to be sufficient to keep them under control. The stem does get woody, but it is nothing that would be of any harm to your mower when the shoots are young. You could go around and cut them lower if you want, but you really can save yourself all of that trouble. I would stop the poisoning if you want to keep the parent trees around though, because the effective herbicide for them is one that is translocated – that is to say, it will travel through the roots – and if you use one of those on the shoots it will end up affecting the health of the parent tree as well. You could kill off the golden goose. Just mow them back and that should keep them in check. In terms of your septic system, what you want to do is to discourage the root system from coming in that way. If you have enough room, I would measure 5-10 feet from the end of the septic bed and dig a trench right across the yard, 18-24 inches deep, and put a physical barrier into the ground. Use something solid like old metal siding that the shoots won't be able to come through or a geotextile or landscape fabric. Then back fill, put the lawn back in place and you will know there is a barrier there that will at least impede those roots. Any shoots coming beyond that point towards the septic system should be few and far between. The other thing that could be helpful is to water the slope away from your lawn when conditions are dry. The sumac can certainly tough out dry conditions but the root systems will be inclined to run towards moisture, which is the attraction of your septic field. They

are looking to survive and will be attracted to the most optimum conditions. If it is wetter in the other direction, that is where they'll head. The other thing I would suggest is that you not fertilize the lawn at all between the septic tank and the sumac for the same reason. You could try fertilizing on the downhill side of the slope however, and again, the sumac would then be attracted by the higher nutrients in the soil and encouraged to move away from the septic field.

Downed by Storm

We were hit by a huge wind storm this summer and I have a Sunburst Honey Locust that is 18-20 feet high and about 4 inches around that got blown over. It seems to have bent about 5 feet up from the ground at the point on the trunk where a year ago it had a huge bacterial infection about the size of my hand. That damaged area was sealed over but it must have left some sort of weakness. We got someone in two days later to get the tree back up and they staked it about 8 feet up on three sides using wires threaded through what looks like rubber hosing, but we are wondering what chance it has of recovering.

If you were able to get the tree back up and staked within two days, the cambium layer would probably have been protected. What generally happens in these situations is that a previously injured spot, like the one you described, is the weak link in the chain and is going to break with stress or pressure of any sort. That being said, if the tree got righted fairly quickly, it will have time to heal over during the remainder of the summer and there is a good chance everything is going to be fine. I would suggest that you leave those stakes on for at least two years to be sure. Wire through hose is fine as a support. That rubber is going to be cushioning the impact of the wire on the stem itself. You will also have to move that wire up or down on the trunk an inch or so – or as far as it will "give" – a couple of times during that two year period. If you can lift them or lower them even just slightly at the end of summer and again at the end of October or early November, come through the winter and then move them again in the spring, that would help. It is just a matter of shifting them up or down within the range possible so that you are not getting a permanent impact point on the stem. Make sure that the wires are loose enough to accommodate any expansion in the size of the tree so there is no chance of the tree starting to grow out into the wire where you will end up with another weak point. There is going to have to be some healing and some growth go on underneath the bark so don't be surprised if the tree is a little bit slower next year. Any encouragement you can give it first thing in the spring would be a plus. If there is not a watering ring around the base of the tree, it would be a good idea to create one now. It's best to have at least a 3-5 foot diameter circle around the base with no grass or other plants growing there. Put compost over the soil as a mulch and that should be sufficient. What you want to do is encourage the tree into good, healthy, vigorous growth again so that it can actually seal off and heal over this damage. The support of those wires for a full two years is going to be worthwhile – too much movement before the weakened area gets healed could cause it to bend or break at that same point again, so do leave those supports in place and it should come along fine.

Hydrangea Transfer

I wanted to transplant a very large, well-established white hydrangea. How should I do that?

Once your plant gets a good hard frost in the fall, trim it back to about half its height.

When you do that, you will probably be able to see the individual crowns fairly clearly and where it can be easily severed. Just drive a spade down through the plant at those points and cut the roots, severing the various pieces of the existing crown. Leave it over the winter and then first thing in the spring, as soon as the soil is workable, lift the whole thing out. The clumps will come apart easily because you have already divided the roots. Add some compost back into the original hole, put one of the clumps back in there and cover it up again. Dig new holes for the others, adding a good quantity of organic matter – anywhere up to 50% – mix the soil thoroughly and transplant them in. Soak the daylights out of them to eliminate any air pockets in the soil. If you find there is winter-kill on some of the stems, trim them back to healthy growth. They are going to do beautifully. In fact they will all do better for the transplanting. It may take them a year to get well established again but now that you have taken away the competition among the individual parts of the original plant and given each new section its own space, they will take off.

Propagating Tree Peonies

I was given about 10 seeds for a tree peony and told it has beautiful balls of flowers but my books say you can only propagate these by cuttings. Now someone else tells me that these seeds would need two periods of cold if I am to have any luck at all germinating them, so I am checking with you to see what I should do.

I have managed to grow tree peony successfully from seed, so it is possible. These seeds absolutely do need two periods of cold. Start in the fall, say late September or early October. Put the seeds into a paper bag labelled with the date and put it in the refrigerator. After 6 weeks you can bring them out and pot them up. Alternatively, if you only have a handful of seeds, you can pot them up into 2-inch plastic pots right away. Bury the seeds to their own depth, soak them thoroughly and put them into the refrigerator, preferably in a plastic bag or covered over the top so that they don't dry out. Leave them for 6 weeks and then bring them out into a warm, preferably sunny location. The sun part isn't essential but you do want light and you do want warmth. They usually do pretty nicely on top of your refrigerator. Do keep the soil moist throughout this period. You are probably looking at another 4-6 weeks here – watch them closely enough to see when the radicals form, that is, when the first shoot breaks out of that seed coat. Once that has happened, give them another week or so out and then moisten the soil, cover them again with the plastic, date them again and it's back into the refrigerator for another 6 weeks. All this will have eaten up at least 4 months, so if you start in mid fall that gets you through to the end of January or beginning of February. Light levels are starting to pick up again by then, so after that second cold treatment, place them into a sunny window and water them as required. Don't ever leave them standing in water but keep that soil constantly moist. You are going to see them go into the next stage and start producing their first set of true leaves. If you find that some don't progress after a month of being out this second time, those can go back into the refrigerator for another 6 week cold treatment. It usually takes at least two cold treatments to break their dormancy and get them to come into leaf, but occasionally 3 might be necessary. Unlike some other plants however, time in the freezer is not required with these and is really not advisable. Too much of a good thing can sometimes be fatal, so stick with the

fridge even if it takes a few sessions in there.

Harassed Hollyhocks

For the last few years something has been eating the leaves on my hollyhocks almost from the time they break ground and what's not eaten eventually turns brown. I do get blooms but that is pretty much all I get. I have been checking the leaves and there are tiny yellow dots on them, but I never see any insects. I have been putting powdered eggshell down, thinking it was slugs. Could it be something else?

It isn't slugs. It's more likely rust. If some of the early leaves are yellowing, pick those off and clean up any leaf or plant debris around or under the hollyhocks. A dusting with sulphur powder on the leaves and on the soil will help to keep this problem in check. Any time your plants start to show signs of the rust again, pinch that part off. Don't put these bits into your compost though – burn them or bag them and take them off the property. If you are diligent, this should get the rust under control early in the season and it won't spread to the rest of the plant. If you can avoid splashing that foliage when you water, that would be a big plus as well. Sanitation is critical to keeping this problem in check so make sure you clean up around your hollyhocks every year, spring and fall.

Promoting a Raspberry Fiesta

What can I do to promote abundant fruiting on my raspberry canes? I just inherited them with this house so I have no idea how old they are. They are sitting here in a clump with a little bit of a trellis around to keep them from drooping over too much. What should I be doing with them?

Look into the clump and see how you could cut it up and divide it into rows 2-3 feet apart. Once you make that decision, start removing the plants in between those rows. Get all the root system out that you can when you remove those plants. With those that remain, cut off some of the oldest, thickest growth as well as any damaged or diseased canes. Be careful not to take off all of the old growth though, because the flower and fruit generates on the second-year wood. Next, trim back some of the younger plants to thin things out but again, don't take out all the young growth because if you do, next year you won't have any second-year wood coming along to produce that year's fruit. What

you really have to do is rejuvenate the patch. So thin it down, get rid of some of the oldest material and some of the surplus new material. Where you have taken out plants, between the rows or elsewhere, you are going to have to get something back in there. Soil would be fine but compost would be ideal. You would be feeding the soil and therefore feeding the raspberries. Next I would suggest 6-8 inches of good clean straw mulch, not against the stems, but in between the plants and between the rows. The big plus with straw is the light colour – it reflects daylight back up underneath the plants and makes it easier to see the berries. It is also useful for the plants because the reflected light gives them that much more energy to use to photosynthesize. When they start to flower, make sure there is enough moisture to not only produce, but also to sustain the berries. Mulching will be helpful here to keep that moisture in the soil. You should find that your raspberries come back quite quickly after this initial clean up. You'll want to continue to maintain the patch on an annual basis this way by taking out the oldest growth and keeping a balance between young and very young growth coming along. If you can do this on an ongoing basis, the patch should produce for you for years.

Scaly Japanese Maple

My Weeping Japanese Maple had some of the leaves curling up at the ends and now that all the leaves are gone, I notice there are oblong scales that are harboring some little beasts. What can I do?

Don't cut it away and don't spray. These are scale insects but Japanese Maples are not receptive to being sprayed with dormant oil, which would normally give you an ideal cure for any scale problem. However, if you get a reasonably warm late fall day, up around 8-10° celsius, mix up a solution of 40-parts water to 1-part liquid soap and then add 8-parts rubbing alcohol. Give the branches with the scale a thorough spraying, especially around the insects. You should use a very fine but strong mist and you want a bit of penetration in underneath, so if you can get in close and blast them, that would be good. Leave that on for 10-15 minutes and then go over the whole thing again with clear water to rinse everything off. Do it again first thing in the spring as the buds are appearing and getting ready to swell but before they have actually started to open, and that should give you a good measure of control. Watch for re-infestation and treat that as required, but avoid spraying young foliage or opening buds.

Dividing Silver Mound

My problem is with Silver Mound. A small plant I bought a few years ago has done very well. In fact, I have divided it twice. It is now immense and floppy and looks like it is going to seed. What do I do to get back to a small plant? If I cut up the roots in wee bits, will I get little plants?

Silver Mound looks magnificent but one of the problems with this plant is that as it ages, or if it rains very hard, it is sort of like a bush of peonies; everything flops over at the same time. Don't hesitate to trim it and by all means, feel free to split it up into smaller pieces. Just lift it out and divide it up. You can transplant it in the fall or the spring, either way it is going to be fine. Be sure to soak everything in well, even if the soil seems moist when you are doing the splitting and transplanting. The last thing you want are air pockets that will dry out the new roots and either slow development or kill off the plant. If you opt for a fall transplant, be sure to leave enough time for the root system to get established in the new location before the ground freezes.

Combating Comfrey

We've got an over-abundance of comfrey outside our house. Every time we dig it up, we take out as much of the root as we can and haul it out to the back of our property but wherever we dump it, it grows. Although my wife likes to do the organic thing, we tried using Round-up on it and that didn't even faze it. We'd like to put down grass but how can we get rid of the comfrey?

When you dig the comfrey up, put it all into your compost instead of dumping it elsewhere. Those big green leaves tend to activate the compost quite nicely, so chop it up, throw it in and just keep it working in there. Unfortunately, if you leave even a little of it in the ground it is going to want to come back, so do try and get as much of it out as you can. Next prepare the soil by loosening it up to a depth of about 6 inches, mix in some well-rotted organic material from your compost and then put down your grass seed. If you are putting down sod, it is probably going to be enough of a light inhibitor to block out any comfrey that might want to come back, but make sure that the joints are tight. If you are seeding, which is not a bad way to go at all, there is going to be a competition factor and it is going to be a little bit harder to get rid of the comfrey completely. You may have to repeat the treatment in small areas here and there to get more of the root

out after the fact, but over time, the problem should be resolved.

Ash Envy

When I was a kid my old next door neighbour had a tree that always had really neat red berries on it. I seem to remember the birds getting drunk on them near the end of the season. My mother always called it a Rowan tree but I think it was a Mountain Ash. I went to a nursery the other day thinking I would like one for my house and the guy there told me not to do it because of this ash disease that is making its way up from the States. Now I wonder if this is true. I would have thought that the Mountain Ash would be hardy. Do you know if whatever it is that is bugging these other ashes is going to be a problem with the Mountain Ash?

I would think not. You were likely steered off because he didn't have one. In fact, Mountain Ash are not the same family as true ashes. Mountain Ashes are Sorbus species and part of the rose family, as opposed to Fraxinus, the ashes in the olive family. Rowan, as your mother called it, is a European Mountain Ash, Sorbus *aucuparia*. There are two native species in Canada. When you do find one, be sure to incorporate a good quantity of organic matter into the soil when you plant it, as well as some rock phosphate or bone meal to stimulate the root development. If you are planting very late in the fall, be sure to stake the tree well so it doesn't get blown around all winter long without the benefit of a well-established root system to stabilize it. That support should also help to protect any of the new, fine roots that would start coming along and prevent them from getting sheared off every time the wind blows. And yes, toward the end of the season, when those red berries start to ripen and over-ripen, they can ferment right on the tree. The birds certainly can get a little tipsy if they indulge, especially the blue jays who I've seen start acting pretty weird after a good meal of them.

Mushroom Madness

I seem to be having major mushroom headaches this year – I have two outbreaks I need advice on. The first one is in a large maple tree with a 2½ foot diameter trunk where a shelf fungus has shown up right at the base where two major roots join. The second is in the middle of my driveway where a bunch of white mushrooms have erupted through the asphalt. What do I do?

It is amazing how strong mushrooms can be. I have seen them lift through a huge slab of asphalt. Heaven knows what the source is but there is definitely a quantity of organic matter under there supporting the mycelia which produced the fruiting body or mushroom you see. Cut them out and remove them from your driveway. Put a little hydrated lime down into the hole and patch the area. In terms of the tree, what you are seeing is indicative of something else going on inside there. There are mycologists who could probably tell you exactly what state of decay the interior of that tree is in just by identifying the type of mushroom growing there. I would have it looked at by a professional arborist because you may be able to take some preventative action. If it is simply a matter of wet wood in the heart of that tree, you could try drilling a hole and inserting a pipe as drainage to dry out the core and that would slow down, if not stop, further rotting inside. That fungus is a good indicator that something else is happening there however, so it would be best to have it checked by a professional. Your tree could be a danger if it is no longer structurally sound.

Pine Blister Rust

I think I have White Pine Blister Rust on my trees. I have been on the internet and it tells me that this type of rust lives on goose-berries or currants. There were some gooseberries planted close to the tree which I have removed, but I still have a number of trees that seem affected. I was wonder-ing if there is any way I could treat this problem short of cut-ting the trees down.

Unfortunately, there isn't any effective treatment for blister rust. On the plus side, the spores are fairly heavy and don't travel all that far. The gooseberries work as an alternate host but they have to be in close proximity. Certain-ly taking out those bushes is the right way to go. If you have wild ones around, it is best to remove them as well. The debris should be taken at least 100 metres away from the original site to ensure that there is no further contact possible. If you can do anything to encourage the health and vigour of the White Pines, they are going to react appropriately and will outgrow the disease. Don't worry too much about fer-tilizer. One feeding early in the season is sufficient but it's most important to make sure they are not under moisture stress for the duration of this growing season.

The rust tends not to be so much of a problem when the trees are healthy and vigorous.

Black Spot on Roses

My well-established rose bush has developed black spots on the leaves and then they turned yel-low. What should I do?

Black spot is a fungal disease which attacks when there is high humidity on the foliage of the plant. If you have a localized problem, you can pick the leaves off and get rid of them. Nitrogen-rich foliage has a greater propen-sity to pick up black spot prob-lems, so be sure you are not feeding with a high-nitrogen fer-tilizer. Black spot will come on to any type of rose but some vari-eties are more susceptible than others. One solution is to spray the rose bush with a solution of 1% baking soda in water, making sure that the soda is completely dissolved before spraying. It would also be helpful if when you prune your roses, you prune them to an open vase shape. This will ensure not only full light pen-etration and exposure, but good air circulation so that the leaves do not stay wet in between water-ings and after rainfall. Also, be sure you do not water the rose bush from above. Instead, water around the base of the plant, soaking it thoroughly to get the water down to the root system and not over the foliage – this will help prevent any future black spot problems. All the debris and affected leaves that come off the rose this year should be collected but do not put this material directly into the compost or use it as mulch. Collect it in a black plastic garbage bag, add enough water to moisten it thoroughly, seal it up and let it sit out in the sun for a week or two so that it goes to mush. After that you can add it to the compost pile, being sure to mix it in well. That baking will help kill off the fungal spores and ensure that your compost does not become part of the problem in future years.

Merits of Burlap

We are in a new neighbourhood about two years old, and the builder has planted trees. We have a Red and a Green Oak about 10 feet apart on our front lawn. They have staked them and then wrapped the trunks in burlap and we have put mulch around the bottom. Is the burlap necessary?

The builders are worried about sun exposure and the burning and drying of the tree tissue, and yes, it is worthwhile. When you are watering the trees, I would

say water the burlap as well, especially on hot days. It helps cool down the bark, which is particularly helpful on the west side. The burlap generally will be loose enough to allow some light penetration but it is effectively working as a shade cloth. It shouldn't get to the point of girdling the tree but if you notice that it is getting fairly snug at some point, you will want to loosen it off a little. But certainly for its first year or two, I would leave it in place. As the burlap weathers and starts to break down, remove it.

Blisters on Broad-leafed Plants

I have had a recurrence of what looks like flat, brownie-beige blisters on many of my broadleaf vegetables like chard and beets, and sometimes even on the spinach. I have planted these in different areas in the past two summers but it still recurs. They are still edible but not very pretty. Any idea what might be causing this?

You can get this sort of effect with cool, damp conditions. It is called botrytis and it is a fungal problem. Sometimes an insect that is piercing and sucking the juice from the leaf will give you the same kind of spotting, but in this case I would suspect that it is the fungus. Getting rid of it will be a matter of not watering over the top of the plant unless it is done early in the day so they have a chance to dry off completely. They need to be at least reasonably dry going into night time when everything naturally cools down. Obviously, a lot of rain will exacerbate the problem – this may have caused it to start with, especially if that rain came with cooler temperatures. A summer where you don't get the usual hot, dry conditions provides the ideal environment for this type of fungus. I suspect a combination of keeping water off the leaves when you are watering and thinning your crop a bit to get some good air circulation in there to keep the foliage drier will help solve the problem.

Re-bloomin' Apple Tree

The tail end of a hurricane came through here this spring and there were no blooms left on my apple tree after all that wind and rain. This tree is about 30 years old and is sitting in full sun on the south-east side of our property. It has had a couple of rough years. A storm blew through at blossom time last year as well and although it was covered in blooms at one point, it didn't produce much fruit that season. This year was looking good before this storm hit, but we've resigned ourselves to another non-productive season. Now here it is almost fall, and be darned if that tree didn't bloom again last week. I have never seen anything like it! Can you tell me what's going on?

I have seen a few trees do this. It usually happens where the tree has been under stress right at the beginning of the season. The conditions after that storm were likely similar to spring conditions, with things cooling off a little but enough heat to encourage some active growth. If you kept getting more rain, the tree would think it's spring again. It would have set its buds but instead of holding on to them in the dormant state ready for next year's spring flowering, it goes right ahead and blooms again in the same year. The result may be that this tree doesn't produce worth a darn next spring. As long as you don't have an early freeze-up, it's not going to be a problem. What you wouldn't want to see now is a lot of warm weather that would stimulate more bud growth with new leaves coming onto the plant. We definitely don't want an extended Indian summer for that tree. If you did get one, you might see some new growth initiation, and that would be bad news because it would not get a chance to harden off before freeze-up. Whatever you do, don't let any fertilizer near this tree, not even if the lawn is getting a fall fertilizing. If the tree needs pruning because of damage from the storm, trim off any broken branches that may pose a danger. Other than that, make sure it goes into dormancy now and loses its leaves. February is a very good time to do any other pruning you might want to do while the tree is in a totally dormant state. The plus of pruning while it is dormant is that the spores are not as active so you run much less risk of any infection that might be caused by pruning. If you miss that window, you can certainly prune before the blossoms are due to come out next spring, but be sure to do it before the buds start to swell. The advantage of taking the material off while the tree is dormant is that the tree won't have to waste energy next spring swelling the buds or leaves you are going to cut off anyway and it can direct that energy elsewhere.

Late Summer Deals on Perennials

I've noticed a lot of garden centres have deals on perennials and for that matter, shrubs and small trees, toward the end of August.

Is this too late to get these planted and well established before winter? It's very tempting to take advantage of these deals but they would be no bargain if everything is dead come next spring.

If you have space in the garden, buy them and plant them quickly. The sooner they get in the ground the better. You want to maximize the time they will have to establish themselves before going into the winter. With potted material, as opposed to transplants, you don't have to worry about whether you have a whole root system intact; it's all there. It's just a matter of getting those roots to spread out and making sure that the plant or tree is going to be stable throughout the winter. Be sure to water them well when you put them in. With the perennial plants, do try to loosen up the root ball a little because if they have been sitting in pots since last spring, or in many cases, even longer, the roots will tend to wrap around and will continue this growth pattern if they are not loosened up and headed away from that tight root ball. Other than that, if the plants are healthy when they go in and have sufficient time to get established before winter, they should do just fine.

SEPTEMBER

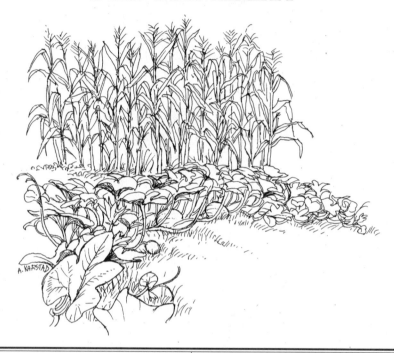

A. KARSTAD

Preserving Jack in the Pulpit

This year one of our Jacks in the Pulpit produced a cone of red berries. Can we preserve them over the winter and plant them in the spring?

Yes, but there is a better technique you can try. As soon as they are dry or ripe, clear an area in your garden right around the location where your Jacks in the Pulpit are coming up, scratch into the soil to about the depth of the seed itself, put them into the soil, cover them back over and mark them. Be sure to put something over the top so the squirrels and mice don't eat the seeds – wire mesh is ideal. They will germinate better here than they would indoors. Lift the mesh in the spring as your new seedlings come up. It's best to label them when you plant because the seedlings don't necessarily look like the parent plant right off the bat. As they establish you can lift them carefully from that location with a good clump of soil and spread them out.

Cutting Back Flowering Brugmansia

I have a Brugmansia that was out on the deck all summer and now it is flowering. When can I cut this back and how far can I go?

If your Brugmansia is flowering at this point just enjoy it. As it continues to flower and as the light levels drop toward the end of the summer, you are going to see more yellowing of the foliage and a general deterioration. That is the ideal time to go ahead and do the cutting. Make sure you leave a minimum of 3 or 4 nodes up from ground level if you decide to cut it back that far, maybe 6-8 inches from the ground. If you have a decent structure to the plant right now, just trimming the branches back to within an inch of the main stem as close as possible to the last node may be enough. Do leave the node on there because that is the point at which it will start growing again. Don't forget to keep it in a good high light situation when you bring it in. Let it dry down between waterings and if it is in a cool, bright room, that could take a fairly long time. As the plant starts to regenerate, new buds will start to form. It only flowers after it has started to develop the side buds but you won't see any active, vigorous growth there until the end of February when the light starts to pick up.

Preparing Bulb Beds with a Clay Base

I made a new bed for bulbs recently by putting down about 8 inches of triple mix soil over a clay base. I planted a variety of bulbs in there and then suddenly it started raining very heavily this week. Now I have a whole patch of water sitting right on top of the triple mix. Is there any way to prevent this?

The water will seep down through the soil very slowly. Soil mechanics are such that no soil will pass moisture from itself to another type of soil below it until that first layer has become completely saturated. Only when your triple mix layer becomes completely waterlogged can it pass moisture on to the clay, and clay being clay it doesn't absorb water well, so the soil stays soaking wet. A more feasible arrangement would have been to put down a layer of triple mix 1-2 inches deep and then mix that in with the clay, then add a bit more soil and mix again, a bit more soil and mix and so on, so you that you have a fairly deep layer of the two soil types combined. That being said, you are still going to have that hardpan clay underneath there at some point. Hopefully not all the rain you get will be as heavy as last week's, but what you want to do with that bed is to start to slope it. You have to grade the top of it slightly downward so water doesn't collect on the top and sit there. You don't want a steep slope either because you do want a bit of moisture to stay and penetrate that area. If you can establish a slight angle to direct the water away and toward a tree for example, that would be ideal. At this point you could develop the slope by adding more triple mix to the bed but be aware that you may have put in some bulbs that want to be shallow. You don't want to be putting 2, 3, or 4 more inches of soil on top of those, so there may be some wisdom in waiting until they bloom and transplanting them before you increase the grade. Over time you will get some breaking down of the clay underneath but this is a very long process. Composting into that soil annually will help, but you have got such a depth of soil there now above the clay that this is not likely to happen any time soon.

Pine Pruning

There is a stand of White Pines in an open area on the north face of our home and I find them very unkempt and wild looking. They are all about 16-20 feet tall, so they provide a wonderful wind barrier in the winter. Is it worth trying to trim them or should we go ahead and replace them with something that looks a little more presentable?

Yes, you can trim White Pines to shape them up. In this case, it's going to be a matter of trimming off some of the tip growth so the trees will fill out in the centre. They respond to pruning in the same way most plants do in that they will initially put out more growth to compensate for what has been taken off. If you are counting on these for a wind break during the winter months, wait to prune them first thing in the spring before the buds start to swell and the new candles start shooting out on the branches. It's best to trim them early so the tree doesn't waste energy producing all that new growth which you are then going to come along and trim off. Prune before they come out of dormancy – that way all the new growth that comes in will be where you want it and this will help with the process of filling out the trees. It is just a matter of giving them a bit of shape and structure as you are going. Try to develop or maintain a conical shape instead of the scraggly form they can take if left on their own. Restrict your pruning to a maximum of 25% of the volume of each tree's crown per year. This will avoid any undue stress on the tree that would result from excessive loss of photosynthesizing or food-producing foliage. This restriction may mean you'll accomplish the re-shaping over the period of a few years, but produces better results in the long run.

Gnawed Beets

When I pulled up my beets, they were gnawed both above the ground and underneath. I also noticed red ants everywhere. Is it possible that the ants are eating my beets? If not, why would there be so many in the area?

The ants will forage and eat wherever they can find as a food source and in this case, it may be your beets. Once the beets have been gnawed on by anything, enough sugar would be exposed to attract the ants, but it is unlikely the ants caused the main problem. There may be slugs or grubs in the soil. If they look like they have been chewed on, this might be field mice, chipmunks, squirrels, rabbits, or even deer. The fact that they have been eaten in the ground as well might suggest moles, but more than

likely, it is field mice. To get rid of the field mice, or voles, as they're called, you could try castor oil. Put a tablespoon of castor oil in a solution of 40-parts water to 1-part soap and spray it along the edges of the beets, but be sure that you rinse the beets before you eat them or you may get some of that taste. Planting castor beans around the edge of your garden can also help discourage the rodents. Likewise, a sprinkling of blood meal can help to deter all of these vegetarian pests, but the smell goes away quickly with rain or watering and will need to be reapplied regularly to maintain the effect of the scent.

Garlic Review

Would you please give us a review of all aspects of garlic planting: bud selection, when to plant, how deep, how far apart, what soil, compost, mulch and how to properly store for winter and harvesting?

One trick to keep in mind when harvesting garlic to avoid the frustration of breaking off the stems is to use a fork when you are pulling it out of the ground. Once you have it harvested, hang the stalks to dry for 4-5 days in a warm place with good air circulation. Shake off any loose soil and skin and then continue the drying for another 2-4 weeks. Once that's completed, store the cloves in a dry area. A temperature range of 2-4° celsius is ideal, but you don't want them to freeze. In terms of bud selection, there is no hard and fast rule. I will usually take some of the nice big ones and get those planted up so that I'll have good, strong plants coming along next year. Like any of the spring flowering bulbs if you plant smaller bulbs, you will get smaller plants and harvest smaller bulbs the next year. These smaller ones take longer to get established and come along but they will still be productive, so yes, you can plant some of the smaller cloves off of the original bulbs. If you plant some larger ones and some smaller ones, you will have a greater variety and a more staggered harvest. It is best to plant garlic in full sun in a well-drained soil and well worthwhile to incorporate a quantity of organic matter into that soil so that it holds the moisture, but you do not want a heavy, wet soil. It should be reasonably well-drained with the capacity to hold moisture when you do water. Watering should be done when the soil 5 centimetres deep is barely moist. Keep the plants uniformly moist until the tops begin to die, then stop watering to allow the bulbs to mature. In terms of spacing the buds, a minimum of 6 inch-

es between the plants in the row is best in a home garden situation. If you are producing them commercially, you may want to squeeze a few more into the rows. Plant the bulbs 5 centimetres deep making sure that you have at least 2½ centimetres of soil over the tips. Garlic should be planted by late August. If you don't get them in until later in the fall, I would recommend putting a heavy mulch over them to keep as much heat in the soil for as long as possible. That will help ensure that the root systems will get well established before freeze-up. The better established those roots get, the better the plants will do in the long run. Even if you do get them in earlier, a covering of 5-10 centimetres of mulch will provide some extra protection and moisture retention in the soil next year. In the spring, side-dress your garlic with compost or blood meal and then replace the mulch up to the edge of the bulbs. I have also successfully planted leftover stored bulbs in early spring with reasonably good results.

Over-wintering Angel Wing Begonia

I have a potted Angel Wing Begonia outside that is 4 feet high and about as wide. What kind of root system does it have? Is it fibrous? Can I cut it back to just an inch or two above ground level. What can I do with it to keep it over the winter?

Angel Wing Begonias have been around for a while, however I believe this one might be a new introduction. You may have a tuber in there. You can cut it back but I would give it a little more than 1-2 inches. Do your cutting down to a node and leave the node intact on the plant. I would take a few tip cuttings from it as well. They will root up in damp sand or even in water. Remove the bottom few leaves that would be in the water and take some English Ivy or some cuttings from a willow and put that in the water with them. The auxins that encourage rooting are produced quite freely in both the willow and the English Ivy. Since they are water soluble, they will be picked up by the begonias and will stimulate the rooting. When you cut it back, you will probably be able to scrape back a bit of the soil from the base of the stem. See if it is coming from a tuber or if you are into fibrous roots, in which case your cuttings will be quite important if you want more of this plant. The original plant that you cut back and brought inside to grow on through the winter should come back with many more side shoots and be even bushier the next year.

Bitter Cukes

Why would our cucumbers be so bitter? Could it be due to a lack of rain?

Yes, the cucumbers would become bitter with a lack of rain. Mulch around the base to hold more moisture in and ensure you keep up the watering. Well-composted manure will feed the plants as well as help to retain the moisture in the soil. Be sure to let them mature. If you are taking them off too young, especially when you've had dry conditions, they will be bitter. If you have already picked them and they turn out to be bitter, one solution is to try pickling them. When you soak them, most of the flavour disappears into the vinegar and brine solution so the bitterness will not be a factor.

Encouraging Chrysanthemums

How do you get chrysanthemums to flower in the garden? My experience has been that by the time they are ready to bloom, it is too late in the season.

That will pretty much always be the case unless you are in a position to start controlling the light levels affecting your outdoor plants. The interesting thing with chrysanthemums is that they tend to flower earlier in a summer when it has been particularly cloudy or rainy through the month of August. What you are seeing is the plant's reaction to the reduced light levels which trigger it to set flower buds. If you are planting early in the season, pinching them back gives you a much bushier plant and therefore the potential for more bud set. If they are in a location that gets 10-12 hours of light instead of full sunlight all day, they will trigger earlier just by virtue of being partially shaded in the afternoon or not getting sun until later in the morning. The other controlling factor is whether or not they are a vigorous hearty mum. If you are using mums that were produced as house plants, these varieties do not always react as well in a garden setting in our climate.

Diminished Harvest

We have four Concord Grape vines growing in our yard and last year we built a trellis and placed these vines over it. Everything was growing along very well over the summer. The whole trellis was covered and we had lots of grapes. Then all of a sudden, they started dropping. We've lost more than half the grapes and I can't figure out why. Have you any idea what might be happening?

It is probably just moisture stress. They very likely were drying out and if there is a lack of water, the first thing the plant will abort is the fruit. The best solution would be to try to amend your soil with compost so it retains moisture a little better. This is the case regardless of whether the soil is sandy or clay-based. In both cases, organic matter is going to make the greatest difference. Mulching around the base of the vines would also be a plus. And water. On a clay-type soil, that is going to mean, long slow waterings. Make sure they are getting the equivalent of about an inch of water over the area per week. If you can give them a couple of inches, they are going to be that much happier, especially in a hot, dry summer. A sandy soil may require a daily watering, depending on how hot and dry the weather is. The plants were obviously flowering well to produce that abundance of fruit initially, so if you can amend the soil, get some mulch on top and water as required, you should get a full harvest from your vines.

Transplanting Dwarf Apples

Our two dwarf apple trees have been in their present location for 3 years and we are getting lots of

233

buds and flowers but no fruit. I want to move them this fall, or would it be better to wait until the spring?

I would let your trees go through the winter where they are and then first thing in the spring, as soon as the soil is workable, move them. You can prepare the new holes for them in the fall and get the trees ready with a bit of root pruning. That would entail driving a spade the full depth of the blade at about the drip line of the tree, and then skipping the width of the spade and driving it in again. Do that for the entire circumference of the tree. What this will do is cut off the exterior roots and stimulate new growth within the pruned area closer to the base. That new growth will be part of each root ball that will be lifted out when you move the trees to their new location in the spring. You will also have that much less root to cut when you go to transplant. Do put a high-phosphate fertilizer into the hole – something like a rock phosphate, super phosphate or bone meal will do quite nicely, or you can use some other fertilizer with a high middle number. Mix it in well with some organic matter and soak it all thoroughly. You want to make sure these trees don't dry out next spring because they are going to be pushing all of

their buds very shortly after they are transplanted and they can't do the bud push without having moisture available. You are going to have to commit yourself to ensuring they have enough moisture for the first few months of the season as they start flushing their buds and getting themselves established. Mulch the soil surface well – starting a few inches away from the trunk out to at least 6 inches past the drip line or branch tips – to help keep that soil cooler and moist throughout the growing season. Once you get them past that initial stage, they should be fine.

Danger of Double Crowns

My Colorado Blue Spruce is only about 5 feet tall but it has started to grow two shoots at the top, each of which is about 1½ feet long. Should I trim one of those points off?

Yes, you definitely do want to prune one of those leaders and the sooner the better. Cut the thinner of the two, the one that looks a little weaker than the other, as close as possible to the point where they split. Clean cut it so that it will heal over and give you a single head. Otherwise you will end up with two heads on the tree forever and that is inherently a weakness. If there is a problem with a heavy snow load, a double head would be susceptible to breakage at that point, whereas if you cut it off and it eventually heals over, the wound will be completely incorporated into the developing trunk as the tree grows and it would not be susceptible to having the two heads pulled apart and possibly breaking off one or both sides.

Mites in Trees

There are three hackberry trees in my backyard which appear to be infected with some type of mite. There are 1–1½ centimetre galls on the underside of the leaves. What should I do?

The best thing to do this fall is to make sure you clean up all of the debris around the base of the plant so that you eliminate any eggs that have been laid ready to infest the tree again next year. Next spring, once the temperature rises to about 10° celsius during the day and before the buds start to swell, treat your trees with a dormant oil application. Start early in the morning and spray over the entire tree trunk from the bottom up, on the undersides of the branches, into all of the crotches and crevices and then spray all of the branches to the point of runoff. This kills both active adults and the dormant eggs which get smothered by the oil coating before the tree comes out of its dormancy. Next summer, if you are still noticing mites, a soap and water solution will give you very effective control but be sure to wait until all the leaves have matured to avoid any possible burning of the new foliage. Mix a solution of 40-parts water to 1-part soap, spray it over the whole tree from the bottom up, do the undersides and be sure you get the crotches as well because that is where the insects are going to be hiding. Once the tree has been completely coated with the soap and water solution, leave in on for 10-15 minutes and then rinse everything with clear water.

Poor Showing on a Thunbergia

All I got on my thunbergia this summer was about 3 blooms. I feed it with 10-52-10 or 15-30-15 and it gets lots of sun so I'm wondering why I got so few blooms? I'm also not sure what I should do with it in the wintertime?

Knock off the fertilizer. Too much food, too much nitrogen available will be at the expense of the flowers. No more feeding it, give it a little trim back in the fall and then bring it in for the winter. Put it into the brightest, sunniest window you have without fertilizing it, leave it in the pot in that good sunny spot and you will probably find that you get a great succession of flowers right up until early or mid November. It may even go straight through Christmas. When the flowering does stop, trim back the stems by up to 50% and water only as needed to keep the soil moist. As the light levels increase in mid to late February new growth will start to appear on the plant as well. Increase the watering as needed and fertilize at half the recommended rate once a month until it goes out again for the summer.

Unproductive Cucumber Plants

This year we grew hothouse tomato and cucumber plants and there were lots of blossoms on both early on. We had them in two patches about 20 feet apart and although we ended up with lots of tomatoes, we have no cucumbers. Have you any explanation for this?

This is usually an insect problem, in that you want lots of bees and wasps and spiders attracted to the cucumber flowers to pollinate them. I have found it particularly helpful to include a couple of marigolds along the rows, or at least on either end and in the centre with the cucumbers. I have also grown the marigolds up on a fence just to take less space, but the critical thing is to get the cucumber plants pollinated. Those flowers were obviously not attractive enough to the bees. Having the tomatoes right next to the cucumbers should not be a problem in itself, unless the tomatoes were flowering heavily at the same time and provided just that much more of an attraction. Even then, the bees should be moving over naturally to any other pollen source available. Next year, if you see that things aren't coming along early in the season, you can hand pollinate. To do that, go out with a feather or a cotton swab to collect the pollen and transfer it from flower to flower. Another thing I would suggest, since both your tomatoes and cucumbers will wind pollinate successfully, is that they should be located in an exposed area where the wind is not obstructed by anything. You might also find it helpful to grow your cucumbers on supports which exposes a bit more surface area and saves ground space. The cucumbers tend to stay a lot cleaner and you don't get slug damage on them. If you do decide to grow them on supports, one thing I would suggest is to plant some pole beans next to and in among the cucumbers. In your case this year, something impeded pollination, so mixing in different plant material would certainly be worthwhile. Add in some flowering plants, borage, dill, marigolds, and maybe even some chives. Get other material flowering more prolifically so that more pollinators will be attracted to the area and you will have a much better chance of success.

Large Tree Fungus

I have a wonderful 25-year-old Silver Maple that provides tremendous shade to our house in the summer but that has developed a really big fungus in what is left of a hollow on the main stem where a branch has been cut. I have taken the fungus away but it grows back quickly. Should I worry about this and if so, what should I do?

I would get an arborist in to take a look. The fungus that you are seeing is the fruiting body of mycelia that are inside feeding on decaying wood. The fact that you are getting a fruiting body says there is a lot of decaying wood in there. It probably needs to be opened and some of that rotted heartwood taken out so that there is good air penetration and drainage from the cavity that has formed inside. An arborist will also be able to recommend what

sort of cabling or bracing the tree may need to keep it stable. You don't want to lose this tree. It is a vigorous grower and is doing an awful lot both in terms of your landscape and the shading it provides through the summer, so definitely get a professional in to have a look at it. If the outer layers on the tree are solid and still intact, the tree will be able to recover from this problem. We can help it by slowing down or stopping the decaying process – by draining any water out and by increasing the air circulation. Once that is done, the tree can continue to grow on without any danger of weakness or collapse. The strength and structure of the tree is actually coming from the live cambium layer on the outside, and that keeps building outward as the tree grows. Think of a coral reef that is continually building on itself. Even if the inside is experiencing some localized decay, as long as the shell around the outside is intact it should be fine, but it does need a professional to take a look at it and make an assessment. I generally recommend that you get two opinions and two quotes on the work before making decisions to proceed with any proposed treatments or solutions. Don't hesitate to ask for references from other customers or examples of work done by the professional arborists. It is, after all, your money and you want some assurance of value before you spend it!

Gusto Gone from Grasses

Our 4-year-old Northern Pampas Grass grew to 12 feet and gave us a spectacular show two summers ago, but this past summer we got nothing more than a couple of 2-3 foot green shoots. We were so disappointed. It is in a garden that gets full sun most of the day, so light can't be the issue. Can you explain what might be happening?

The use of ornamental grasses has really taken off over the last couple of decades and that's largely because of the spectacular showings many of them give, as well as the number of varieties that have become available. Pampas Grass is from Argentina and starts growing later in the year, which means it flowers later in the summer. It bursts into growth just around the time your spring flowering bulbs and early season perennials are dying out. The new growth of the Pampas Grass fills in the voids quite nicely and can help to cover up the dying foliage of the early season plants. Because it prefers a warmer climate than ours, it will not be as rampant here, so it is easier to contain and control. A warm sunny location is essential and most of the trouble you run into with them stems from the fact that these plants are sensitive to extreme cold and should have their crowns protected during the winter. Mulch liberally with 4-6 inches of straw or leaves in the late fall and remove it the following spring. Although the Pampas can tolerate drier conditions, they won't reach their full potential in terms of size, height and seed head production unless they have regular, thorough waterings, so maintaining the moisture level is essential for that spectacular growth.

Cana Keep This Plant Over Winter?

I bought this plant called a new Cana Tropicana, variation "Fusion". I originally got it for the foliage but then it surprised me with fantastic flowers. I planted it in a half barrel and it did beautifully. Now I'm wondering if it could be over-wintered, and if so, how you would do it.

Yes, you most definitely can keep these over winter. Don't lose this one. You want to bring it back because undoubtedly you are going to have a larger tuber next year which means more shoots. You may have to split it but wait to see what happens over the winter. These have wonderful flowers and can sit in water quite easily. People haven't really discovered the Canas yet. At a pond side or as a shallow water plant in a garden pond or even just a damp area, this is an ideal plant because they love lots of moisture. What you want to do now is keep it growing and photosynthesizing as long as possible to store as much energy as it can. The first frost is going to knock it back and at that point, cut off the foliage, lift the tuber out of the barrel and let it dry out in the sun for a day or so. Don't worry about taking any of the soil off it. It's best to let it dry on the tuber. Once everything has dried, the easiest storage is either in dry peat moss or in vermiculite. Take a plastic bag, put in a couple of inches of vermiculite or peat at the bottom, put in the tuber and then cover it over with a good quantity of that material. Store it in a dark, cool location. A temperature just above freezing is ideal. Come the end of February or early March, you can pot it up, water it well and get it going inside. Make sure that it gets good regular waterings and a light feeding is certainly worthwhile. Later in the season you can either transplant it back into your half-barrel, making sure you keep an intact root system, or leave it in its pot.

Water it accordingly. Manure tea works beautifully for these plants and you should also put a good quantity of compost in the soil when you plant it. There are a lot of different varieties of Canas out there, including much shorter ones, and a full range of flower colours and coloured foliage. I've seen some that were actually potted up in water with an inch or two of pea gravel over the surface of the soil to hold it in the pot and keep the soil from staining the water too much. They were plunked right into the edge of the pond and looked beautiful.

Fully Girdled Tree

I live at the edge of a wood and there is an oak tree with a trunk about 8 inches in diameter on my property that porcupines have girdled almost all the way up to the top. They went up about 8 feet, stripped off the bark all the way around, skipped about 18 inches and then went the rest of the way to the top. Is there anything that I can do?

Everything on the tree above that first girdling is finished. There is no sense even trying to do any grafting or building on that, especially at that kind of height because it is going to be too weak for anything to take after being stripped out that extensively. There is really no hope of saving anything above that point. So what you are going to be faced with is an oak that now tops off at 8 feet. I'm assuming there are lateral branches below that and some of them will start bending skyward, which may take a while, or they may decide not to and just put up some shoots from the top side of the uppermost branches that are left. Your best approach at this point would be to remove any of the branches above the section that has been girdled. Cut them off in small pieces so they come down safely, then start bringing the trunk down, stop-

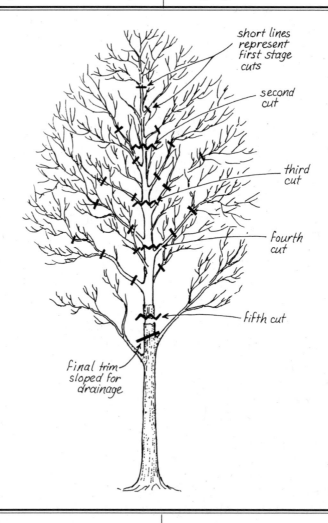

short lines represent first stage cuts

second cut

third cut

fourth cut

fifth cut

Final trim sloped for drainage

ping maybe 6-8 inches above where you want your final cut. Then, do a last careful cut by hand. Clean cut around the edge of the trunk through to the heartwood with a very sharp knife and on a slight downward angle so that any water that hits it is going to run off to the side and down. You will be taking off that last small height of wood without all the extra weight above it, so it's not going to tear any of the bark down the trunk. Once that's done, the tree will callus over and start to seal itself off. With that done, the oak that you now have with an 8-inch diameter base can continue growing and developing. It will never be a magnificent looking specimen in terms of its original form, but if all goes well you should end up with an aesthetically pleasing and well-established oak at the edge of your property.

Divided Over Clivias

I have a couple of pots of very healthy clivias that are desperately root bound. I was just about to bring them in from the deck to start drying them off for the year and I wonder if this is the time to divide them or do I wait until spring?

As long as you're feeling up to the task, fall would be a good time to get going on them. Knock them out of the pots and take the garden hose to them. Flush away all the soil from around that root system and you should see some pretty clear indication of where they can be divided. Once you've split them, re-pot them into new pots that are large enough to give a minimum of an inch on all sides around the root system and preferably a couple of inches if you want them to develop a bit more. Soak them thoroughly and then leave them outside until there is a danger of frost. The cool nights won't harm them at all and the extra bit of light during the day is certainly going to help them get re-established. Make sure you let them dry down between waterings while they are outside. If you can get them into morning sunlight with an east facing exposure, or mottled sunlight throughout the day, there will be a little less stress on them. Let them re-establish outside initially and then bring them in and put them into a cool spot. They don't have to dry right down through the winter. In fact, if you cool them off and slow them down, you will often get another set of flower buds showing up sometime in December through to early February. At that point you can bring them out, give them more light and water, enjoy them and once the flowering is done, put them back into those slightly cooler conditions. That way you will get another flowering through the summer when they go back out next year.

Hardy Holly

I received a 4-inch holly plant last Christmas and it survived through to the spring, at which time I planted it in the garden. What do I need to do to see it through the winter?

The development of a winter hardy holly is one of those horticultural success stories. Some amateur gardeners in the New England states selected out and cultivated a strain of holly plant that has proven to be able to withstand winter conditions. Not all of the hollies that are sold as Christmas plants are winter hardy in our area however, so err on the side of safety and give it winter protection. Just before winter build a cone around the plant with evergreen boughs. Mulch over it with dry leaves. Oak leaves are particularly good for this because when they dry they stay intact, curl up and hold air in, all of which provides better insulation and protection around the plant. If you are dealing with anything other than oak leaves, alternate the layers of leaves with evergreen boughs – other leaves, such as those from the Norway Maple will mat down as they get wet and you will get a very heavy, thick, clumpy mass around the plant that can do more harm than good. The objective here is to get an insulating layer around the plant to bring it through the worst of winter and provide some protection.

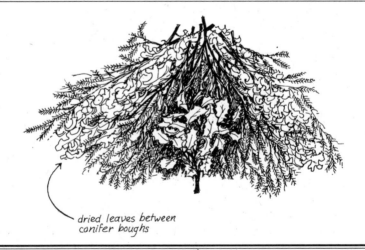

dried leaves between
conifer boughs

The other thing you can do to help is to add snow around the plant after a fresh snowfall to give it that much more protection. With adequate coverage, it should come through the winter with flying colours.

Stow-a-ways

We bring some of our summer flowers and herbs indoors for the winter and every year we seem to bring in an assortment of ants or wood bugs or earwigs as well. Is there anything we can do to cut down or eliminate this problem?

There are a few things that you can do that will help. First, set all of your plants on a solid, dry surface and turn them over, being careful to support the plant so it doesn't fall out. What you normally see when you do this is an open hole in the base if it's a clay pot, or several holes if the pots are plastic. It is possible that these openings have been used as an entrance and exit for visitors. Rinse the pot off with water to eliminate any woodlice or earwigs that might be hiding on the bottom. After giving the plant a good watering, knock the pots off the plants and inspect the root balls all around the sides and bottom. You should have a spray bottle filled with a 1:40 soap and water solution handy in the event you see something moving that you would rather leave outside. If you need to add more soil to the pot because some of it has been evacuated by the 'visitors', put a bit in the base before you sit the root ball back in. With a good inspection and a bit of cleanup, you should be able to get those plants indoors without bringing anyone else along.

Cranberry Pruning

My 6-year-old High Bush Cranberry is about 9 or 10 feet tall and growing well but it doesn't produce many flowers or berries. Should I be pruning it back or fertilizing it? What is the best time to prune it?

Generally, the best time to prune a cranberry is right after flowering, unless you want to keep the berries on for the birds. That usually means leaving them on the bush into the winter, if they last that long. If the birds clean them off earlier you can certainly trim them back in the fall. If not, first thing in the spring is fine. In terms of production, they need high light. Keeping the soil moist, adding compost and mulching over the surface will make all the difference in the world. A light feeding could be done, but I wouldn't even bother. These ones stand up beautifully on their own as long as they are getting enough nutrient in the soil. Composting and mulching over the surface should be sufficient as long as they are in high light.

Lime-soaked Red Oak

Last spring, I treated my apple tree with liquid lime sulfur for over-wintering insects. While I was at it, I also sprayed my 9-foot Red Oak tree. I thought I had killed it because no leaves came out. Later in the year, it put out new sprouts all the way up the trunk to the branches, but still no leaves. I don't know if the tree is finished or if there is anything I can do about it.

Let the oak grow on at this point. Lime sulfur isn't recommended for oaks, as is clearly indicated on the product label, and what probably happened is that you sprayed it at just the wrong time when the buds where starting to swell. It likely burned off all those young buds, so you killed them back, and the oak is now putting what energy it has left into dormant buds or secondary buds along the main stem. The tree has had a bit of a setback but with the size it is, it certainly has time to shape up into a fine specimen. You may eventually look at doing a bit of specific pruning to get the kind of shape you want.

With a lot of sucker growth like you have, it doesn't always develop into a nicely branched specimen, but I wouldn't be too concerned about that for a couple of years yet. Let it grow on. If you can get half inch or so of compost around the base and out a couple of feet over the soil surface, and then put some mulch on top of that to ease any moisture stress, that would be a plus.

Love Me Tender

I have a Yellow Flax Lily, Linum floridanum I think is the name. Apparently it falls into a category called "tender perennial". How should I keep it over the winter?

This Yellow Flax is native to moist or dry woods on the coastal plain from about south eastern Virginia to Florida. It is also grown in Louisiana and north in the Mississippi Valley as far as southern Illinois. Obviously, with that heritage it is going to be "tender" anywhere in the northern regions, but it can survive in the garden in the extreme southwestern parts of Ontario or on the west coast and in very sheltered microclimates with heavy winter mulching. That would mean a covering of 10-12 inches or 25-30 centimeters of peat moss or friable compost. A much more reliable technique for over-wintering is to lift the plant and pot it up in mid September. Give it a thorough watering before digging it up and another once it is in the pot. Leave it standing outside where it was growing until it gets a couple of heavy frosts to kill back the foliage on the longest stems. Cut these dead stems off and leave them in the flower bed where there is a chance that any ripe seed will germinate next spring. Put the plant into a cool, bordering on cold, dark location, ideally between 0-10° celsius, and leave it there until the end of February or mid March. Then bring it out into a good bright window and give it a thorough watering. Don't water it again until it starts into active growth and the soil dries down. Water as required thereafter but never supersaturate the soil or let it stand constantly in water. Once the danger of late spring frost has passed, transplant it back into your garden and enjoy!

No Success with Spraying

My three ornamental apple trees seem to be losing their leaves every summer. The leaves curl up and then just fall off. I tried a number of insecticides and this seems to work but it is never really 100% successful. Is there a proper time for spraying the trees?

What you want to do is twofold. First, sanitation. Some-thing that is coming back every year and attacking the tree can do so most easily if it goes through its wintering stage on the fallen leaves, so clean everything up as thoroughly as you can each fall. That material can go into the compost but don't put that compost back around the apple trees unless it has composted for a couple of years. Normally, I say leave it one year but you want that extra time as insurance when dealing with fruit trees, and even then make sure it is well rotted before you use it. The compost has to heat up really well to kill any pathogens. Get everything cleaned up in the fall and then next spring, I would suggest an application of a dormant oil spray. The time to apply it is on a day when the outdoor temperature is above 10° celsius. Try to choose a bright, sunny day so the oil dries on the tree. Do it early in the season before the temperature gets up too high and before any of the buds start to open. There are two reasons for this. First, you don't want to be injuring the buds, and second, as soon as the buds start to swell the insects and the diseases start getting active as well, so you have to catch them before they start moving. Timing is critical. That dormant oil application along with improved sanitation in the fall should take care of your problem.

Cultivating Fresh Litchi

Last summer they were selling fresh litchi in the produce section. If you peel the outside off, the inside is like a cherry with a nut right in the centre. I planted some of those nuts and now have two plants about 8 inches high, but I have absolutely no information about them. I don't know if they are trees or shrubs or vines or what they need or if they will take 40 years before bearing fruit. Do you know anything about these?

I know they are originally from southern China and southeast Asia and are considered a delicacy. I believe it is a tree or a large shrub and will need indoor protection. I am sure that they are not hardy here or somebody would be growing lots more of them. I would expect with that kind of fruit production this is a full-light exposure plant, so put them in a south or a west window, ideally within a foot of the window or right in the window itself, and certainly outside for the summer. You are going to have to keep increasing the pot size as they develop and you may have to pinch the tips at some point to get some lateral branching on them. You can use a soluble fertilizer with them or, if you have some available, add compost to the soil either as a top-dressing or mixed in with the soil when you re-pot them. The organic matter in the compost would certainly give them a more balanced and ongoing feeding. Combine that with a 3-3-3 soluble organic fertilizer. A fish emulsion or seaweed fertilizer would do nicely. Feed them from about mid to end of February until the middle of October. The lower overall metabolism of the plant during the darkest months of the year doesn't require extra fertilizer and this break also ensures that any possible build up of soluble salts in the soil is dissolved and used with the regular waterings. As always, I would suggest that you apply the fertilizer at about half the recommended rate with every fourth or fifth watering and use clear water for all of the waterings in between. I believe a cool, dry period is required to induce flowering, so let the plants dry down a bit more between waterings in the winter months. Once flowers have been produced, make sure to increase both the watering and the ambient temperature.

Starting Birches From Seed

Beavers have destroyed several of my young birches but there are a few adult trees left. Is there a way to collect the seeds and start my own plants so that I can replace the trees that are gone?

You'll want to watch for the seed heads developing on your mature birches and as they ripen and begin to fall you have two options. The first and often the simplest option is to clear any debris away from the area around the base of the tree. This is done strictly to expose the soil surface where some of the seeds will hopefully land. If you can rough-up the soil surface lightly with a straight rake – as opposed to the fan rake you used to clear the debris – you will increase the chances of successful germination that much more. Once the seeds have fallen, sprinkle a light covering of leaf litter or compost about a 1/8-1/4 inch deep over the area in order to maintain high humidity around the seeds. Once the seeds germinate and start to grow, which is usually around mid to late summer, get a hose or sprinkler out to them if you can and water them as needed. This will help improve the success rate of your seedlings. Be sure not to move the seedlings until the following spring. Birch will only transplant well when dug in the spring. As soon as the soil is workable and before they come out of dormancy you should dig the seedlings up, move them to their new location and soak them well. Make sure you keep them well watered and they should come along nicely. Now the second option is to collect the ripened seeds in the fall and sow them in an area that you have already prepared. A light covering of soil or screened compost about 1/8 inch, is sufficient and keep the soil bed moist, but not soaking wet, until the seeds germinate. Once they've germinated, nurse the seedlings along as required and then transplant them the following spring.

Rusting Magnolia

I started a magnolia from seed 3 years ago and it is now about 2 feet tall. It was in a large pot but didn't do very well there so I transplanted it to the garden. Now the leaves have a rust colour on them. When I transplanted it, I made sure that it was well watered and I continue to water it regularly. It has a well-developed root system which I loosened up when it made the move. Have you any idea what is going on?

Loosening the roots around the outside edge was certainly a critical step. There may be a problem with this plant not getting enough moisture into the original root ball, therefore any watering that you do now should be a slow

How to Plant Bulbs

Bulbs are generally planted in early to mid fall. Be sure to have the pointed end of your bulb facing skyward and the flatter, root-producing end facing down. Depending on the year and the timing of the freeze-up, bulbs can usually be planted later into the fall but the outcome is not always as certain. With larger bulbs you'll want 6 inches of soil cover above the bulb to get them through the winter successfully. If it is not possible to get them that deep, you'll need to mulch over top. Mulch is good in any case because it will hold the moisture and the heat in the soil for a little longer, allowing more time for their root system to get established. Smaller bulbs require less soil — a minimum of 3-4 inches over the top should be sufficient, unless you are looking at crocuses, where a scant couple of inches will suffice. Do not expect a uniform flush with the crocuses in the first year because they tend to set their individual timers more precisely as they establish. As a result, the first year tends to be a bit sporadic. All the rest of your bulbs should come along once they are in the ground. A bit of bone meal or bulb fertilizer tossed into the hole to give them a boost when you are planting is worthwhile as well. Make sure the soil is moist and water them in after planting. Then leave them. If you can mark the area, that's usually helpful since most people forget where they have planted by the next spring. If you have not done this with your older bulbs, you may find you are running into some of them when you are planting again this fall. As they appear next spring, mark these established patches as well so you are not digging them up when you are working in the same beds with your annuals and perennials. If squirrels are a problem in your area, try laying down some chicken wire over the beds to provide some protection against them digging and eating or re-locating your bulbs.

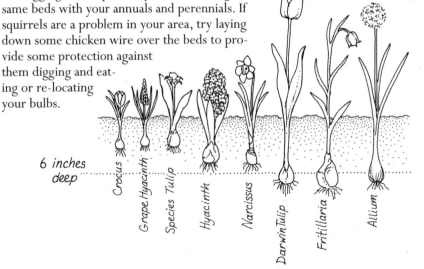

6 inches deep

Crocus

Grape Hyacinth

Species Tulip

Hyacinth

Narcissus

Darwin Tulip

Fritillaria

Allium

trickling of the water. You could use a 5 gallon pail with a hole in the bottom that leaks slowly. Ensure the hole is right next to the trunk of the tree so that it is seeping down through the old and possibly pot-bound root ball to get the moisture to it. Initially, do not rely on the new roots to get out and around. Continue this watering as needed through the fall until freeze-up and it should grow well next spring.

Cure for a Spindly Hibiscus

My 5-year-old hibiscus has absolutely wonderful double peach blooms. I put it out on the patio in the spring and bring it in at the end of the September, but it has gotten spindly. It is about 7 feet high and I feel that it is pot-bound. Is the fall a good time to re-pot it?

If it really is pot-bound, it certainly could be worthwhile to re-pot. The easiest way to do that would be to take it outside, knock it out of the pot, get the garden hose and just flush as much soil off the bottom and the sides of that root ball as you readily can. If it has been in the same pot for the last 5 years those roots are undoubtedly pretty tangled up. Give them a really good blast. Anything on that root ball that is

white is fine. Anything that is brown in the root system, try and flush it right out. Your new potting soil should be mixed with about 25% clean sharp sand. Don't be tempted to pinch that sand from the box along the side of the road because road sand often has salt in it as well and that can be disastrous. You can get a sharp brick sand or sand for a children's play box at a garden centre or even at a hardware store in season. An earthenware pot is very nice for them because it breathes. You don't need a very large pot but if you had one that was about 14 inches, I would certainly go up to that. If you have hollowed out the root system at the bottom of the root ball you may find you need to put a dome of soil in the bottom of the pot, so mound it in the centre and then sit the root ball onto that. Add your soil around the edges and pack it in. Water it extremely well. You are going to find that the sand carries your soilless mix down into the voids in the root ball. Make sure that all those air pockets are well filled and be prepared to add more soil as needed. When you have finished the process, let the plant drain outside. If you get this re-potting done this fall you may want to do a bit of hair cutting on your hibiscus before you bring it in since it is heading into a semi-dormant period anyway. Be careful with the watering. As the light levels start to pick up again towards the end of January to mid February you are going to find that you have all kinds of new growth coming out. If you want a nice bushy head just pinch the tips off the new growth once they develop 2 or 3 sets of new leaves. The plus with the hibiscus is that they flower from new growth. The more new growth you get, the more flowers you will have. If all goes well you should have a pretty good showing on it by the end of May, just in time to put it out again for the summer.

Permission to Attack Azalea

I have an azalea which I haven't done anything to in years and it is badly pot bound – the roots are so tight that I would have to attack it with a knife to get it out. So I just soak it and put it back again. Now it has split the pot. What can I do?

You could attack it with a knife. Even if you could make 3 or 4 incisions around the root ball, equally spaced around it, you could cut through and loosen things up that way. A less drastic alternative would be to take the plant outside and just spray the daylights out of that root ball with the hose. Flush as much soil away from the roots as you can and there will be two benefits. First, because you are using water, you are keeping the root system saturated and moist so you are not going to kill roots off by drying them out. Flushing the soil away also means that the roots are still intact and can be untangled after the fact – as opposed to cutting through them and forcing the plant to callus off and generate new roots. You are going to untangle as much as possible and do any pruning that might be necessary if some are too leggy or too tightly wound together. Then put the plant back into a good clay pot. If you keep your azaleas for a long time, it is well worthwhile. A good light peat-based mix is fine but if you could add some pine needles to that or crumble dried cedar foliage in with the soil to add a bit of acidity, that would be ideal. It will also give you a nice friable mix that drains readily but holds sufficient moisture for them. You have to pay attention to the watering with azaleas because they do not like to stand in water constantly. On the other hand, they do need to have a sufficient amount of moisture in the soil, so it is the balance between air and water in the soil that guarantees their success. With that in mind, keep the soil moist, but never soaking wet.

Fungal Eyesore

Last August our mulberry tree started getting black mouldy spots. The leaves shrivelled and by the end of the season it seemed every leaf on the tree was affected. This year the black mouldy spots were back again by June. We tried taking off the affected leaves, we tried pruning, we tried spraying with a fungicidal spray and as the summer progressed every leaf had them again and the tree looked awful. So my question is: is there anything I can do to prevent this happening next year and can this tree be saved from looking like a total eyesore?

What you want to do this autumn is collect all of the leaves, twigs and branches that fall off the tree and take that litter away from that area and preferably off the property. If it is possible to burn them that is ideal. You may have some Apple Scab in the area which will also attack mulberries, or there is a possibility that it is Black Spot, which comes from roses. The fact is that both of these can come from apple trees or roses or even Mountain Ash if that is around as well, and the spores are fairly readily airborne. Unfortunately an oil spray is not going to give you control for the disease problem you have. What you would have

to look at is a lime sulphur treatment. Better still is a Bordeaux mixture treatment which is a lime/sulphate mixture with copper added. The addition of the copper greatly improves the effectiveness of the solution and was actually discovered by accident when someone mixed the lime/sulphur solution in a copper pot. You can spray with either of these at the time of the outbreak, in the fall and again the next spring. All that being said, the best way to get control of this problem is general sanitation. Remove any dead leaves, dead branches, or fallen material from underneath the tree and keep the site clean. That eliminates one critical stage in the life cycle of the spore. There is probably some other affected specimens around that will continue to transmit it, with it being airborne, but if you can reduce the volume that is in proximity to the tree, the mulberry should be fine.

Pruning Clematis Vines

I always wonder if I should be pruning my clematis vines back in the fall or in the springtime? Mine are mostly the Jackmaniis. What do you recommend?

The Jackmanii, like many of the large flowered hybrids, can be cut right back to ground level.

You can do it in the fall but many books recommend that you don't do it until the spring. I find it doesn't make a huge difference. One of the benefits of waiting until spring is that you have some animation and structure left in the garden throughout the winter. Another is that if they are up on a trellis and if there are feeders around, birds will use them for shelter between trips to that feeder. If you do opt to trim them back in the fall, leave some length on the vine, say 2 feet, as opposed to taking them to the ground. In the spring, you can see what particular vines or branches have been winter-killed a little more easily and cut those ones off. Since the Jackmanii come back from the ground with no problem, they can be cut right back in the fall if that is desired. The others, the "Nelly Moser" for example, don't want to be pruned to ground level. Clematis are divided into 3 main groups when it comes to pruning, which seems complicated, but really isn't. Group "A" are the clematis that flower from growth produced in the previous growing season. These should be pruned right after they flower and then they will flower next year on this year's new growth. Group "B" flower twice in the growing season. The "Nelly Moser" is in this group, flowering on last year's growth early in the spring and then again in the summer on this year's new growth. Weak and winter-killed shoots should be pruned early in the spring, then when growth starts the remaining stems should be cut back to a pair of strong, active buds. Group "C" includes the "Jackmanii" and many of the popular, large-flowered hybrids that flower on the shoots that grow this season. These get pruned back to within a couple of sets of buds of ground level once new growth starts each spring.

Over-wintering Asparagus

I put in a new asparagus bed this spring and it did gloriously all summer. How should I get it ready for winter?

Mulching is certainly worthwhile, especially in the colder regions, in that it is going to eliminate or greatly reduce any freeze-thaw cycle during the winter. Fortunately the roots of your asparagus are down deep enough that they won't be affected by the cold, but the added protection is always welcome. You can leave the fronds on them – the plus of this is that you know exactly where the plants will be shooting from next spring. The fronds will also help collect snow around the base of the plants and that will act as insulation. On the other hand, the 1-2 metre long stems can be unwieldy, snap off in the winter and get a bit messy so you might want to trim them to 8-12 inches from the ground. Leave the stubble and you will know where things are going to come up, as well as ensure there will be some retention of snow around them. If you have some compost ready, you can side-dress around them now. It's helpful to do that every fall so that the organic material is breaking down and working into the soil before winter and also ensures that it will be immediately available to them as a nutrient source the next spring. You can also compost again in the spring if you like and that would give them just that much more nutrient. In the case of asparagus, don't worry too much about piling compost over the crowns since it won't impede the new growth. The spears will emerge right through the top-dressing next spring. If you like your asparagus blanched, pile the compost or mulch just a little higher and then harvest down below that surface next year to find the whitest stems. If you are in doubt about when to start digging into the compost mounds to harvest

those white spears, wait until you see the very first tips start to show through the top of the mounds and you'll know the ones below are ready.

Gladiola Grief

We planted 200 gladiola last year and they came up and were about to flower – then they all died. I was told by a local greenhouse that it was Gladiola Thrips. How can you prevent these?

One of the first lines of defense against thrips is to soak your bulbs in a soap and water solution overnight as soon as you buy them. It won't hurt the gladiola corm at all, but it will kill off any thrips and their eggs along with them. Get them into the ground as quickly as possible after that and that should take care of any early problems. Unfortunately, the story doesn't end there since thrips are airborne and can turn up later. Unlike many of the other insects, these are attracted to the colour blue, as opposed to yellow, so one method of control is to hang blue sticky strips in the garden. The thrips will be attracted to them and get stuck, taking them out of circulation and obviously limiting their ability to reproduce. You can also monitor them this way and know whether you have an infestation on your hands, so this technique is well worthwhile. Thrips are readily killed with the "1-part soap to 40-parts water" solution, however they fly very quickly so you will need to use a fine spray and go over the whole plant several times for this to be effective. Rinse off the solution with clear water within 5 minutes of the application. The earlier you can apply this treatment after you spot the thrips, the better, because these insects often bring a virus along with them that will infect your glads but you also don't want to be spraying the petals of flowers when they are just opening. One last thing to keep in mind: the thrips you had last year may well have carried a virus that over-wintered in that immediate area, so I would recommend changing the planting location of your glads this year and keep moving them every year thereafter. If you had 4 different beds and rotated them through so at least a couple of years would pass between each planting, that would be ideal.

Preserving a Flowering Begonia

I have a very beautiful, very large double begonia – a Tuberous Begonia – outside in a large plastic planter. It is about 4 feet long and about 2½ feet across and it is so gorgeous, I would love to keep it over the winter but have no idea how I could do that. Is this possible or are these really seasonal plants?

As long as you have a good bright south window, keeping this plant over winter shouldn't be a problem. Bring it inside, put it into that window and make sure it is sitting up at window height. That may mean getting it up onto a table or a support but be sure that it is getting all the light that it possibly can. Water it as required. Don't let it dry out completely but make sure it is drying down in between the waterings. Give it a quarter turn every day so you are changing the side of the plant that faces the outside and therefore the direct sun. You decide whether you want that turn to be clockwise or counter-clockwise, just make sure it gets a quarter turn in the same direction every day. If it starts to deteriorate with the lower winter light levels, don't hesitate to trim it back. I find that putting the plant on to a one metre high stool, rather than a table, works quite nicely. The plant can drape over the sides and it is easy to turn the whole stool a quarter rotation a day.

Multi-coloured Marrow

This year I planted Spaghetti Marrow, or Vegetable Marrow, and now I have quite a few of them. It has been a little bit on the chilly side this September so I have already picked them. The odd thing is that on the same vine, one would be green and one would be yellow. Why is that and why didn't they all turn yellow?

It's just a question of giving your melons enough time to ripen. You want to leave them out as long as you can and if there is danger of frost, cover the vines to protect the squash. If there has been a frost and you didn't get any cover on them, the squash leaves get wiped out very quickly. If this happens, you will need to go out the next day and cut everything that hasn't ripened. Store the melons in a dark, dry, warm place but make sure it's not too hot. Normal room temperature is fine. Actually, under the bed was the traditional place to store squash because it was away from any direct heat in the house and it would be dark. Anywhere that would duplicate that environment, like a cupboard, would be fine. Even a brown paper bag will work well for this. The ripe yellow vegetable marrow will generally store better than the un-ripened ones so be especially careful that the green ones stay dry, dark and warm. Obviously, you will want to use the yellow ones first and as the others ripen they should be fine.

Over-wintering Herbs

There is some sage, parsley and thyme outside in pots that I would like to keep over the winter. I don't have any sunny windows so I bought a 4-tube fluorescent grow light and I'm wondering what I have to do to give these herbs the best chance of success?

Fluorescent tubes create a cool light so there is no danger of burning the plants. Get the grow light as close as you can over top of these plants, at a maximum 1-2 inches away. You need that intensity for herbs. If some pots of herbs are much shorter than the others, elevate them on inverted pots to get the crowns at a uniform height. You must also be careful with watering. Water them as required but don't ever keep them sopping wet. The thyme and the sage need to dry down a bit more between waterings than the parsley if they are to keep any intensity in the volatile oils within their leaves, which is where all your flavour comes from. If you end up with beautiful greens but there is no taste to the plants it sort of defeats the purpose. So just water them accordingly. Trim things back from the top so that you are getting good light exposure down through the plants and if they are getting tall, pinch the centre part of the stem off and use those bits when you cook. The ideal approach would be to use the largest stems and tips first and encourage new lateral growth that way. Go easy on the fertilizer. If you have well rotted compost available when you bring in your plants, put a couple of trowels full into a nylon bag or an old nylon stocking, tie it up and let that sit for a couple of weeks in a 2-gallon pail of room temperature water. After that, once every 2-3 weeks water your herbs with half compost "tea" from the pail and half tap water. That will provide all the nutrient that your herbs need. If you replace the amount of liquid you take out of the compost tea pail with room temperature water each time, you should be able to keep a supply going throughout the winter. I would suggest covering it – although it usually isn't a problem indoors, it can start to smell a little heavy. If it gets too rich, bottle the stuff up in any sort of container and put it in the fridge or keep it somewhere cool. The left over com-

post in the bucket can be pitched into the garden or onto the compost pile, depending on the time of year.

A Plague of Grasshoppers

I have about 1000 asparagus plants and in late August I was plagued by grasshoppers. They just flew in and devoured the ferns. Initially there were only a few but then the situation got much worse and I'm worried they will have laid their eggs and when those eggs hatch, the larvae are going to attack the roots. How can I get rid of them?

If the infestation happened in August, at least the plants have had a chance to photosynthesize and store the energy. Putting up lots of bird houses and encouraging as many birds as possible to come around would be helpful. Bluebirds, in particular, would work well here so if you can afford to put up a minimum of 3 bluebird houses, all the better. You should also try to attract tree swallows, which will do an equally good job at insect control. The only problem with tree swallows is that they will not establish their nests within 100 feet of each other, so there is no point in putting up swallow houses any closer than that. If you are putting up 2 houses less than 100 feet apart, one should be for the bluebirds. The more birds, the merrier, because they have a lot of feeding to do and it saves you a great deal of time and effort if they can do some of the cleaning and picking off grasshoppers for you. Purple martins are also an excellent bird to have around but they tend to take their food on the wing as opposed to at ground level so their utility with this problem is limited. The more diverse the bird population you can attract, the greater the chance you are going to have of a more efficient, broad-spectrum insect control.

Mouldy Grape Vine

I am concerned about a sick Concord Grape vine. It is about 8 years old and almost 50 feet long. The upper part of it is exposed to the sun and the other half is in the shade. We have had marvellous harvests from it every year except this past year. It was going fine and then all of a sudden it developed what appears to be a mould or a fungus. It is a whiteish colour and seems to be growing on the surface of the mature fruit and extending onto the stems of the grapes. I don't think I've seen any on the leaves as yet. The fruit shrivelled and some has turned black. They also become small and hard very late in the season. Some seemed to survive but we got only about a tenth of the produc-tion we normally do. Have you any idea how to treat this?

Any time you have a particularly cool, wet summer it provides the ideal conditions for any number of fungi to take hold on grape vines. It's not always bad news. In fact in some Mediterranean countries, there is a botrytis that attacks the grapes late in the season and it is actually sought after because it draws moisture from the fruit leaving a higher sugar content. You get a much sweeter grape from an infected plant than you do from the healthy ones. However, the cool, wet conditions required for that botrytis are detrimental to the plant earlier in the season and this is why you really need to have good air circulation around your vines. Having them up on a trellis or pagoda certainly helps – the leaves get better exposure to the light and all kinds of air circulation. While the leaves dry, they also shade the fruit and the stems underneath and that provides the high moisture conditions necessary for a number of moulds or fungi to start growing on your plant. The result is that the fruit deteriorates too early and you get a significant reduction in the level of production. Pulling or cutting off a handful of leaves around every cluster of grapes in mid to late summer is effective in controlling the problem, but be sure to leave a leaf or two over each bunch to prevent sunscald. You may have to thin out the vine so that you are getting a bit more light and air penetration underneath the support system. However, the development of these fungi is really more dependent on the climatic conditions of a given year. It is always a good idea to thin a little, just to make sure you are getting good air circulation and light penetration. It may prevent this happening again and at the very least, it would give you ripened fruit earlier in the season.

How to Prepare the Soil for Bulbs

Being a farmer I am a little embarrassed to find myself asking a gardening question, but here it goes. I ordered some crocus, tulip and iris bulbs from an online store and they got here but I have never planted bulbs before. I was wondering what the proper way would be to get the soil ready for them.

Not many farmers come in to contact with bulbs, so no need to be embarrassed. With smaller bulbs like the crocus, you are going to need to get them down a couple of inches into the soil in the fall, preferably in a sunny location or one that is going to

be sunny early in the spring. You can actually plant these under deciduous trees or shrubs as long as there is light penetration early in the season. As the trees come into full leaf later on, they will get less light and that's fine, but they do need that period of full sun to get going. In the case of the tulips, you want to make sure that you loosen the soil thoroughly. Amending it with organic matter will be well worth your while on two counts. It feeds the soil, which in turn will feed the bulbs over time, and it also helps create a soil that is loose and friable enough to drain well. No bulbs really like to grow in water. If tulips and daffodil bulbs get wet they rot and you are not going to get any production from them. Corms on the other hand, want a moist soil, but they don't want to be sitting constantly in water. Being a farmer, you probably have ready access to manure. On the whole, that'll make good compost, but make sure it is well rotted and well aged. It needs to have been piled for a minimum of 2 or preferably 3 years – that long is necessary with tulips because fresh cattle manure can often cause or is capable of spreading tulip blight; so avoid it if it is young. The alternative would be to mix fresh manure into the soil in the spring and leave it to rot. Turn it regularly all summer and then plant the bulbs there the following fall. If you are in any doubt about the age, stay away from that manure and use other compost or mix a bit in with the other compost. The potential for burning roots with fresh manure is also fairly strong and it could finish off the entire root system. So if it's well aged, don't hesitate; if it's not, hold off.

Transplanting a Silver Maple

There is a seven-year-old Silver Maple tree that is about 12-14 feet high and 2½ inches round that I would like to take with me when I move. When should I move it and how should I go about doing it? I do have the property I am moving to now so I can move it at anytime.

You can prepare the hole now, remembering that since the tree is 2½ inches in diameter you will need at least a 3-4 foot root ball. Let the maple go into its dormancy this fall and once it is in full dormancy, you can lift it and do the transplanting. Soak it in at the new location and let it come out of dormancy there next spring. The other alternative would be to do it first thing in the

spring before it starts to come out of dormancy, however that is particularly difficult with maples because they become active as soon as the temperature gets up to + 5° celsius and a lot of sap is pumped up into the tree at that point. This is what makes the maple sugar run successful, but in your case, that would be more detrimental for the tree. Do put a little rock phosphate or bone meal into the hole to stimulate root development and ensure that you water it well in the new location. Compost and mulch is always a plus.

Hyacinths Fail to Bloom Again

I keep trying to grow hyacinths in my water garden and only once or twice have I gotten blooms. What do I need to do to get a bloom every year?

If you could start your water hyacinths up a little earlier, that should help. Don't wait until summer to start them growing in the pond; get them going inside in late winter and let them grow on for a few months before they go into the pond. A small tub or large plastic dish filled with water and placed in a good, bright, sunny window will do nicely for this. As the plants start expanding, you will probably see offsets begin to develop; these can be separated and put out later as another grouping. If you can organize all this in the higher light of late February, the plants will be that much more mature by spring and will flower more quickly when they are put out in the pond in mid to late May.

OCTOBER

A. KARSTAD

Over-wintering Explorer Roses

I am a new rose gardener and I have a question about over-wintering roses. I have a David Austin shrub rose and an Explorer climber. What should I do to get them ready for the cold weather?

Both of these roses should be hardy and go through the winter without too much of a problem. Generally speaking, I recommend that people not prune their roses until the spring. The reason is you don't know what may be winter-killed and you will inevitably experience some damage even with the hardy roses that you are growing. Imagine that you have 5 stems growing on one of your rose bushes and 2 of them get killed in the winter. Come spring you know which 3 stems you'll keep for that year. On the other hand, if you prune them back in the fall and leave 3 stems and 2 of them get killed over the winter, you are left with only 1 stem. So to increase your odds, do the pruning in the spring. It is also worthwhile to get a good heavy mulch over the soil in the fall to protect the root system. If you can mound it up around the plants and go a foot or two up the stems, and the higher the better, it gives that much more protection. Having said this, your best defense against winter when it comes to roses actually happens at the time that you are planting. If you can ensure that the graft point or bud union is at least 4-6 inches below the surface of the soil, then even if the entire plant dies back to soil level during winter, what will rejuvenate in the spring is the 4-6 inches of grafted material. If the new growth comes directly from the root system, it isn't going to give you the rose you expect but rather one from the original root stock and it won't bear any resemblance to the grafted plant you purchased.

Propagating Butternuts

My butternut tree is beautiful but it is definitely growing in the wrong place. It's too near the garage and I think that the roots are compacted, so even if I were to leave it, it would likely die soon anyway. I have a few nuts but most of them went to the squirrels. Is there any way that I can propagate this tree because it is too big to transplant and I may soon need to take it down?

Competing with the squirrels can certainly be a problem, but there is also the issue of canker in the Black Walnuts, and more in the butternuts. If you can get some of the nuts from the tree, they do propagate pretty well. What you want to do is get those nuts into a cage in the ground so that the squirrels can't get them out or won't take them out inadvertently as they look around for the ones that they have buried. It is helpful if you can take off the outer hull to start with and you will get to the very hard shelled walnut or butternut inside. You'll want to run that shell back and forth over something fairly rough. A rasp works most effectively but if you don't have one, even the concrete curb can be used to grind it down somewhat. You don't want to go all the way through that outer shell. This is a very heavily ridged nut so grind it down just to the point where it is getting to be quite smooth. If you do this on just one area of the shell, that will be enough. What you want to do is weaken that nut shell sufficiently so that the water will be imbibed or drawn in there and break that outer layer down more quickly. As the seed starts to germinate it will slowly do the rest but it needs a hand for the water to penetrate it and start the process. Once you've got an area smoothed out, plant it down to its own depth into the soil. I would try about half a dozen of them spaced about 6-8 inches apart in a grid. Cover over the whole thing with half inch chicken wire with the sides bent down at least an inch or two into the soil and put something like old bricks around the edges to keep it in place. It may take a couple of years for them to germinate, but when they do, they will shoot up first thing in the spring and you will need to lift up that wire screen. Generally the danger of the squirrels coming along and taking the nuts will have passed, but you can't always count on it, so just raise the screen with some supports underneath and wrap the sides. When the plants get to be 2-3 inches high, take off the protection. Now is the time to transplant. Dig a full spade depth deep down beside the individual nuts and lift up. You are going to find a big tap root there and you want to transplant it with that tap root intact. Leaving enough space in between the nuts when you first plant them makes it easy to get a trowel or a small spade down there now. The root will probably be 3 times the length of the shoot because it has developed first and got well established. Another alternative is to plant the nuts in pots, one nut per pot, and sink the pots completely into the soil and again, do cover them over. Use a 6 inch diameter full depth pot as a minimum for this procedure to ensure adequate space for that tap root. When it is time to transplant you can just lift the pots out of the soil and remove the root ball intact.

Harried Over Hibiscus

I think I really am a hopeless gardener. I have two hibiscus my sons planted out in the garden for me. I brought them into the house thinking that the cold weather would be bad for them, and now they are losing all their leaves. I guess bringing them in was a mistake. Should I plant them out again?

No, keep them inside. Find the brightest, sunniest window you've got and put them there. When you water them, give them a good watering and then don't water them again until they almost dry out completely, so you are sure they are using all the moisture. Two things are happening to them. They are going through transplant shock because they now have less root system than before, and they are also going through a light change shock coming from the outside to the inside. Even in a bright, south-facing window, it is still a shock.

They are getting maybe 10-20% of the light they would from the direct sunlight outside, so they slow themselves down. The first thing they do in reacting to this change is to drop what flowers are there and start yellowing and dropping their leaves. That is not a problem. The plants will re-establish themselves and you will get new growth. They may sit without doing much for a couple of months but as the light levels come back up again next spring, they will start back up into new growth. Trim them back during this semi-dormant period to a structure and size that you can live with comfortably indoors. The buds develop on the new growth, so you are also going to get more flowers with this pruning and that's another plus. Next spring, have your sons plant them back out again and then sit back and enjoy.

Over-wintering Geraniums and Begonias

I have about 4 dozen geraniums, both annuals and perennials, and about 50 begonia bulbs. Everything is still in bloom and I want to save them over the winter to plant out next year. What should I do?

Leave the perennial geraniums where they are, they will be fine. With the annual geraniums,

you will need to get them out of the ground before the first frost hits. With that number, you should consider how many you can handle comfortably for the winter and select the best ones. If you have 4 varieties and you can handle a dozen plants, it will mean keeping 3 of each variety. Dig up the healthiest, most vigorous plants and transplant them into pots. Place them on a sunny windowsill, water according to need, and no fertilizing until about the end of February. When you want to start picking them up again, increase the frequency of watering and give them a light feeding. You can take cuttings, but again, early February to the end of February will be the time to do that. As far as the Tuberous Begonias are concerned, you can leave them in the garden and let them flower as long as they will for you. When they get hit by frost, lift them immediately. The soil will not freeze as quickly as the foliage, so at that point, if you lift them out, the tubers will still be intact and unharmed. Cut off any of the leaves or blooms that are still on them. If it is a good sunny day, spread them out, let them dry in the sun for the day, and then knock the dry soil off of the tubers. If it is a miserable day, lift them, cut the blooms or leaves, bring them indoors to a dry location and let them sit for a day or two to dry out a little bit. Again, knock any surplus soil off. Once they've been dried either indoors or outdoors, you can layer them in a plastic bag or cardboard box. Put a couple of inches of dried peat moss on the bottom of the bag or box, space the tubers out on top of that and then put a 1-2 inch layer of the dry peat moss over top. Vermiculite also works extremely well for this; in fact, I find it is in some ways better than the peat moss. Over the winter there will be a minor exchange of moisture back and forth from the tuber into either the vermiculite or the peat moss. I find with the vermiculite, if the bulbs are well isolated from one another with a couple of inches between each of the tubers, if one starts to rot or deteriorate, it tends not to spread to the others. While peat moss can work well, I find I have better luck with the vermiculite. Continue alternating bulbs and either material for successive layers until you fill the bag or box, then seal it and put it in a cool dark location until late February or early March. At that point it is just a matter of taking them out, triaging through to make sure everything is healthy, and then planting them up in individual pots. Once all danger of frost has passed, you are ready to plant them outside. They should come through beautifully and that early start indoors in the sunny location means they will produce flowers much sooner for you once they get outside.

Danger of Black Spotted Leaves in the Garden

Every year my husband goes around and collects leaves from all over the neighbourhood and digs them into our garden. Some of the leaves have black spots and I read that these are a fungus and that putting these into the garden was not a good idea. What do you advise?

Yes, it is tar spot and it tends to be much more prevalent when we have very wet summers and conditions are ideal for its reproduction. The standard recommendation to clear up this problem is to rake up all the leaves and burn them so that you are killing off the fungus. You can also chop them up and put them into a good, active working compost, one that gets fairly hot with a lot of nitrogen in there to make sure things are breaking down. If it composts down, it is fine to use that organic material in your garden the next year, although it's best to wait a couple of years if you are using that compost around the more susceptible fruit trees. Usually the pathogens in the compost, the good ones, will attack the fungal spores and kill them. Sprinkling these leaves directly onto the garden and digging them in without composting could create a problem unless you dig them in deeply and cover them over with soil so that those spores are not going to be released again first thing in the spring. If you do that, it means you can only work to a very shallow level in your garden the next year. You have to be careful to get your planting in on the top of the old leaf material and keep some soil cover over top. Certainly that organic matter down in the soil is going to be worthwhile and you can speed up the process in terms of breaking that leaf material down by using it that way. However, if your husband is going around and collecting the leaves, it might be safer in the long run to compost them first. Let them heat up and break down in a compost pile before putting them onto your beds and you will likely avoid any potential problems.

Decline of the Potted Hostas

My problem is trying to save the lives of four hostas I have. They thrived all summer long in pots on my balcony. I brought them in at the beginning of the cold weather and they are just not making it. I know that the large plants can winter over in the garden, but these are all in small 4-inch pots. They look as though they are dying. As a matter of fact, one of them is down to 3 leaves. Is there anything I can do to save them?

Yes, but you'll have to put them back out onto the balcony until they have gone through a few good hard frosts. Those frosts are going to kill off the leaves and force the plants into dormancy. Once you see the leaves are dead, bring the plants back in, trim off the dead foliage, get them into plastic bags and put them into a cold space. I know finding a spot that is cold enough to store plants can sometimes be a problem if you are living in an apartment, so if you have no garage or other cold storage cupboard to leave them in, pop them into the refrigerator. Just make sure that they are closed up and separate from the other things in the fridge. Leave them there for a minimum of 6-8 weeks, 12 weeks would be even better, but 6 weeks as a basic minimum. Once you've done that, bring them out into the coolest room you have. It's fine to put them right up close to a window if it's cooler there.

Keep the soil barely moist and they should start back up again as house plants. Once all danger of frost has passed it will be safe to put them back out on the balcony for the summer but initially, out during the warm days and back in during the cold nights works as well. I know it might be tempting just to leave them out for the winter, but in a 4-inch pot, the freeze-thaw cycle could damage them. That being said, they really want to go through that dormancy period and feel like they have had some winter, so you have to try and create it for them. After a stretch of constant cold, they should come along just fine for you. One final suggestion would be to move them up into 6-inch pots for the next season. They'll still need some winter protection, but they will have that much more room for the root system to develop.

Icelandic Poppies Frozen Out

I have not had success over-wintering Icelandic Poppies. Do you have any advice?

Poppies need reasonably well-drained soil with some moisture retention as well, so put a little organic matter into the soil. You can help the process by col-

lecting seeds from your poppies once they are ripe and ensuring that they are scattered around liberally. The important thing is to get the seeds established before winter. If you can, mulch over them in the fall to bring them through the winter but get the mulch off as soon as the snow recedes in the spring. When you do the mulching in the fall, put some evergreen boughs over the top to hold the mulch in place and provide a little more protection and hopefully they will come through the winter nicely.

Hardy Hazel

I need some advice on my Harry Lauders Walking Stick. I don't remember its proper name, Crooked Hazel or something. It's rather large, about 5 feet tall, and quite spread out at the bottom. I was wondering if it has any chance of going through the winter?

The common name for this is Corkscrew Hazel and yes, it can go through the winter. I'd suggest you hold off on doing any pruning until the spring, though, because if you get some winter-kill, you will want to take that out and you can only remove a maximum of 25% of the plant in any given year. As long as your tree has a good, well-established root system, it should be fine for our winters. Even if we have a severe winter and you get some damage, normally these trees will come back just fine. Mulching with 8-12 inches of compost over the root system will get Corkscrew Hazel successfully through even the harshest regions of Zone 4. Just be sure to remove that mulch first thing in the spring, prune anything that has been winter-killed or is in the way and your tree should do fine.

Activating Acorns

About a month ago we were visiting cemeteries on a genealogy hunt and we came across old acorns all over the ground. We put some in coffee cups with a little dirt. Then at home we put them in 4-inch pots and I am wondering how to carry them through the winter. Do they have to go dormant?

Yes they do. If you have the bed space available, dig a hole, sink the pots in up to the rim and then just mulch over and leave them there. The pots will make it much easier to lift them out and keep the root systems intact next spring. Let them stay there for the winter and when the soil is workable in the spring, lift them out and bring them indoors. Gradually increase the light and heat level when they come inside – the easiest way to do this is to put them into a cool room first and then into a warmer room. You will give them a head start by bringing them inside but they do really want to have a dormant period and they are much safer coming through the winter in the ground in their pots than they would be elsewhere.

Tree Rescue

I inherited a 12-foot pine tree that is probably beyond help. A neighbour dug it up with a backhoe so it didn't end up with a lot of root ball and most of the soil was lost. I thought that maybe I could save it and I have been keeping it alive over the summer by watering it every 2 or 3 days. But the needles are drooping and the crown died during the summer heat when I let it go 4 or 5 days without water. I have seen trees droop like this before and then die on me in the winter. Is there any way I can save this one?

The critical thing here is not to stop watering, as needed, right up until freeze-up. The only way it is going to have a chance of getting through this winter is to have a good store of water in the needles because they will continue to transpire and lose moisture all winter long – all of the evergreens do. The only way we can avoid the desiccation that signals death is to make sure the moisture reserves are topped up to the maximum right through the fall. In other words, get everything you can into the store house and hope for the best. Other than that, a wrapping of burlap will cut the wind, and in cutting the wind the tree will not be transpiring as much. That would certainly be helpful. It should be a very loose wrap, making sure there is good circulation inside the wrapping as well. If you put stakes around the sides at the tips of the branches and wrap the burlap around that, that would be ideal – or you could put snow fence around the base and wrap with that, just to break the wind in the lower section. Above that, you could make a teepee with stakes and wrap burlap onto that, as long as the wrapping is loose and open so the air will actually flow through. You don't want to get a build up of heat around the tree through the winter either. You might also try adding a handful or two of rock phosphate or bone meal to the soil at the base to stimulate root development, but you don't want to be pushing any other growth on it at this point. Apply that phosphate or bone meal right at freeze-up and then add another application over the surface of the soil after it freezes so that when things start to melt in the spring, the first nutrients the tree picks up will be rich in phosphorous or phosphate to stimulate root development. The critical thing will be getting a good root mass built up on this pine again so that it can take in the moisture and nutrients it needs to be self-sustaining.

Preparing Young Trees for Winter

I was told that I should put burlap around my new Japanese Maple for at least the first couple of winters to protect it. Is this true and if so, should the burlap go to the full height of the tree or just around the base?

What you are looking for in terms of protection with a young tree is mainly to shelter it from the snow load. If you don't it could get smashed, so you might want to put something solid like an A-frame over top of it. If you do, make sure there is enough space at the top point to allow for good air circulation. Alternatively, you could protect it with burlap. What you want to do there is put at least 3, and ideally 4, posts just beyond the tips of the branches and wrap the burlap around those. The burlap is probably about a metre wide so if the tree is taller than that, lift the burlap wrap up so you are getting protection at the top of the tree.

Mulch the bottom of the tree with lots of leaves and try to get them up the stem as high as the bottom of the burlap. If you have a hard time keeping the leaves in place, add a few branches inside the burlap to hold them in and that should do it. Mulching is the most critical thing you can do to ensure the root system survives the harsh winter conditions. Once winter arrives, you can give that tree some added protection by collecting and building the snow up around it to break the wind. This is especially important on the north east side with that being the predominant wind direction throughout the winter months. Exposure to that wind will dry out the branches. The other concern with trees in winter is the potential for frost damage, so if there is any bark exposed on the trunk you want to make sure that you are shading it somewhat. You don't want to get excessive heating on the south or west side of the tree that will allow the sap inside to thaw during the day, only to have it refreeze and expand when the sun goes down and the

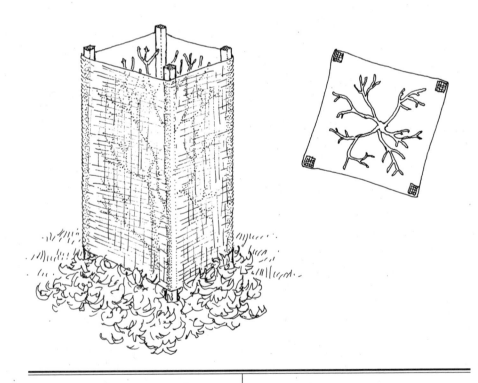

temperature drops, cracking and rupturing the bark. If you are worried this might be a problem, stand up a plank on the south side and that should prevent any excessive heating. Come spring, if you have piled the leaves and mulch up high around the base in the late fall, you will need to completely remove that from the trunk. Having said this, leaving an inch or two of mulch over the soil surface year round helps to retain moisture and as it breaks down it will provide nutrients to the soil and the tree. Remember, no mulch should be in contact with the trunk of any trees.

Mitigating Mealy Bug

My Mandevilla plant is looking very sick. I have it supported on three bamboo stakes but it is still full of large pink blossoms. We had it on our porch until 3 weeks ago when we brought it indoors. Since that time it has developed white powdery objects that are about the size of a rabbit pellet and if you press them they are yellow inside. What might that be?

Welcome to the world of mealy bugs! Most common insecticide sprays will not be effective simply because they are not able to penetrate that waxy, fuzzy, powdery, coating that develops over the outside of the mealy bug. Rubbing alcohol can be used to wipe them off, but you will have to repeat the process a few times. You can get a reasonable level of success using soap and water, 40-parts water to 1-part soap, and adding 8-parts rubbing alcohol. Be sure to spray into all of the cracks and crevices including at the ends of the bamboo stakes. A real concerted effort has to go into spraying those spots where the masses of insects look almost like pellets. After a thorough spraying, wait 10-15 minutes, and then rinse the whole thing down with clear water. If you can get the strong jet from a spray bottle or better still, a good hard mist from a hose, this should be strong enough to peel off those insects. Unfortunately, they will sometimes stick onto your plant even after you have killed them – if you don't take them off you're never quite sure if they are dead or alive. Keep an eye on your plant for the next few weeks because you will likely have a few small outbreaks. With these smaller infestations, a cotton swab dipped in rubbing alcohol works beautifully, but remember to flush off the alcohol with clear water afterward as well. The whole process can take a few weeks from start to finish but if you keep at it, eventually all of your mealy bugs will be eliminated.

Tender Perennial Care

I have a tender perennial that I believe is a first cousin to the Brugmansia. The first year we had it, it stayed out in a pot all summer but didn't bloom until after we brought it into the house and put it in the basement. This year we planted it into the garden itself and we got 5 blooms, but now that it's time to bring it in, it has thousands of buds. It's also huge. Can I lift it with the buds on and if so, should I put it back in the basement or into a window?

You can lift them with the buds on. Bring it in and enjoy the flowering inside. Datura or "Angel's Trumpet" are other names for Brugmansia. The cousin you have has smaller blue flowers and is commonly called "Flowering Potato Plant". They are both in the potato and tomato family, Solanaceae. You will probably have to cut it back a bit to handle it more comfortably and pot up. Leave it upstairs in the sunniest window available until it stops flowering. When all the flowers are gone, let the soil start to dry down and once it's done that, put it in the basement. Keep it barely moist and cool in this semi-dormant stage. About mid-January, bring it back up again and put it into a sunny window. You can wait as late as early March if space

is a problem earlier. Start picking up on the watering, but water only as much as it uses. Having cut it back, it will start into new growth as the light levels pick up in the spring. By getting it up and going early you'll get a head start on the growing season so that when you get it outside, after all danger of frost has past, and plant it in the full sun, it will be that much closer to its first bud initiation. You should be able to get it to flower all through the summer. Be careful with any fertilizer – you don't want it exposed to too much nitrogen. If you get nitrogen near these flowering plants – when you fertilize the lawn for example – you will get good green foliage but at the expense of flowering. If you fertilize it at all while it's indoors, use a soluble fertilizer with a low first and second number and a higher third number. Generally a 1-1-3 ratio is perfect; there are a number of fish emulsion or seaweed fertilizers out there, as well as the standard run-of-the-mill solubles. I would recommend using half the strength suggested by the manufacturer but apply it twice as often. Instead of once a month, feed it every couple of weeks or at every other watering with a half-strength concentration. If you plant this one directly in the garden, you might want to give it some additional fertilizer to get the roots sprouting, and in that case you will need a 10-30-10, or a 10-52-10, just to give the plant a little boost. But sun is really all it will want. It will be just as happy to stay in its pot provided you can provide all the water it needs and keep it in full sun.

Fallen Leaves on Turf

My brother tells me that a carpet of leaves left on a lawn over the winter will have a negative effect on the grass. How true is that?

Generally, it is not a good idea to have those leaves stay on there. Leaving a carpet of leaves on the lawn over winter does a couple of things. It traps in moisture and fungal spores and it encourages moulds to develop under the leaves that will eventually attack your grass plants. So if you can get rid of the leaves, all the better. The ideal way to do this is to run over everything with your lawn mower in the fall so that the leaves get chopped up into finer pieces. You can rake up the surplus bits, but the small bits will fall between the blades of grass and act as mulch. In this form they are actually beneficial in that they will be broken down by the micro-organisms in the soil and add nutrient to feed your grass. The rest that you gather up can be put on to your flower beds or around your shrubs. Any left over after that goes into the compost. It will break down there and can be used the next year to top-dress the lawn.

Propagating Black Walnuts

I was told that I have one of the few Black Walnuts that exist in the Haliburton region because they are not supposed to grow this far north. It's been a fabulous season and I've got about 300 walnuts off it. I'd like to know how to plant some of these to get more of these Black Walnuts growing. Can you tell me what I should do?

This is the ideal way to propagate that type of tree in your area. It's always best to use nuts off a local tree so you know there will be a greater hardiness built in. After you harvest the nuts, get some rubber gloves and peel the outer hull off those you want to plant. Rinse them off and you should be at the hard inner shell of the nut itself. With a good solid file or a rasp, take the individual nuts and scratch up one edge of each of them until you're almost down through the shell. Soak them in warm water indoors overnight and then plant them out, burying them to their own depth, in other words, not more than an inch or 2. It doesn't matter which way the filed side goes in – the purpose of the filing is simply to allow moisture to penetrate the shell. The seed inside will eventually swell and break the hull, the radical will implant itself in the soil and the stem will make its way towards the light. You could also try putting each nut into an individual pot – a 4-inch plastic pot would do nicely – and then bury each pot to its own depth below the surface of the soil. Once you've sunk the pot, you'll want to put wire mesh or some chicken wire over the whole thing and weight it down so it stays in place. The mesh will keep out any squirrels who will think they have planted the nuts and will gladly eat them. Mesh or wire should also be placed over the top of any nuts you plant directly into the ground. First thing in the spring, take the mesh off and wait until you see germination happening in the individual pots. When you do see the stems and leaves coming up above the edge of the pots, you can take them out and transplant them into their desired location. Mark these spots so you can keep an eye on them and avoid stepping on or inadvertently mowing over them. Plant them at the same depth, water them

well in the new location and they should grow on fine from there.

Rosemary Revelations

I have tried to keep my rosemary plants in the house over the winter and that didn't work. A white powder appeared on them and they died. The next year we left them outside, buried them with leaves and then put compost on top but that didn't work either. Do we just give up?

No, don't give up. Bring them into the house for the winter, put them in the brightest, sunniest window you can find and water them as needed. But be sure to check the moisture levels regularly. One day of sunshine can dry out a rosemary plant. If you let them dry out that will be the end of them. We have to remember that our homes, especially in the winter with central heating, can be dryer than a desert. Even though rosemary generally wants hot, dry conditions when indoors they are restricted in the amount of moisture they can find by the size of their pot, so you have to be checking the moisture level regularly. It doesn't hurt to mist them every once in a while throughout those winter months as well. That white powdery substance that appeared likely came about because it was too hot and dry to start with, so the misting would certainly be advisable. If the powdery mildew is really widespread, trimming back the rosemary and applying a light treatment of a 1% baking soda and water solution will give you a measure of control. Make sure there is good air circulation around the plants and let them regenerate. If the mildew problem arrives early in the season, you may not see any regeneration for a while. For example, if at the end of October or early November you start to see the powdery mildew show up you may not get any regeneration until the end of January or even into February; however the plant will hold its own. Also make sure the plant never stays sopping wet. That will result in a whole other set of issues. As for trying to over-winter your rosemary outdoors, unfortunately it will not survive in this climate. One thing you can do to help them along and make life easier is to use clay pots for the winter and then bury them in the ground, pot and all, the next summer. The big advantage here is that when you lift them out to bring them back in for the next winter, you are not disrupting the root system too much so there is little or no transplant shock. That is a plus because with less stress on the plants when they come in-

side they will be able to better tolerate the transition.

Leave the Leaves?

What should you do if your garden gets covered with leaves? Do you leave them there for mulch or do you clean them up?

If you want to see those leaves disappear a little bit more quickly from your lawn, run the lawn mower over them and chop them up. By creating smaller leaf bits you are exposing that many more edges to all of the micro-organisms in the soil that feed on them and break them down, and that will effectively accelerate the natural process. The one caution is if the leaves are already affected by some disease such as tar spot. In this case you want to take as many of those leaves off the lawn as possible so you don't give that disease a place to over-winter near the host. Likewise, if the leaves get soggy and haven't been chopped up they are going to mat down and create a soggy wet blanket over top of your lawn. No light will be getting through to the grass and you can get into some rot situations. If there are leaves in your gardens, you can rake them out onto the lawn, chop them up with your mower and then blow them back onto the beds. As a mulch this will provide some degree of protection to the roots during the winter and you probably won't have much left there by the spring. Diseased leaves can, in some cases, be used on the beds, especially if you have been incorporating lots of organic matter into your soil over the season – but it is essential that you work that leaf material down into the soil to make sure those spores are well buried. If you have a healthy active soil there are actually pathogens there that will attack and eliminate the disease spores that arrive with the organic leaf material. But if you have any doubts, bury those leaves into your compost. It is an awful lot of work cleaning those diseased leaves out of your garden, but if you have had problems with apple scab on your apple tree or black spot and powdery mildew around your roses for example, get that stuff out of there and break it down in an active compost pile. When you do re-apply it to the soil as mature compost you'll be getting all the benefits of this rich organic material without any of the problems associated with diseases.

Maple Makeover

The 15-year-old maple tree in my backyard had some ice damage and the branches are pretty uneven. I want to prune it up so that both sides are equal but that would take off about half of the growth. Will that kill it?

No, but that would be a pretty severe setback for a tree. You could try taking off a quarter of the growth on the side you think needs to be trimmed back so that the other side gets a bit more light and a bit of encouragement. As it starts growing out, you will eventually get the two sides back to that balance point. It may not be perfectly symmetrical for a while but like most things, beauty is in the eye of the beholder. A less-than-perfect shape can sometimes add an interesting feature to the landscape.

Recycling Swimming Pool Water on Gardens

Can we use the water we have in our pool at the end of the season to water our gardens?

Yes you can. Once pool water has sat in full sun for a day or two, the sun's ultraviolet rays will have rendered the chlorine inactive. All it takes is that exposure to full sun. In fact, in some places like Phoenix, Arizona – where it is against the law to have a grass lawn in front of your house because of the shortage of water in that region – they have developed commercial watering systems specifically to re-use pool and household grey water. People still try to cultivate gardens or ground-cover using native plant materials and this is one way they can maintain them without putting any extra strain on the very limited water resources available in that area. Even in regions where water shortage is not an issue, re-using that large volume of water on plants and gardens makes very good environmental sense. As long as you let it sit for a bit it poses no danger whatsoever to your plants. On the contrary, they will be grateful for the extra moisture to help take them through the winter ahead.

Fallen Leaves on Alternate Ground Cover

I have a heavily shaded yard where I have established periwinkle and thyme for the ground cover. It's not easy to remove the leaves. Is it alright to leave the leaves on top of these plants?

Yes, it's fine to let those leaves stay where they fall. That will certainly help to protect the ground cover through the winter. There is the possibility that a very heavy mat of leaves will not break down enough over that period and result in some of the plants underneath getting smothered. To help avoid this, wait until your leaves dry down and take a stiff fan rake to them. Even a light raking will help break them down and allow those leaf fragments to come into contact with the soil. Then ideally the organisms that are there will continue the decomposition process and other workers in the soil, particularly the earthworms and the ants, can incorporate that material more fully for you. If you still find clumps left in the spring, especially wet clumps, give the yard another light raking and the ground cover will come back very quickly.

Composting Leaves with Black Spot

My maple tree has leaves that have been affected by black spot. What should I be doing with the fallen leaves to ensure this problem does not continue next year or affect my other trees?

Leaves affected by black spot, or what's more commonly known as "tar spot", should be composted. It's best not to put this fallen material directly onto your flower beds unless you have a good quantity of compost already in that soil and are prepared to work those leaves well down into it. Once you've buried them, the pathogens in the soil will break down any diseased material. If you decide to compost the leaves make sure they are going into a good, hot working compost because that is essential to ensure the materials get completely broken down. If you can run the lawn mower over them first and chop them up to smaller sized pieces before you put them in there, that would be helpful. The added plus in doing that is you are also going to get some grass clippings mixed in with the leaves which will supply a bit more nitrogen to the compost. Give them a good soaking when they go in. Those tar spots are where the fruiting body of the fungus will develop and the spores will be ejected from them next spring just about the time when the leaves start to unfurl on the trees. It's very uncanny timing on nature's part. If those spores are in proximity to the trees they will infect them with the fungus. If they are incorporated into the compost and confined in there, heating up and breaking down, you eliminate the problem.

Persecuted Ponytail

My Ponytail plant was infested with scale insects so I took it out on a cool, fairly bright day in September and because it was too large to wipe down with alcohol by hand, I gave it a good dosing of soap and water. I used a high concentration of a fairly strong soap and I soaked it over and over, but rather than taking the soap off, because I was afraid that the scale problem would just continue, I left the soap solution on. I brought the plant back in and now probably 80% of the leaves have died. It has either gotten scorched by the sun because I left it outside for a good part of that day or they've died because of the soap solution. With Ponytails, if I cut off 70 or 80% of the leaves I don't believe it will rejuvenate. The plant is only sending out green shoots at the top, which is about 2½ feet up the plant, and the rest of the trunk is just covered in dead branches. What can I do?

Trim off the dead leaves. The new growth is going to come from the top. The plus with the Ponytail, much like a fountain, is that it comes up the middle and then spills over the sides and droops back down. As your plant recuperates and continues to grow on, the foliage will hang down and cover the bare sides. Quite possibly you had a combination of effects going on there, from the strong soap not being rinsed off to the effect of the strong sunlight, which would have been quite a shock. There is a sunburn factor, as well as a bit of chemical burning from the soap solution, however your plant will come back. If it is putting out new growth, that's a good sign. Give it a light feeding this fall, half strength, then let it stabilize until the light levels start to pick up, so no more fertilizer until the end of February or early March. Then continue with the half strength feedings every 5th or 6th watering after that and it should be fine. Generally speaking, we follow that pattern from the end of February or early March on to the first of October and then give the plants a break through the winter. So no feeding, and water only when the soil dries out during this period. That large bulge at the base of the stem stores water and is your indication that the plant likes to dry out between waterings. It also accounts for the other common name for this plant, "Elephant's Foot".

Alternatives to Composting Tar Spot

I know that you recommend that we put leaves with fungus or tar spot into the compost pile but I don't have room for a composter. I usually just chop them up and dig them straight into the garden. Is that a no-no when the leaves have tar-spot?

That would depend on how deep you are digging those leaves into the garden. If they are worked well down into the earth, about a foot deep, and then have a layer of soil over top of them, it shouldn't be a problem. What you are in effect doing is composting those leaves in the soil itself, without the possibility of the fungus coming back to the surface and re-attacking. Generally you should be fine with that. If you are simply chopping them up and throwing them down onto the beds with healthy leaves to let the worms eat that down, then you would be running the risk of the disease coming back. A better option would be to throw them into an active compost, but since that is not possible in your case you could just pack them into plastic garbage bags, add enough water to moisten the contents and then set them in a sunny location until next spring when you can incorporate this material into your beds.

An Evergreen Maple

I live in a really old area of town on a beautiful tree-lined street and am fortunate to have a maple tree on the boulevard just in front of my house. I don't know how old it is, but it never changes colour in the fall. It stays green while all the rest of the trees turn like they should. The leaves also seem to fall very late in the season. How do I get them to turn that beautiful red colour?

I can almost guarantee that you have a streetlight in front of your house – and that tree is not getting the proper light signals. When trees change colour, they are not responding to cold temperatures, as many people often think, but rather to a shortened day length. Your streetlight is on a photocell that comes on when it starts to get dark, so the tree thinks it is still summer. In some situations this can be a real problem. If you have a heavy wet snowfall in the late fall or early winter and it lands on a bare tree, the snow just slides off. But if you have a tree that still has its leaves on like this one, that heavy wet snow can get held on there and the weight of it can pull branches down and even split the tree in half. I've seen it happen. Unfortunately, there is nothing you can do about this unless you can have the light turned off. It is just a matter of the placement of the tree and the amount of light it is getting.

Plant Raining Leaves

I have a Schefflera arboricola that is literally raining leaves. Have you any idea why this might be happening?

If you've been watering this plant a lot, stop. Over-watering is one of the biggest enemies of the *schefflera* and its smaller-leafed cousins. They just do not like to stand in water. Do water it thoroughly but make sure it is drying down in between each watering. The symptoms of too much water are exactly the same as the symptoms of no water. The leaves often brown off. The fact is that if the root system is drowning, it cannot take in moisture and sustain the foliage on the plant, so it actually amounts to the same thing. This one should come back without too much difficulty. Take those browned-off or dead leaves away. Don't leave them on the soil as a mulch because any disease or pest that is present will usually be on the foliage and it will get back onto your plant. Disposal into the compost is perfect because any diseases won't survive one good frost out there. If you would like to build the foliage that has been lost back up and get a bushier plant, wait until the plant re-establishes itself. As it is putting out new foliage and starts back into active growth again, pinch the tips off of each of the stems. If you want to take cuttings from these, then take them about 3 inches back and cut just before a node so that you are leaving the node intact on the remaining stem. This is where the new growth will come from. The cutting you removed will root up successfully either in floral foam in water, or just in water. Cover the bottom half inch or so of the stem with water and once the root starts growing and gets to be 1/2 -1 inch long, plant it up in its own pot and keep it moist until it's well established.

Drastic Hedge Reduction

We just moved into a house that has a cedar hedge growing between our property and the road. It's over 10 feet high and 60 feet across and it provides way too much privacy. What I would like to do is cut it down to about 4 or 5 feet but if it's going to be ugly for a long time and possibly not survive, I would just as soon take it right down and start over from scratch with new trees. What would you suggest?

Taking the hedge down to 5 feet is going to be tough but it is worth a shot to try and keep the established plants. The best time to do this would be very early in the spring before any new buds start to break. Run a string from one end of the hedge to the other to establish the new height and then bring those tops down. Hold off pruning the sides just yet. The reason is they are going to act as a wind break for what is happening on the inside and you want some winter protection for a little while yet. At the end of March or in mid April, go ahead and trim the sides. Try to get back to a conical shape but you don't want to trim any further in than the point where you can see green leaf on the branches. In other words, you want to bring it in as much as you can but still have a surface of foliage. Angle the sides about 10 degrees from bottom to top so it is wider at the bottom and narrower at the top. You are going to have a very open flat top on these at first but new growth should start filling back into that area quickly, and in the interim the sides will get much thicker. Make sure the trees are not lacking for moisture and a feeding of compost around the base will help. If you apply about an inch of that compost it will act as a mulch as well. With 60 feet of hedge to trim, I don't think the job will get done all in one weekend. Try to do a bit at a time to get it all back to where you want it. Keep in mind that with any cedars up to 10 feet tall, the stems half way up are going to be too thick to cut with pruners. Use a sharp pruning saw and cut the stems as close as possible to the node or branch nearest your height-marking guideline. I have used a battery-powered reciprocating saw successfully for this type of pruning, but be sure to hold the tip of the saw, before the blade, tightly against the trunk to avoid unwanted vibrating.

Conserving Crocosmia

Should I take crocosmia out of the ground for the winter and plant them again next year, like I do with the Canna Lilies, or can I leave them in the ground over the winter?

You should remove them. The good news is that they store very readily. Allow them to get hit by the first frost so that they will maximize what they are photosynthesizing and storing in terms of energy. The first frost will knock the foliage back but there should be enough warmth in the soil to prevent any harm to the bulbs. Lift them out at that point and lay them in the sun for a day to cure. At the end of the day, cut the spent foliage off and then layer them in a bag with an inch or two of vermiculite or dried peat moss under them. Be sure to space the bulbs well. Another layer can be added on top of the first one but make sure you have a couple of inches of buffer between each layer of bulbs and over the top. Seal the bag and place it in a cool dry location for the winter. Come spring, they can be planted back out in the garden once the soil has warmed and is again workable. If you would like to try for an earlier flowering, start your crocosmia in pots indoors 4-6 weeks before you would normally plant them outdoors at the end of May or early June.

Christmas Cactus Blooming at Halloween

I have a large Christmas Cactus that blooms beautifully every year. The problem is that it blooms 2 or 3 weeks earlier each year and is now so far ahead of schedule it is blooming for Halloween. How can I get it to bloom at Christmas time?

I am assuming that since it is flowering this profusely and regularly it goes out for the summer. If that's the case, when you bring it in – even if it is covered in buds – place it in the coolest location possible, although it will still need a bright spot, and don't water it at all. If you put it somewhere where it is warm and dry, the buds will start to open on their own, and if it is warm and moist, they will open fairly quickly. So a cool, dry spot is essential to controlling that bloom. A week or two before you want to start the buds swelling and opening, move the plant from the cooler location into a warm, bright spot and increase the moisture level.

You should see the flowers start to appear in a week or two, right on schedule for the holidays. I have, however, heard other theories as to what actually controls this flowering. A former colleague of mine was convinced it was the smell of the turkey roasting that was the real trigger.

Lost Dwarves

The four dwarf apple trees in my backyard are in danger of losing their dwarf status because they are all about 10 feet high. They are sending up what I think are called water sprouts through the crown. How should I deal with those?

Any time around the end of February would be an ideal time to get on with this job. You can take up to 25% of the total volume of the crown off the tree, so just clip those sprouts out. Cut them right back to the branches they are coming from. And if you take those cuttings, cut them again and put them into water, they will start to grow for you. You will get that wonderful lime green colour at the start that will eventually darken up. That darker foliage from the water sprouts makes a beautiful piece to have inside for decoration. If you are not interested in that, they can either go into the compost or into the fireplace.

Protecting Large Rose Bushes

I was given a rose bush some years back and this summer it bloomed with pink flowers that look like wild rose, so I imagine it must be some antique variety. It has grown like mad. Some stalks on it are 14 feet high and it is still putting out new shoots. Some of these have 7 leaves and some have only 5 – somebody told me that next year it would not produce on the ones with 7 leaves. It's obviously very hardy but what is the best way to protect it during the winter now that it has reached this size?

Roses will sometimes produce on a shoot with 7 leaves but the flower will be smaller and this is usually an indication that the plant has reached its reversion point, which is when it starts producing from its root stock as opposed to producing from the grafted stock. Once you get to 9 and 11 leaves, this reversion is more predictable; 3 to 5 is usually well within what has been tamed. It may just be a little atavistic, showing more of its grandparent's qualities as opposed to its parent's, but it is obviously a very hardy and healthy rose. If it is supported well and it is not going to experience any excessive ice or snow damage throughout the course of the winter, leave it the way it is and prune it back in the spring. If it is getting this kind of length, this may be a Rambling Rose, in which case it will flower from the second year growth as opposed to flowering from the new growth. It is probably an older variety of rose so you don't want to be too drastic when cutting it back because if you cut off all the new growth it is definitely not going to flower. When you do cut, try to be selective in taking out the new growth so that you are controlling what will keep growing and where it is going to grow. That way you are more likely to have the flowers where you want them. The pruning will also produce a bushier plant by stimulating the growth of lateral buds rather than single long stems. ·

NOVEMBER

Marriage Hopefully Hardier than Azalea

We were given a huge azalea as a gift 2 years ago. We put it in a north window where it is fairly cool and it has bloomed solidly for 2 years. Well this spring, I decided it was time to put it into the garden. So I prepared the soil with lots of pine needles and things and put it in there and it did well over the summer. But now my wife is after me. She is very angry with for me putting it out there because she thinks it is going to die this winter. I think it is going to be all right but to tell you the truth, I don't really know that for sure. I have covered it up with about 2 feet of leaves from the maple trees so it is well protected right now, but I am wondering if I should leave it there and take my chances or bring it back in while the ground is still not frozen. What would you recommend?

Are you counting on living with your wife for a couple more

285

years? If so, I would lift it and bring it in. They will take a light frosting and they can stand a light freezing as well, but the florist azaleas just don't have the hardiness of the native varieties. They are not bred to be an outdoor plant. You could get very lucky and bring it through the winter successfully, but I don't think it is worth the risk. The soil mix that you have it in seems to be ideal if it has come through the summer that nicely. It should be a fairly fibrous mix with a good quantity of organic material. What you want to do is take a pot that is large enough to accommodate as much of the root and soil as you can lift out and water it thoroughly when you bring it in. Try to keep it in a cool, lower light spot for at least a month to allow it to acclimatize to the drier conditions indoors. Do keep an eye on it. Make sure it is drying down between each watering, but not drying out. Misting the foliage will help. It will be a shock coming indoors when the central heating season is already upon us. It is awfully dry inside right now compared to the conditions it has had outdoors so it will have to acclimatize to those drier indoor conditions again. The north window will be an ideal spot for it. You may be eating crow for a while, but at least you should be able to save the plant.

Wrestling Rabbits

Over the last 23 years we have managed to create a perfect habitat for rabbits on our 10 acres. They've pretty well denuded a couple of nice trees, including a Serviceberry, my firethorn trees and the euonymus. The last year was bad, this year was worse and I hate to think about next year. We have tried a number of things, including wrapping the shrubs in burlap and spreading around the dirty cat litter. Is there anything else you know of that works for sure?

Certainly wrapping the trees with burlap will help, as will the cat litter in the short term. Rabbits dislike the smell of cat but the scent does wear off over time, so you would have to keep spreading that old litter around on a fairly regular basis. Your best bet would be a physical barrier, something like plastic tree wrap or chicken wire that can be loosely wound around the trunk of your trees and shrubs in the fall. You can take it off for the summer if the rabbits are less of a problem then. Moth balls around the base of your shrubs is often recommended as a deterrent but we now know that naphthalene, its main ingredient, is one of those nasty chemicals that you don't want to be introducing into the environment or handling yourself.

Aside from it being a known carcinogen, it's also a neurotoxin and can be particularly dangerous to young children or domestic pets, so I would avoid it entirely. Instead, try a little foul tasting material on the trunks of the trees. Something like Tabasco sauce can work nicely. With 10 acres of land, any of these measures would be quite a challenge, but all that space is also why the rabbits are doing so well. On the plus side, you shouldn't be surprised to see an increase in the fox or coyote population in the next little while. Nature tends to take care of these imbalances by bringing in more predators, and assuming that humans don't eliminate those natural predators, that should eventually bring that rabbit population back down to normal levels.

Love that Liquorice

I bought a Liquorice plant as part of a hanging basket this summer. It was the first time I've owned one and I found it so beautiful mixed with a scarlet and a white begonia; it made a lovely contrast. Now I gather that Liquorice plant is from Helichrysum family but I cannot even find out whether it is an annual or a perennial. I brought this hanging basket in at the end of the summer and after a few weeks it is still looking very good. I have taken some cuttings from it, some of which look quite healthy. Am I likely to be able to keep it through the winter?

You have *Helichrysum petiolare* which is native to South Africa where it forms a mounding ground cover. It's actually a spreading shrub with hairy gray leaves and stem. There are two other varieties: the "Limelight" has pale yellow-green foliage and "Varigatum" is gray and cream colour. Try to keep this plant in a good bright light and dry to moderately moist when it is indoors. It will undoubtedly slow down with the lower light levels of winter but that's not a problem. It's from Zone 9 so don't let it get too cold. With a little care you can probably bring it through the winter. You are going to get younger, more vigorous growth from the cuttings, which are best taken in summer or fall. In the process of taking these off and trimming it back, you should initiate some healthy new growth next spring and rejuvenate the parent plant as well. You have to consider this plant as an annual because the winter would definitely kill it off, but you can nurse it along as a perennial indoors and with any luck keep it going again for next summer. Similarly, the begonia can also be cut back to produce a fuller plant in the hanging basket and those cuttings also used to produce new plants.

How to Keep a Date Happy

I would like to know how to grow an indoor date plant. Last year I grew one about 18 inches high and then it died. Obviously I was doing something wrong. Can you walk me through the proper steps?

What it needs is all the light you can give it, so putting it in a south window, right up at window level, would be ideal. Use a normal soilless potting mix but I would recommend that you amend that by mixing in about 30-40% sharp sand. A clay pot works best here so that your plant can dry down readily. The sand amendment is going to give you freer drainage and you also want to make sure the root doesn't sit in water for any length of time. When you water it, soak it thoroughly. You can even sit it in a container of water and let it soak thoroughly for 20 minutes to half an hour, then let it drain and put it back in that sunny window. Don't water it again until it has dried down. Managing the moisture level will be the critical thing here, as will ensuring that you have it in a pot that is large

enough to accommodate it. As your plant fills a smaller pot with roots, take it out, tease out the roots so they are not just wrapping around in the form of the pot and put it back in a pot one size larger at a time. With enough sunlight, appropriate water management and sufficient space for root development, you should have no problem achieving success. Lower temperatures of 10-12° celsius during the winter months and reduced watering, making the soil barely moist, provides a helpful rest period. When active growth begins again in spring, increase the watering accordingly.

Bloomin' Rosemary

I've had a rosemary plant for 6 or 7 years that I keep in the garden all summer and then move inside to a cool corner. This year it is in a 16-inch pot and it's about 4 feet high. I stopped spraying it and put a cold humidifier underneath it. Now it is covered in blue flowers. What happened?

A combination of things have occurred here related to the age and maturity of your plant, a good growing season and the increase in humidity around it. A cooler temperature is fine through the winter months. If it gets too big, don't hesitate to trim it back, dry it and use it. It will shoot again for you quite quickly and successfully. Rosemary can also make a nice topiary specimen. If you are moving the pot out to a bright patio, you can shape it into a nice ball or any other shape. You can always trim the tops or offshoots back. If you take cuttings from this plant, be patient. They take a while to root up and you should use at least a #1 rooting hormone. If you are going to try to root them in water, use floral foam and add some English Ivy or any cuttings from the willow family in with them. If you use willow, bring it in a few days beforehand and cut them as you normally would just in front of a node; put them in the water and let them start coming along first – then do your rosemary cuttings. Use the water from the ivy or willow cuttings to moisten the damp sand or vermiculite that you use for rooting up other cuttings. You will get the benefit of the additional rooting hormone that comes from the natural auxins in the willow or English Ivy which is water soluble and will be readily picked up by your other cuttings.

Woeful Oleander

I have two oleander trees that I brought in from outside and there are three problems with them now. There are white crystals in the soil; the leaves have dried on both of them and most have fallen off or will fall off if you just walk by, even though I have been watering them religiously once every 4 or 5 days; and lastly, there are little white bugs or something that looks like cotton batting clumped in certain parts of the leaves and trunk. There is also a bad smell coming from them. Is there any hope or are they too far gone at this point?

Poor plants. I'm afraid you may have drowned them. Stop the watering. Any leaves that fall off, collect them up and remove them completely. They can go out into your compost if you have one outside but don't leave them anywhere where toddlers or small children can get into them since oleander leaves are poisonous. In terms of the white clumps, that's mealy bug. I would give the plants a good shake and take as much foliage off as you can. If there is not too much mealy bug on them, you can get rid of it by dipping a cotton swab in rubbing alcohol and touching the individual clumps of insects. Just wipe them off with the alcohol-soaked swab. If there is a large infestation of them, then the plants need to be sprayed. It would be best to put them into the bathtub, mix up a bottle with 40-parts water, 1-part liquid soap, and 8-parts rubbing alcohol and give them both a very good spraying. Working from the bottom of the plant upwards, spray to the point of run-off and allow that soap solution to sit on the plant for 10-15 minutes then re-spray the entire plant twice, again from the bottom up, with clear water. The problem with spraying is that you don't get to see that the problem is cleaned up the same way you do with the cotton swab, but it's the only way to treat it if the bugs have spread all through the plant. Now in terms of the watering, hold off and wait until the plants are drying out and the pots start to feel fairly light when you lift them before you do any watering at all. That will allow the soil to dry out sufficiently and in the process of drying out, will draw more air down into the soil. Roots need oxygen to breathe and if they don't have air in the soil, they drown, just like people do, so that could have been what has stressed these plants. It's more a matter of watering them thoroughly when they need it and letting them dry down in between waterings as opposed to putting them on a regular watering schedule every 4 or 5 days. In the case of oleanders, even in full sun, they can go 5-7 days between waterings with no problem at all. Those thick, leathery leaves conserve moisture well and can go

quite a while without water which is why oleander is often the plant of choice to be used to landscape medians or boulevards in places like southern California. If you can regulate the moisture and eliminate the mealy bugs, you should start to see them come back along in the next few weeks.

Deer Diner

I have deer nibbling on the bottom of some of my small cedars and now all of the bottom branches are gone. Will they grow back?

Your cedars can grow back over time but they will not start that recovery as long as the deer keep coming back to feed on them, so you really have to deter the deer. There are a number of things that they don't like in terms of smell. One recipe I have heard of that seems to be successful is a couple of eggs in a litre of water. Run the eggs and water through the blender, add a teaspoon of soap and put it into a sprayer. Any liquid soap or dishwashing detergent will work – it's just in there to make the egg solution stick and spread. Spray that on the trees that the deer have been eating. Unfortunately, just because they have previously been feeding on these younger cedars, it doesn't mean they will not bother with your others if they find something unattractive on the little ones. It's best to spray the entire area while you're at it and hopefully they will get completely discouraged and move on.

Recommendation for Drainage Materials in Pots

I am wondering how you feel about having drainage in the bottom of pots as opposed to using rocks or perlite in the bottom. What exactly is perlite and is it a natural substance? Do you recommend using those self-watering pots?

Perlite is a siliceous rock that has been expanded through heating. It has certain properties that allow it to expand up to 20 times its original volume – sort of like popcorn – which explains why it is so light for its mass. On the question of drainage, it is certainly healthier for the plant to have the water drain out. Even if it means having to take your pot out to be drilled, it's worth it. As for adding a layer of rock or perlite on the bottom, that raises another interesting property of soil. What happens with any soil mixture, whether it's outside in the garden or in a pot, is that the moisture will not move from one type of soil to another type of soil until the first one has become completely saturated. This is true

even if the first layer is sand, although in the case of sand a saturation point is reached quickly. If you put some sort of drainage layer like perlite underneath potting soil, the soil will stay quite wet because moisture will not pass through until and unless it is at its saturation point. So effectively, what you have created with a drainage layer is a barrier that holds moisture in rather than helping to drain moisture out. This is why it is far preferable to have a hole or holes for drainage in the bottom and one kind of soil throughout the pot. Now with the self-watering pots, that is a different situation. What happens with those is you have a layer of soil in a pot and a reservoir below so the water that drains out can be captured. As the soil dries out, this system has the capacity to wick moisture back up from this water reservoir and let it disperse throughout the soil. These can work quite successfully in some applications such as window boxes and balconies where dripping pots can cause problems below.

Stunted Pine Tree

I have a indoor Norfolk Pine that may actually be three trees because there are 3 trunks coming out of a 10-inch pot. We have had this plant in an east-facing window for almost 7 years. It has en-

dured a house-sitter who over-watered it, after which we had some yellowing, but it recovered completely. This past year there is new growth on top of these 3 trunks, but a lot of yellow and brown needles are falling off. I just recently saw somebody who has had a tree for about the same amount of time, but in a south window and it is 6 feet tall and healthy and green. Mine is pretty stunted by comparison. Are those 3 trunks contributing to its stunted growth?

Yes, in a minor way that could be a factor in that there is less space and a bit more competition for the moisture and nutrients available in that pot, as well as competition for the available light. What has happened with yours is that it has finally arrived at a point where the available light is not anywhere near what the plant needs to sustain itself at its present size. Being opportunistic, the plant is putting out growth at the top where it knows it has more chance of getting light and there is less shading from the other branches. If it invests its energy there, it assumes the return is going to be high. Lower down where those needles are browning, there is too much shade from the rest of the plant and it can no longer sustain those branches successfully. You are going to continue to have a problem unless you

can raise the light level. If putting it into a south or west window is not an option, what you can do to sustain it a little better is to lift it up so it is right at window height and get it as close to that window as possible. A table or pedestal would work nicely here. Give it a quarter turn every day so there's an even distribution of light to the crown of the plant. Come summer, once the danger of frost has passed, put the tree out into mottled sunlight. You could even give it a couple of hours of direct sunlight each day, but you don't want it in full sun all the time. It will have to come in again at the end of the summer, before there is any risk of frost, and go back into the brightest window you have available. With that east window you do have a few hours of direct sunlight – it may be enough to hold on to some green foliage and branches on the lower part of the tree for a while, but I'm afraid in time you will eventually lose them.

Basil Lover's Lament

I cut some basil stems last fall and now I have two drinking glasses bursting with greenery and roots. I am hesitant to pot them up because last time I tried this they quickly began to turn black. What's a basil lover to do?

What a basil lover has to do is go ahead and pot up those

rooted cuttings! Your past problems probably happened because the stem rot had already started while your cuttings were immersed in the water. Stems will eventually start to rot if left submerged too long. When potting up the rooted cuttings, you want to avoid damaging the fragile root system as much as possible. Untangle the roots gently and put the plants into a large bowl or saucer, covering the roots with water while you work. Choose a pot that will just comfortably accommodate the root system, that is to say, not too big. Using a peat-based soilless mix, hold the plant by a bottom leaf over the pot with the roots at the desired depth, then fill in around them with the potting soil. Press the soil gently but firmly into place around the roots and water thoroughly but slowly from the top. You can dampen the mix first if you prefer. After thoroughly watering, gently press the soil

Fertilizing Indoor Plants

I generally recommend that people fertilize their indoor plants using half the amount of fertilizer specified by the manufacturer on the package, but applied twice as often as prescribed. In other words, if the manufacturer recommends you feed 10 milligrams of their fertilizer once a month, I would suggest giving your plant 5 milligrams every 2 weeks instead. This gives the plant the same amount of nutrient, but allows you to introduce it more gradually over the same period of time. This will eliminate any possibility of burning and it doesn't push the plant as hard. We often think that a bright, south-facing window is giving our plants as much light as they would get outside. In fact, a window location, even facing directly south, gives about 10% of the light. The whole metabolism of the plant is slowed down indoors, so our tendency is to give it an extra burst of fertilizer to get it going again, but the plant just can't use all that nutrient. By introducing the fertilizer gradually, you also avoid any build-up of salts or soil toxicity due to the high fertilizer salts content. The clear waterings in between will flush out any excess fertilizer. With the gradual introduction, there is also a much greater chance that the fertilizer you are applying will be picked up and actually used by the plant. So I'd suggest you use half the manufacturer's recommended dose, twice as often, and your plants will be all the happier for it. Now if your available light is less than full sun, say in a north or east window, use half the recommended strength fertilizer but only once a month. Remember that any feeding of your house plants should be done only in higher light level periods, so only fertilize from mid to the end of February until mid-October at the latest.

around the edges again and top-up with soil as required. Remember, only bury as much stem below the soil line as is necessary to keep the cutting standing up straight. Place the potted cuttings in a bright location, but not in direct sun, until they can get over any transplant shock. That should take about a week and be sure to keep the soil constantly moist during that time. From then on, water them only when the pot is drying down. After that first week, move the plants further into direct sunlight. Once the cuttings start showing new growth and become a little root-bound in their pots, move them up to a bigger pot, but only one size at a time, until you're ready to plant them out for the summer again. For bushier plants, you'll want to pinch out the growing tips and that will awaken any dormant lateral buds, which in turn will start growing, thus producing a denser head. Don't hesitate to harvest and use the leaves as needed, but if you can use the tips first, that will stimulate more new growth.

Recommended Plants for Low Light

My son has an apartment with very little light but he would like to get a plant. Could you recommend something, preferably something that would flower?

In terms of flowering plants that will tolerate lower light, the choices are very limited. Aglaonema will stand up in that light and perhaps more consistently, the Spathiphyllum, Peace Lily or White Flag Lily, as it is often called, will also do well. You often see these two in shopping centres or in interior landscapes because they can tolerate the lower light levels and are one of the very few that will flower successfully in those lower light conditions. A Spider Plant may produce well. It is important to let it hang because it will not flower until it is pot bound and ready to start throwing off some offsets or pups. Another possibility would certainly be the ferns, but you would want to go with something like the Foxtail or *"Asparagus meyerii"* fern. It will give you flower but rarely a heavy conspicuous flowering. If just a green plant will do, a Boston Fern will do quite well in that situation.

Dismal Datura

I have a plant called Datura, at least I bought it thinking it was. I managed to keep it alive, barely, for 2 years. Obviously I'm doing something wrong. Can you tell me how I should be treating my plant this winter so that it isn't in such a sorry state this time round?

Datura

You have to accept that this plant is one that will not be delighted with winter regardless of what you do. It's nothing to do with you. It's simply a plant that wants to die back into semi-dormancy and then come back in late February when the light levels start to pick up again. So bring it in, put it in the sunniest window you can to start, water it only as needed and enjoy the last of the blooms. Eventually it is going to lose its leaves. When it has dropped them all, get it into a cooler, but still bright and sunny, place. That should be at about the end of November or December at the latest and that's also the time for you to do your cutting back. For the next few months, keep the soil barely moist. By the end of February, in that sunny window, you'll see that it is going to start back into new growth, at which point start to pick up the

watering. Give it a light feeding of half strength 10-52-10 or 15-30-15 followed by half strength applications of a soluble flowering plant food every fifth watering. It will probably re-flower for you some time around the end of May. By that time, you will be ready to put it back into the garden again.

Recommendations on Watering with Treated Water

I have never heard any advice about watering house plants with water that has been through a water softener. I'm wondering if some plants are more sensitive to the added salts and whether it is a good idea to use it.

Some plants are definitely more sensitive to treated water than others, orchids, for example, being one of them. Generally the concern comes from the build-up of salt on the plant as opposed to the impact of any individual watering. If you can use rain water from now on and leach any of those excess salts out, it is usually not a problem. Often the plant will adapt by developing a slower metabolism but you wouldn't notice a big difference. Where it is noticeable most often is with seedlings. They have a tender fibrous root system and you can run into problems with the salt content. Rain water is certainly the preferable choice for any plant and at the very least, use it from time to time to help flush out the salts that will build-up in your soil from your "softened" water.

Attack of the Dreaded Black Knot

After the leaves fell off my Schubert Chokecherry this year, I noticed these huge growths that look like cankers or a fungus or something all knotted up. I am wondering what to do about it. Is this going to kill my tree?

It's called black knot. What you need to do is to cut off any branch that has been affected at the node that is right below, and hopefully a comfortable distance from, the black knot. Clean cut it. After each cut, disinfect your pruner or saw by dipping it in rubbing alcohol or alternatively, in a 50% solution of chlorine bleach and water. Make sure you are dipping it between each cut. The plus with rubbing alcohol is that it will air dry quickly – you don't want to be cutting while the blade is still wet. The chlorine solution takes much longer to dry but is also effective. Work very thoroughly through the tree to cut out all of those knots and get them into a bag. If you have a woodstove or fireplace, you can collect them in a paper bag and burn them. If you don't have the facilities to burn them, then they should go into the garbage rather than into the compost. There's not too much you can do to prevent black knot coming back but keeping the tree in a healthy condition will certainly help. If you have compost, a side-dressing of that around the base of the tree with several inches of mulch over the surface will make all the difference in the world. The compost will provide all the nutrient that the tree really needs. Other than that, it is just a matter of constant surveillance. Any time you see the black knot showing up, cut it off. Keeping the crown fairly

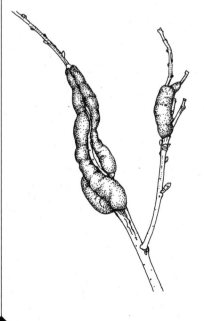

open so that the tree gets good air circulation will also help. Black knot is caused by an airborne spore that can come in from elsewhere, so keeping the tree healthy and constant surveillance are your best defense.

How to Water Hibiscus

My 2-year-old hibiscus produces wonderful flowers, but since I brought it in for the winter the buds that form just seem to fall off. I thought that maybe I was over-watering it, so I let it dry out until the leaves began to droop and then gave it another really good watering. Is the watering the problem?

Flowers are always a little bit more expendable to a plant than foliage. They will tend to drop flower buds before they lose any leaves. This could happen if the plant had drunk a bit too much, however that doesn't seem to be the case here. Barring that, it may just be the light level. If they go into a bright location when you bring them in from the summer, they will usually keep coming along and flowering in the fall until they get toward the end of their viable production. Unless you have a really bright sunny location for them, they go a bit into a semi-dormancy. This is an ideal time to trim them back.

As the light levels increase, they gradually come out of that state and will flower from the new growth that has been put out. In your case, what you have is probably a combination of lack of light and maybe stretching it a little too far in between waterings. It is good to let them dry back a bit, but they should always have some degree of moisture. Letting them dry out completely makes it more difficult to get the soil to take up the moisture again. It also puts that extra bit of stress on the plants and they have to recuperate again before they start growing on. Water down from the top of the plant so that you know it is soaking down thoroughly through the root ball with no dry pockets. Water until the excess comes through into the saucer; leave that excess there for 20 minutes and then take away any surplus. That way, if there is still a need for moisture, it can be wicked back into the root ball and absorbed by the peat moss. After 20 minutes, it will have taken all it needs so it is safe to throw away any water that remains.

Amaryllis Advice

I have kept two large amaryllis plants going for about 5 years. I leave them out year round in a bright window and they always have gorgeous flowers on them.

There is no sign of any bud on them yet but they have all these leaves. I am wondering if I should cut them off before the new flowers start coming along? They have also had a secondary growth for the last 2 years and I am wondering if I should encourage that?

Don't remove the foliage. They look very attractive with it on, although we find it unusual to see them with flower and foliage at the same time. If the relative humidity or moisture conditions are higher when an amaryllis starts into bud, you will get foliage along with the flower. I generally recommend to people that they don't take their amaryllis out of dormancy until the flower bud shows up because sometimes it makes it a little harder for the bud to come along. Other times, they won't come fully out of dormancy in that they start back into active growth but the flower embryo just sits there and doesn't show up until some time in midsummer. That being said, you already have them out and growing now. The bulb has expended an awful lot of energy and food reserve to produce foliage so let the foliage work. Keep them in a bright, sunny location and water only as required, making sure that they are drying down in between the waterings. Once the flower

stem shows up, you will find it uses more water so you can increase the frequency of watering. With regard to a secondary growth off of the first bulb, what I would recommend is that you grow these in full sun as long as you can this year. When you get to early or mid-August at the latest, it would be worthwhile to cut off the water and let the bulb go back into dormancy. Cut off the old foliage once it has all yellowed and dried and put the bulb into a dry and cool, but not cold, location. When it has been there for at least a month, take it out of the pot. What you will probably find is that there is a side bulb developing off of the parent bulb. Just take that off from the main bulb. You can sever it with a knife but they will usually break away quite easily. Pot up the smaller bulb and bring it up into the light and let it go. Leave the larger, parent bulb in the dark. Don't bring the parent bulb out until it shows you the flower bud and then bring it up and let it grow on again. That dormant period is certainly helpful for the plant although as you have seen with yours, it is not absolutely essential for re-flowering. Dormancy allows the plant to slow down a little bit and the developmental stage of the flower comes along while it is still dormant. That is the point at which the bulb wants to get back into active growth. This process best mimics the normal cycle of the amaryllis.

Deer Deterrents

I have had a problem with deer trotting into the backyard and munching on my 10 year-old Japanese Yew shrubs. They have stripped the branches down to where they look like little scarecrows. Is there any particular deterrent I can use? Can the yews be cut back and will they rejuvenate?

It's best not to cut them back because they take a long time to grow. I am nursing a pair of Japanese Yew myself that the deer got to and it is a heartbreaker. The plus is that, at 10 years, your plants are well established and will have a better bud count. Once the deer stop damaging them, they will come back more strongly than younger ones would and do fill in quite nicely. I would recommend that you set up a physical barrier to protect these plants in the winter. Putting some supports into the ground and wrapping chicken wire around and over the top of them. You can also use plastic mesh over the top, which is a bit cheaper – the sort of thing that is sold for stringing up sweet peas and morning glories – but you'll want something a bit more solid around the edges. You can usually take the plastic or chicken wire off in the late spring because by then the deer tend to find enough elsewhere to satisfy their hunger. Another short-term deterrent is blood meal around the plants – do this first thing in the spring and through the season just to keep that smell around, or if you have a cat, spread the used kitty litter around the base of the shrub. The smell is not appealing to the deer and does discourage them somewhat.

Propagating Azaleas

I have had really good luck this year with several azaleas and one in particular has been spectacular. It has lots of flowers and it looks to be a different variety from the others I have. I am wondering if I can propagate it or has it been grafted?

Quite possibly it has been grafted but that doesn't mean you can't propagate it. Your cuttings would be tip cuttings from last year's wood, with new growth coming in from this year. A #1 or #2 rooting hormone should be sufficient and you can root those up successfully in damp sand or vermiculite. You want to keep the foliage dampened but not constantly wet throughout the process. Either spray it regularly or put a plastic bag over top, but remember to open it occasionally to get some air circulation. Be careful not to put the bagged plant in the sun either or it will bake. Whichever approach you take, you want high humidity around the cutting while it starts to root up. Now the other thing you can do is to take those cuttings and put them immediately into water. Cut them off at a node, leaving the node intact on the plant, and then re-cut to the next node nearest the bottom of your cutting. The easiest way to do this is on a cutting board with a very sharp knife. Leave the node intact and put it directly into the water with some cuttings of either English Ivy or even better, willow. Once the azaleas callus and start rooting you can transplant them – a fairly light peat moss and sand mixture would do nicely here. As they start coming along just move them up one pot size at a time. Having taken the cuttings from the flowering part of the plant, it will develop on its own root stock and you will get the same colour flowers.

Bulging Basement Floor

The two Sugar Maples in my backyard are doing extremely well, but that may well be my problem because I have a bulge in my cement floor which has been growing gradually over the past 6-7 months. The maples are about 40 - 50 feet high and they are about 25 feet from the basement wall of my house. Could that bulge be a root from one of these trees that is coming through my basement floor? And if it is one of those roots, is it just a question of digging it out in that area? I'd rather not lose the trees.

A root coming up through the floor like that would be a bit unusual for Sugar Maples. Red Maples would tend to be more of a problem because they like wetter conditions. A Silver Maple would definitely be a problem, but 25 feet from the wall and coming up through the floor is questionable with Sugars. You are going to have to do something about the bulge in the floor in any case, so when you cut it out, that is time to do an ID of what is there. If it is a root, do get an arborist in to identify it. Don't assume that it is your maple. An ID on the tissue will be able to confirm what type of plant it is or they'll be able to tell just by the size and shape of the material. If it is your maple, find the source of the invasion and how it is getting in through the floor. There are tree guard materials you can use that are specifically designed to redirect roots. That being said, roots don't normally penetrate solid surfaces so I suspect if it is a root, there might have been a problem with the foundation of the house to start with, maybe an open crack just under the surface that it could get into. There might also be something attracting it there, like a water source. If that's the case, it would be a matter of tile draining which would deflect the roots away from the wall. Those trees are worth preserving so if you can find the cause and repair it or deflect the roots away from the house, that would certainly be worthwhile.

Propagating Plants with Aerial Roots

I was given a Monstera clipping with long aerial roots and a stem with two leaves. After I potted it up one of the leaves fell off, the bottom turned all black and then the other leaf fell over. I pulled it up and discovered the roots had all rotted away, so I cut the bottom off. Is it possible to use what's left, that is the stem and the two leaves, to try again?

Those adventitious or aerial roots have adapted themselves to grow in the air, so they really don't stand up as well when they're planted down into the soil. However, if you had laid them on

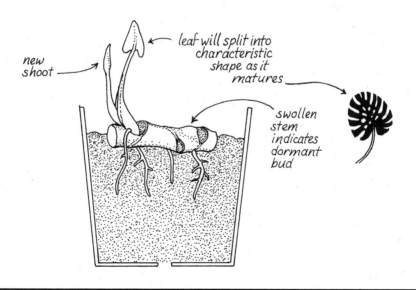

new shoot

leaf will split into characteristic shape as it matures

swollen stem indicates dormant bud

the surface of the soil, they eventually would have put down further roots beneath the surface and that would have been fine. For that reason, it is better if you can get a cutting while those aerial roots are fairly short so you can lay them right onto the soil readily. Propagating from the leaf at this point is not going to be successful, but if you have a section of stem, it's really quite easy. Take that stem and cut at the node on both ends of the section that you have and lay it on the surface of the soil or bury half of it just under the soil, much in the manner you would plant an iris rhizome. If you are seeing any swelling at any node along the stem, put that piece facing up. If there is no swelling, put it off to the side. Do keep the soil moist. The aerial roots will develop and eventually put out roots that will grow down into the soil. It will swell a bud at one or more of the nodes and start growing back up from that point without too much trouble.

Cyclamen Mites in African Violets

Our African Violet was doing beautifully, but recently the leaves in the centre have started to dry up and get very hard. Have you any idea why this might be happening?

That would be cyclamen mite. If you want to avoid using one of the heavier chemical treatments, you can get rid of them simply by soaking the plant in a soap and water solution. Mix up a room temperature solution of 40-parts water to 1-part liquid soap in a pot or bowl. Water your plant well and then holding it by the pot, invert the whole thing into the soapy water, making sure that the soil surface gets submerged and the solution comes into contact with all of the stems and the leaves. Once you have soaked everything, remove it and allow it to sit with the soap solution on it for 10 minutes or so, and then flush all of that off again with clear, room temperature water. Shake the plant off and remove as much water as you can. Put the plant into a fairly bright spot with good air circulation. The best time to do this treatment is early in the day so that it can dry off completely before night. You are going to have to repeat the process 3 times over a 10-day period to break the egg-hatching cycle of the cyclamen mites since the eggs are not killed off by this process. Once you've finished the treatment, your plant should pick up quite quickly and you will probably see some new leaves and vigorous growth starting up. It would also be a good idea to give it a feeding of African Violet food or any soluble fertilizer for flowering houseplants. It will have been shocked by all this and that feeding will encourage the new growth along. Any fertilizer with a 1-1-3 ratio, such as 10-10-27, would work well here. Use it at 1/2 - 1/3 of the manufacturer's recommended rate of application and continue feeding about every fourth watering from March through to October. Continue to water as needed through the winter months, but no more feeding until March.

Dividing a Mature Plant

My croton plant is about 20 years old and 7½ feet tall. I have an 8 foot ceiling and I'm trying to figure out how I can cut it off before it grows through the roof. The plant has about 3 feet of woody stem and then there are branches from about the 4 foot mark. Can I just cut it off somehow and plant that cutting to start a new one?

There is a way to do this. Start where the leaves come directly off that stem. At that point, with a sharp knife strip off a piece of bark about a half inch long by 1/4 of an inch wide on all four sides of the plant either between the nodes or at the nodes, having removed the leaves completely. Cut only deep enough to remove the

cambium layer. Next, get some sphagnum peat moss and wet it thoroughly. Apply a little #1 rooting hormone to the areas on the plant where you have removed the strips of outer bark. Rooting hormone can be found at any nursery or garden centre. Next take some plastic cling wrap and use it to secure the wet sphagnum moss around the plant at that point. Tie it off top and bottom with elastic bands. Keep the moss damp by opening up the top of the plastic wrap from time to time

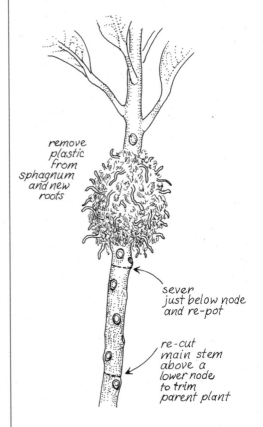

remove plastic from sphagnum and new roots

sever just below node and re-pot

re-cut main stem above a lower node to trim parent plant

and adding water as needed. When you see roots growing out an inch or so through that moss, cut the plant off just below those new roots. Remove the wrap and moss, then plant that upper section up into a new pot. Your original plant will take off again by activating dormant buds along that now bare lower stem and both should grow on pretty quickly without too much trouble at all.

Deep Freeze for Penstemons

I have been trying to grow penstemons from seed. Last winter I followed the instructions on the seed package that said to give them a cold treatment between - 4° celsius to +4° celsius for 2-3 months. So I put them in my fridge and didn't get a single one started. I would like to try again and all the sources I have looked at say they should be easy germinators, so I am looking for some advice here. How should I get these going?

Success here depends on the freshness of the seed and what you did for the cold treatment. You probably would have been a bit more successful if you had thrown them in the freezer for a few weeks and then into the refrigerator. Give them a couple of weeks in the freezer, 4-6 more in the refrigerator, and then soak them overnight in room temperature water before seeding. The other thing you could do, if you get them early in the fall, is to leave them in an unheated garage for a few weeks when temperatures are below freezing and then bring them in and put them into the refrigerator. Cool germination is a requirement so find a cool spot after you remove them from the refrigerator. These are hardy seeds. If they were growing outside and self seeding they would be going through much more severe cold treatment than you are giving them. In fact, harsh conditions such as freezing are often a determining factor in their success.

Germinating Ginkgo

I picked up some seed pods from a Ginkgo tree in my neighbourhood. They look like little yellow apples and I have no idea what to do with them. I was just going to try planting them but the ground outside has already started to freeze so I'm wondering if I should bring them inside from the garage and start them indoors?

Outside is a really good place for these because if you bring them indoors to a warm place, boy do they smell! The best thing at this point would be to decide where in your garden you want them to be and bury them down to about their own depth as soon as possible. If you have some area close to the house that has not yet frozen and is still workable, that would be easiest. If everything has frozen, you can pot them up, but I would say at this point you would be best to get a spade or a pick and break that cover to put them down into the warmer soil below. Be sure to leave the hulls on. As they rot down, the moisture and microbial action will help get through the hard seed coat facilitating germination. Line them out with 3-4 inches between each individual seed. Put the frozen soil back on top and give it a light watering to harden up the top again. This will save you from putting chicken wire over to keep the squirrels out because they can't dig through the frozen surface of the soil. Mark the spot and don't give up if you don't get results next spring. Just leave them in the ground another season and watch for growth. As they develop, lift the individual seedlings. Make sure you dig deeply beside them to get as much root as possible. Transplant them to a sunny location and water them in well.

Impatient for Clivias to Flower

About six years ago I planted two clivias from my mother's seed pod. She told me they wouldn't flower for about 5 years but that fifth year came and went and nothing happened. I'm getting a bit impatient. Is there anything that can be done to help them along?

They will flower when they are pot bound and I am assuming you have left them in the same pot for quite a while now. Let them stay a little bit on the dry side, but give them a thorough watering when you do water them, and cool conditions are ideal. A little less light is fine for them, but a cool spot is essential. In the course of this cool treatment what you may see is that buds start showing up at the base. Look down in between the leaves to see if any buds are there. If some are evident, move the plants out into a higher light. Give them a thorough soaking and let them grow on. If nothing happens by the end of March or so, bring them up into a slightly higher light anyway, water them again and keep them growing on. They can go outdoors into a shady location in the summer after all danger of frost has passed. Clivias are quite happy to be outside and this does help with bud initiation. And no feeding them until they start to produce flowers for you.

Re-forcing Bulbs

I would like to know something about forcing bulbs or bringing them on a little bit early. I have a cold porch and if I can get them into flower in about January, they can flower for several months so I get a lot of time out of them. I have been trying to sort out the ones that I grew last year because I have had very mixed success from some of them. A lot of them are completely gone and I'm wondering what the best way might be to get them to come back?

It is possible to re-force bulbs, but not always with total success because they do need that recuperation time. They need to grow on after flowering for a long enough period of time to allow sufficient energy to be built up in the bulb through photosynthesis. It's this energy that allows it to produce the flower embryo within the bulb itself for the following year's bloom. Often the stress of being forced out of season and not having more ideal conditions – the combination of cool temperatures, regularly moist soil, and constant sun exposure that it would get if it flowered in season

– is such that the bulb cannot recuperate fully in one year. Once they are planted outdoors after forcing and are naturalized, they will often come back, if not in the following year, then the year after. It is a matter of giving them enough sun and nutrient to produce another flower bud. I never recommend trying to force spring flowering bulbs a second time because spending your time and energy on gardening deserves good results and for the best return, you need to force large, healthy new bulbs each year.

Saving Outdoor Rosemary

I was given two rosemary plants last summer. They are great big ones, about 3 feet tall and I have them in big pots. I brought them into the porch, which is not heated although we put plastic over the screens and I've put a little heater in there just to try to warm it up slightly – but there will be days when the soil freezes. I've tried this before but I have never been able to get the rosemary through the whole winter inside. Is there anything I can do to save them?

That freezing is going to be a little rough on the plant, although from my experience they can take a light frosting down to about -5° celsius. They prefer to stay just above the freezing mark through the winter months. That being said, if you have a cool, but not freezing, location, it is always going to be easier to keep them through the winter. If it is possible, bring them indoors off the porch into a cool room, with good light exposure. Make sure they dry down between waterings, but do check them regularly and don't let them dry out. This is where most people have problems with rosemary indoors. Our houses often have lower humidity levels in the winter than a desert and plants can dry out very quickly. Putting a humidifier in with them would certainly be worthwhile. If you have a wood stove, keep them out of that room. Or if you have forced air heating, make sure they are away from any direct draft of hot air. With a cool location and a bit of benign neglect you will probably find them coming through the winter and flowering for you at the end of February and possibly through into March. They produce a beautiful small blue flower that is pretty much as fragrant as the foliage. If you collect a bunch of those flowers, boil them up and then simmer them for a while, that rosemary scent will travel right through the house. You can harvest continuously as long as the plants are growing ac-

tively, which they will do above 5° celsius.

Exposed Cyclamen Corm

I removed two cyclamen that we have had for 2 years now from their plastic pots this past spring and planted them out in the garden. They flowered all summer. I repotted them in September in clay but I note that the root is now actually about an inch above the soil. Is this a tuber?

I assume when you say "clay" you mean a clay pot as opposed to clay soil. I say this because cyclamen must have a porous, free-draining soil in order to develop a good root system and avoid rot problems that are inevitable if they sit in constantly wet conditions. This is why a clay pot is preferable to a plastic one since the clay pot actually breathes – that is to say it wicks away excess moisture from the soil and allows air to permeate and come into contact with the root system. The corm, which is technically somewhat different from a tuber, should be at least partially exposed to avoid crown rot. In fact, it is happiest when sitting on the surface of the soil with only its roots in the soil mixture. The plant is a bit more stable if the corm is partially buried and this isn't a problem as long as the soil isn't constantly wet. You may find that while your cyclamen is growing indoors it will fill the pot with roots to the point that it pushes itself up and out of the soil a bit more. This isn't a problem. When you replant it into the garden next spring, after all danger of frost has passed, place it at the same depth as it was in the pot. When you repot it to bring it in at the end of the summer it is inevitable that the root system will be disturbed. Clean cut any broken roots with a sharp knife. Rinse some of the soil away from the root ball around the bottom, sides and top. Add some fresh potting soil, place the corm into the pot and fill in the sides and around the top so that it is again sitting at the same depth. This will provide some fresh soil for the winter growth but also avoids any excessive buildup over the corm itself. Cyclamen will be happiest if you can put them in a window that cools them down to about 45° fahrenheit or 8° celsius at night. You may be able to simulate this temperature change by pulling the drapes in the evening so that the plants are between the windows and the drapes rather than exposed to the inside room temperature. That temperature drop at night would certainly be a plus for them.

Cat Scat

How can I stop my cat from peeing in my Umbrella Tree? It's gotten moldy on top of the soil and I'm worried this is going to hurt my plant.

Your cat is going to go back to where the scent is and to where it has enough surface area to be able to scratch up the soil. If you can get it out of the habit of using your Umbrella Tree pot, it usually won't go back. The easiest way to control the problem is to kill off some of the scent. Cat urine is slightly acidic so the next time you water, loosen up the soil and sprinkle baking soda over the surface. You'll want to use slightly warm water to help dissolve some of the soluble salts that are in the urine itself. Scratching up the surface of the soil will ensure that the mold or moss that is starting to form there won't have the conditions it likes. The baking soda won't eliminate the moss but will certainly stop it from spreading. If the baking soda treatment doesn't deter the cat, you are going to have to put some sort of physical barrier over the soil. Normally I'd recommend mulching with organic matter over that surface, but in this case, it's not going to stop the cat from digging. You will most likely have to use something a little more solid, like pebbles or marbles. Keep in mind that you tend to get less evaporation from the soil surface with any kind of mulching and that means that you are going to have to push back whatever you have on there and check the moisture levels in between waterings. You'll find you will probably have to water a bit less frequently. Aside from the unpleasant aesthetics, as long as the plant has rooted, the urine won't actually hurt your umbrella tree. In fact, it might have some benefit. The plant will be picking up the ammonia from the urine and that means a shot of nitrogen, so stand back and watch it grow.

Potential Wall Cracking Properties of Walnuts

My walnut tree is only 15 feet from the house and growing like mad. I asked another gardening expert and she had said not to cut it, but I want your opinion on that. I am wondering if the roots of the tree would damage the basement.

No, that is the big plus with walnuts. They are not invasive in that manner. When they come up to an obstruction, they generally have enough sense to veer away. Some of the maples, willows and poplars might try to push on through, but not a walnut. If you are concerned that some of the branches might become a problem, especially near roofline, you may want to be tipping some of those off to encourage them to spread away or to promote more growth on the other side of tree. The advantage of the walnuts though, is that they are a long lived, slow growing tree and generally quite beautiful, besides attracting all of that wildlife. They also produce a very good natural dye that can stain you hands for several days, so you will find that once it starts producing nuts, especially if they are rotting a little, you will not want to handle them without gloves.

DECEMBER

— A. KARSTAD

Encouraging Christmas Cactus to Flower

Our Christmas Cactus is three years old and the first year we had lots of blooms; last year we had a couple that seemed to fall off early and this year, there's nothing. What am I doing wrong?

Your plant may not be getting enough sunshine or it may be getting too much fertilizer. As far as the feeding goes, use about half the recommended strength of a soluble 10-10-10 or 20-20-20 fertil-izer every fourth or fifth watering. The fish emulsion fertilizers work very well here. You don't want too much nitrogen in there, so 3 or 4 clear waterings between the feedings should be fine. Follow this pattern from about the end of February or early March through until the fall, with the start of October being the absolute maximum, and then stop the fertilizer. Allow the plant as much light as possible year round and that will help to initiate the flower buds. It would be happiest with a western or southern exposure. Christmas

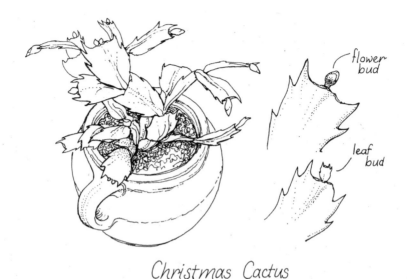

flower
bud

leaf
bud

Christmas Cactus

Cactus can grow quite successfully inside in a bright location year round, but they are even happier if they go out into the garden for the summer . Wait until all danger of frost has passed before you put it out and make sure you put it into a partially shaded location for a week or two at first – an easterly location with early morning sun would be ideal – and then move it out into full sun once it's had time to adapt to the higher light levels. Though it may not seem so to our eyes, which adapt very quickly and effectively to changes in light levels, the difference in light intensity between a sunny window sill indoors and a partially-shaded spot out in the garden can be more than tenfold. Plants need time to adapt to these increases; otherwise they can get as badly burnt as we sometimes do early in the season. At the end of the summer bring the plant back inside before the first frost and keep it in a cool, bright location until you want it to flower. Keeping it cool and dry is the only way to hold the flower buds back from opening. If it is warm and dry, the plant will still use its stored moisture to open the flowers and will suffer a great energy loss in the process. Keeping it cool is the secret to holding those blooms at bay. When you want the cactus to bloom, move it into a warmer spot and increase the moisture level. Once the flowers are out, the plant will require significantly more moisture to sustain all the transpiration from those delicate blooms, so keep an eye on it and be sure to water it before the soil dries down completely.

Transplanting Larger Norfolk Pine

I purchased a Norfolk Island Pine at Christmas and I now realize that there are actually 11 different trees in the pot – each about 2 feet high. Can I plant some of these outside next spring and if so, will they survive the winter? Then I'd like to split up the rest into groups of 2 or 3 and keep them for our Christmas tree next year. What size pot should I use and what should I feed them?

You could take a chance and try planting some of those trees out this summer but I wouldn't expect to get them through the winter. They are not winter hardy in our region. Having said that, splitting those trees up into groups and transplanting them indoors will work quite effectively. The plus with the groups is that you will get a denser needled or green area and the crown will look much fuller. It is preferable to divide them into clusters of 3s rather than 2s in order to avoid the flat-sided appearance given by 2 conifers growing side by side. If the clusters fit into 6-inch pots, start there and once the roots have filled up those, move them up a size. If they are already too big for the 6-inch pots, go to a 7 or 8-inch azalea-size pot that is 6 inches high, but with an 8-inch diameter at the top. And here again, do not move them up to a larger pot until the roots have filled that first one. After transplanting, you can use 1/3 strength 10-52-10 fertilizer to help stimulate the roots – or anything else with a low first and last and high middle number. Some of the fish emulsion fertilizers on the market that come in a soluble format will work nicely. The essential thing is to cause as little disruption to the root system as possible. You can minimize that disruption by thoroughly soaking the pot before you start taking the root ball apart and by keeping the roots covered with a damp cloth or a piece of plastic bag during the process. Water them in after transplanting and do not water them again until they dry down – but don't wait until they are completely dried out – then give them another thorough soaking to help establish the root system. Do not set them back into full sun right away. They'll need bright light, but not direct sun, for the first few weeks until they have adapted to the transplant. Then back into full sun they go and you should have a nice range of Norfolk Island Pines for next year's Christmas.

Poinsettia Pointers

Every year I buy several poinsettias at Christmas time. Can you tell me the proper way to look after them?

There are few basic points that will increase your odds of success with poinsettia. First and foremost, make sure your plant is wrapped before you leave the store. Even a few minutes expo-

A Word About Poinsettias

I don't think there is any other seasonal plant more popular in North America than the poinsettia. The Aztecs cultivated this plant — and considered it a symbol of purity — long before Christianity came to North America. Joel Robert Poinsett, the United States' first Ambassador to Mexico, introduced the plant to the U.S. in 1825. A capable botanist, Poinsett found the plant growing and flowering on the hills around present-day Taxco. He supplied his own greenhouses, some botanical gardens and some horticultural friends. The cultivars available across this continent today are from scaled-down strains of that native Mexican shrub which normally grows to a height of 2-4 metres. Poinsettia (euphorbia pulcherima) gets such common names as Mexican Flame Tree, Christmas Star and Lobster Plant. First noted for the bright red bracts that surround the comparatively inconspicuous yellow flowers, the palette of available colours has grown steadily over the years. Poinsettias can be found in a vast array of tints and shades of red, from deep burgundy to pale old-rose red, as well as in a wide range of pinks, whites and mottled combinations of all three of these basic colours. A few years ago the industry even introduced a golden yellow variety with the idea that it would be attractive for decorating both at Thanksgiving (American that is) and at Christmas time. Tradition dies hard though — it didn't catch on at all and I've never seen or heard of them since that initial introduction. Dick Veerman, a friend and horticultural consultant in the greenhouse business, told me a few years back that we in Canada grow enough poinsettias to provide one for every household. That translates into millions.

A. KARSTAD.

Poinsettia

sure to freezing temperatures will frost-burn or even kill it. It's also best if your car is warmed up and make sure you're heading straight home. Unwrap the plant as soon as you get home. The ethylene gas that is released when the leaves are bent in the wrapper is actually somewhat toxic to the plant and can cause the leaves to drop. The longer a plant is in the wrapper, the longer it takes to re-adjust and lift its leaves again. If it has sat bound up in a sleeve or wrapper in the store, expect to find drooping leaves when it is unwrapped. Once you get your plant set up, check for moisture and water it if needed. If there is a plastic or foil wrap around the pot, make sure there are drainage holes at the bottom so the plant never sits in water any longer than it takes for the soilless mix to absorb what it needs. If you should get busy over the holidays and let it dry out too much, this plant will let you know very quickly. If you discover it completely flagged – and what a sorry sight that is – just water it well and it should pick back up within 30-45 minutes. Bright filtered light – the kind you get from behind sheer curtains – is ideal, but it's not essential if the plant is only being used as a seasonal decoration. No feeding is really needed; these plants have usually been

force-fed in the greenhouse since they were potted up as cuttings in the early summer. Enjoy your plants and when they're done or you've had enough of them, send them to the compost. Or if you prefer, hang on to them, let them grow on and keep them around for next year. Not only do they make a very acceptable indoor green plant when the coloured bracts are removed, but they can be great "space fillers" in a flower bed.

Cocktail Query

Can I grow a tree from the pit of an olive?

No, not successfully. The olives have been marinated long enough that the pit is rendered useless. It would be a bit like trying to grow a maraschino cherry tree!

Miracle Tree

About 7 years ago I put a big seed – I think it was a lemon but it may have been a grapefruit – into some soil and it sprouted. After about 9 months, I planted it into a little pot. Low and behold, 7 years later, I have a tree about 6 feet tall. I had been told that it would never grow because I am living on the north side of a condominium but the tree loves me. It's about an inch in diameter at the base with 3 feet of trunk and about 5 branches on the next 3 feet with these beautiful green leaves. I once measured one that was 8½ inches long and 3 inches wide. It's sort of like a miracle tree because it just sits in front of these patio doors on the north side where it only gets a maximum of 2 hours of light in the late afternoon from May until August. I never feed it and there's so little room in the pot I can't even get the moisture gauge in. I'm pretty sure it should be dead. What do you think?

You probably have a lemon tree. The fact that it came from a piece of commercial fruit and germinated is more exceptional than the tree itself because these seeds often do not ripen fully before the fruit is harvested for shipping north. However, it obviously worked. If it can go out onto the deck or balcony through the summer, after all danger of frost has past, it will do that much better. That being said, it is obviously getting enough light to sustain it. Trimming it back will force some of the dormant buds into growth along those lateral branches as opposed to it throwing all of its energy into one leader. It would also force more buds to come along and with a higher light level in the summer, you might get it to flower, although generally you need to have 4-6 hours of direct light a day in order to get flowering. In terms of watering, if you could get at it just a little before the leaves start to droop, that would be worthwhile. And after 6 years, it is definitely time to move up to a larger pot. Don't go larger than one size up at a time. Loosen up the roots on the outside of the root ball and take away as much soil from the top and sides as you can. It would be happier in a clay pot rather than in a plastic one because the clay breathes a little bit more. It would also be worthwhile putting in all new soil when you make the change. Generally all of the citrus are heavy feeders and they can deplete a soil, so filling it with fresh soil after you loosen those roots would be beneficial.

Holiday Tree Division

I bought a small potted Norfolk Island Pine for a Christmas tree and I now realize that there are actually 4 trees in there. Should I separate them?

Yes, separate them after Christmas. Use the smallest size pots that will accommodate the root system, so if the plant fits well into a 4-inch pot don't use one that is 6 inches. They'll establish themselves much more successfully if they are snug. Use any of the commercially available potting mixes and you can add 25% sharp sand to that if you happen to have some handy. The bags sold in hardware stores for kids' sand boxes work fine. Once the trees become root-bound you can move them up one pot size at a time. Next year, with any luck, you will have four Christmas trees instead of one. I have done this a few times with small trees that I have brought in to decorate at Christmas and they have come through this process quite nicely. Give them a good bright light, not necessarily full sun, although if they can get it they will do that much better. Water them thoroughly when you do water. Make sure they dry down between each watering but don't let them dry out completely. You'll end up with four trees for the price of one!

Reviving Rosemary

I am sure you are familiar with the decorative rosemary bushes that are being sold in grocery stores as Christmas trees. I bought one a couple of weeks ago and it was dry so I gave it a good soaking and then drained it. Over the past few weeks it has been dropping needles and now it has these two big patches that are brown and not very attractive. I do want to save the plant and use it for cooking and maybe put it outside in the summer. I don't care that it doesn't look like

a little Christmas tree anymore, I just want to know how I should keep it alive through the winter and what would be best to do with it through the summer?

Keep the rosemary in a bright sunny window. This plant doesn't mind if it is a cooler window, and in fact, it would be much happier if it is a cooler window. A south or western exposure would be ideal. Watch the watering: make sure it is drying down between each watering because waterlogged soil in the winter months can cause a lot of root rot problems. Do not spray or water over the foliage. Rosemary bushes are fairly susceptible to powdery mildew and the spores are pretty much everywhere, especially with these plants that have been commercially grown and may have already been exposed, so avoid wetting the foliage if at all possible. It's also good to remember that when plants such as rosemary or bay are kept in relatively dry conditions they develop a higher concentration of volatile oils in their foliage – if you are hoping to use some of this plant in cooking, this would be an advantage. Make sure the plant is drying down, but you do have to keep an eye on it because they can dry out fairly easily and you don't want them dropping needles. The brown spots that have developed may be some damage caused by shipping or possibly drafty conditions in the grocery store where you bought it. The plant may also have been frosted at some point, so there are a few possible causes, but it will certainly come back. In the spring, after all danger of frost has passed, bring it out into mottled sunlight. You can gradually work it into full sun conditions without too much trouble but the watering obviously has to be increased when it is in the fuller sun. Again, check before you water to make sure it has dried down. In late August you should be moving it back to a slightly lower light level just to acclimatize it a bit before it comes back inside, and again, you have to bring it in before the frost. Keep in mind that some yellowing and dropping of needles is to be expected. Like any evergreen, rosemary will lose some of its older leaves from time to time and these will usually yellow on the plant before they fall. These yellowing, older leaves generally start showing up in the centre of the plant where the light levels are a bit lower and their appearance usually coincides with the generation of new growth at the outer, brighter tips of the branches.

Oh Christmas Tree, Oh Christmas Tree

We normally buy a pre-cut Christmas tree, but the last couple of years we have had really bad luck with the ones from tree lots. This year we have decided to go out to a tree farm and cut one down. We'd like to get our tree the first weekend in December, but I have no idea what to do to prevent the needles from starting to fall off the week before Christmas. Have you any advice?

The big plus this year is that you are going to cut your tree yourself. Often the pre-cut trees have been harvested between late September and early November and are fairly dried out by the time they are transported and sold at Christmas. When you get your tree home, trim off the lower branches and re-cut the trunk just before you put it into the stand. Add room temperature water, although if you do this on a freezing cold day warmer water would be even better. Make sure it is in a stand or container that holds a good quantity of water and that it is constantly supplied with water. That is really all you need to do to have it hold its needles. If you happen to be on a well and there is a possibility of algae build-up, it would be worthwhile to add a tablespoon or two of chlorine

318

bleach to every couple of quarts of water to provide a bit of an algaecide. Make sure that the lower side branches are not inhibiting the tree's ability to sit down deep into the container. Cut any off that are below the waterline and that should give you a bit more absorption. Make sure you check the water level daily and replenish it as needed, especially through the first week when it is acclimatizing to the new indoor conditions. If you keep it moist, it should take you right through the holiday season. I've actually had a few of my fresh-cut Christmas trees swell up their buds and put out new shoots while fully decorated in our living room.

Amaryllis Encore

My children have been given an amaryllis the past few Christmases and they really enjoy watching them grow. Is it possible to keep these bulbs and have them re-flower again the next year?

Yes, these will regenerate. When the plant has finished flowering, cut the flower stem back to about 2 inches above the neck of the bulb; once the re-maining stub has dried out completely, give it a quick, firm tug to detach it from the bulb. Let the plant grow on in full light. If you want it to flower again for next Christmas, you will need to force it into dormancy by the end of August. Start letting it dry out about the middle of July. If the plant is outside, make sure that it doesn't get any rain water. Have it dry out completely, let the leaves wilt back and then cut them off about 1-2 inches above the bulb. At the end of August, put the dried plant into a dark cupboard or closet and leave it there until you see the bud start to show up, usually about 6-10 weeks later. Don't take it out of the dark if only leaves start to show. Once the flower bud appears, take the plant out of the cupboard, place it in full sun and after an initial soaking, water it only as required. Be sure it's drying down somewhat between each watering. The re-blooming can be sped up or slowed down by playing with the ambient temperature and light levels. Warmer, brighter conditions will hasten the flower opening; cooler, lower light will slow the flowering down.

INDEX